Undressing Religion

Dress, Body, Culture

Series Editor **Joanne B. Eicher**, *Regents' Professor, University of Minnesota*

Books in this provocative series seek to articulate the connections between culture and dress which is defined here in its broadest possible sense as any modification or supplement to the body. Interdisciplinary in approach, the series highlights the dialogue between identity and dress, cosmetics, coiffure, and body alterations as manifested in practices as varied as plastic surgery, tattooing, and ritual scarification. The series aims, in particular, to analyze the meaning of dress in relation to popular culture and gender issues and will include works grounded in anthropology, sociology, history, art history, literature, and folklore.

ISSN: 1360-466X

DRESS, BODY, CULTURE

Undressing Religion

Commitment and Conversion from a
Cross-Cultural Perspective

Edited by

Linda B. Arthur

Oxford • New York

First published in 2000 by
Berg
Editorial offices:
150 Cowley Road, Oxford, OX4 1JJ, UK
838 Broadway, Third Floor, New York, NY 10003-4812, USA

Berg is an imprint of Oxford International Publishers Ltd.

Library of Congress Cataloging-in-Publication Data
A catalog record for this book is available from the Library of Congress.

British Library Cataloguing-in-Publication Data
A catalogue record for this book is available from the British Library.

ISBN   1 85973 475 8 (Cloth)
       1 85973 480 4 (Paper)

Typeset by JS Typesetting, Wellingborough, Northants.
Printed in the United Kingdom by Biddles Ltd, Guildford and King's Lynn.

Contents

Contents

Acknowledgements

My fascination with the complex interplay between culture, religion and dress was stimulated by my move to Hawaii in 1993 where I had to quickly learn to negotiate my way through a primarily Asian culture. The conceptual shift into conducting research in and on Asian cultures was facilitated by Bronwen Solyom who has patiently led me through the complex maze of religion, politics and culture in Southeast Asia in general and Indonesia in particular. Her devotion to these cultural interchanges has been most helpful in my attempt to grasp the complex nuances of the interplay between culture and religion and their ultimate expression in the material culture of Southeast Asia.

I am grateful to several people for their help in bringing this volume to print: Joanne Eicher and Kathryn Earle both encouraged me to develop this anthology, as well as an earlier volume (*Religion, Dress and the Body*) in this series. Janis Okino was my able editorial assistant on both volumes, and kept us on schedule. Chapters were submitted to blind peer-review. Eighteen anonymous reviewers provided helpful insights and they are to be commended for their devotion to the referee process that evidences a selfless devotion to quality scholarship.

Finally, I thank all of the people who provided information for the studies that led to the chapters in this volume. Most of the informants were anonymous. Due to the promise of anonymity that we ethnographers and qualitative researchers make to our informants, these people cannot be named. They are, however, the most vital aspect of the research; their interest in the subject and cooperation with the researcher ensures the reliability and validity of qualitative research.

Notes on Contributors

Linda B. Arthur is Associate Professor of Textiles and Clothing and Curator of the Historic Costume Collection at the University of Hawai'i at Manoa. Even before her doctoral work at the University of California, she focused her research on the intersection of gender, ethnicity and ideology and the impact of these social locations on women's appearance. While her publications in the past two decades have been on exclusive groups and ethno-religious groups in the United States, Dr Arthur's current research focus is on ethnicity and identity in Asia and the Pacific. Dr Arthur has recently published a book on Hawaiian dress entitled *Aloha Attire: Hawaiian Dress in the Twentieth Century (2000)*, as well as an earlier volume from Berg's *Dress, Body Culture* series, entitled *Religion, Dress and the Body (1999)*. She has another book on the development of Hawaiian textiles under contract.

Inwoo Chang is an assistant professor on the faculty of the Clothing and Textiles department at Inchon University in Seoul, Korea. Born and educated in Korea, she received her PhD with a specialization in the history of Korean costume from the Graduate School of Dong-kook University and is a scholar who specializes in Korea's costume from the Choson Dynasty.

L. Kaye Crippen is currently starting a marketing consulting firm. Most recently she lived in Indonesia and had a research permit from Lembaga Ilmu Pengetahuan Indonesia (LIPI). Previously she was Director, Southeast Asia for Asian Markets Research and co-authored *Asian Festivals and Customs*. She taught new product development and marketing in the MBA program at the National University of Singapore. Dr Crippen has a multi-disciplinary background having worked as a research chemist in textile fibers and international marketing at DuPont. In addition, she was the area co-ordinator at the University of Houston and was an Associate Professor at California State University at Los Angeles.

M. Catherine Daly is on the faculty at the University of Nebraska (US) in the Department of Textiles, Clothing and Design and is also a research associate with the Center for Afghanistan Studies at the University of Nebraska at

Omaha. Her work focuses on human rights issues and textile craft economies related to Afghan women and the politics of their appearance. In 1998 she was a Fulbright Scholar teaching at the National College of Arts in Lahore, Pakistan and conducting research in the Afghan refugee camps and the development agencies that support Afghan women living in Peshawar, Pakistan.

Shannen Hill teaches Art History at the University of Denver and is a Ph.D. Candidate at the University of Wisconsin-Madison. Her dissertation is entitled "Making martyrs: Bantu Stephen Biko's changing legacy in South African visual culture". Her research interests include intersections of art and political activism, violence and representation, and contemporary visual expressions in South Africa and Cuba. She has published on censorship in the visual arts, biographies of African and African American artists, reviewed books and exhibitions of contemporary African art, and co-authored a video on art from Cameroon.

William J. F. Keenan is a senior lecturer in Sociology in the Department of Social Sciences at the Nottingham Trent University, England. His research interests include symbolic traditions and cultural identity and postmodern transformations in higher education. He has published extensively on religious symbolic culture in the spheres of death and dress. He is preparing an edited volume in this series for Berg; it is entitled *Dressed to Impress: Looking the Part.* He has served as a national subject quality assessor in sociology in Great Britain and has taught at the university level for thirty years.

Lynn A. Meisch received her PhD in anthropology from Stanford University in 1997 and joined the faculty of Saint Mary's College of California, Moraga, as an assistant professor of anthropology. She has conducted fieldwork in Colombia, Ecuador, Peru and Bolivia since 1973 and published on such topics as *artesanías,* traditional Andean textiles, costume and ethnicity, globalization, tourism, the indigenous rights movement and the prevention of intractable ethnic violence in Ecuador.

Patricia M. Mulready is presently associated with Sloboldkina House, Glen Head, NY, in archival and development capacities. She was formerly Program Director for fashion, retailing, consumer studies and education graduate and undergraduate programs at New York University. She also taught at the University of Maryland Eastern Shore and the University of Delaware and was an adjunct faculty member at Hood College and Queens College. She has led/participated in numerous research studies, most notably as the Principal

Investigator for the original *Glamour* Magazine psychology of fashion survey, also contributing to the follow-up work in 1994.

Elisha P. Renne is an assistant professor in the Department of Anthropology and the Center for Afroamerican and African Studies at the University of Michigan (USA). She has conducted research on textiles in several parts of Nigeria, including the Niger delta area (Kalabari Ijo), Southwestern Nigeria (Bunu and Ekiti Yoruba) and Northern Nigeria (Hausa). Her work focuses on the ways that textile traditions in Nigeria are selectively preserved and altered. Her Book, *Cloth That Does Not Die: The Meaning Of Cloth In Bunu Social Life*, was published in 1995 by the University of Washington Press (Seattle). Dr Renne has had articles published in *African Arts*, *Economic Development and Cultural Change* and in several edited volumes including *Dress and Ethnicity and Clothing and Difference*.

Faegheh Shirazi is an assistant professor in the department of Middle East Languages and Cultures at the University of Texas at Austin, Texas (USA). Her major area of interest is the subject of material culture and its influence on gender identity and discourse in Islamic societies. Clothing, particularly the Islamic Veil (*hijab*), is the main focus of her research. She also focuses on the issues related to women, rituals and rites of passage as they relate to material cultures in contemporary Muslim societies. She is the author of scholarly articles in diverse journals such as *Critique: Journal of the Critical Studies in The Middle East, Journal of the International Association of Costume, Ars Textrina, Material History Review Journal* and the *National Museum of Science and Technology*. Her most recent scholarly work includes a recently finished manuscript (in press 2001), *The Veil Unveiled: Visual, Political and Literary Dynamics of the Veil*.

Joseph Stimpfl is an associate professor of anthropology and director of the Center for International Studies at Webster University in St. Louis, Missouri (USA). He holds advanced degrees from the University of Missouri and the University of Pittsburgh. His research interests focus on Southeast Asian culture and society with particular emphasis on Malays, Southeast Asian refugees and ethnic conflict. He has conducted research in Singapore, Malaysia, Indonesia and Thailand.

Emma Tarlo is a lecturer in the Department of Anthropology, Goldsmith's College, University of London. She has done fieldwork in rural and urban Gujarat and in Delhi. Her most recent work concerns the lives of people displaced from Delhi (cf. *Unsettling Memories: Narratives of the Emergency* *in Delhi*, forthcoming with Hurst.) Her chapter in this volume is an extract from her book *Clothing Matters: Dress and Identity in India* (1996, London: Hurst and University of Chicago Press). We would like to thank Hurst for permission to reproduce this extract and the British Academy for funding the research on which it is based.

Susan Tselos received her Master's degree in Museum Studies from John F. Kennedy University in California (USA). Her specialization on Haiti has involved twelve years of research on the material culture and sacred arts of the Vodou religion. She has lectured extensively on the material culture of Haitian Vodou and has written articles on the topic, including one in *African Arts* (Spring, 1996 issue). Susan has curated several exhibits on the material culture of Haiti. She has collected numerous pieces of sacred art from Haiti which now reside in the permanent collection at the Fowler Museum of Cultural History at UCLA. Many of these pieces were included in the Fowler Museum's exhibition "The Sacred Arts of Haitian Vodou" which closed a four-year tour at The Museum of Natural History in New York in 1999.

Haekyung L. Yu was born and educated in Seoul, South Korea. She came to the United States for graduate school and earned her MS degree in textiles from the University of Wisconsin-Madison and her PhD at the University of Maryland-College Park. She taught at Indiana University in Bloomington, Indiana for three years before returning to Korea where she is an associate professor in the Department of Clothing and Textiles at the University of Inchon. Her research interests are in marketing the economic aspects of textiles and clothing. Recently she has been working on several projects involving the ethnic dress of Korea and other Asian countries.

List of Illustrations

Introduction

The interaction between religion and culture is fascinating. In an earlier volume in Berg's Dress, Body and Culture series (*Religion, Dress and the Body*, 1999) we explored the ways that the body and by extension, dress can be evidence of the social control of identity in America's ethno-religious groups. In most of the cultures included in that volume, dress was a visible and powerful agent of social control. However that is not the case in the current volume. In *Undressing Religion: Commitment and Conversion from a Cross-Cultural Perspective,* we examine the interaction of religion and culture in other parts of the world where dress provides evidence of both adaptation to cultural change and expression of religious identity.

Religions have provided ideological support and institutional resources for a number of significant social change movements throughout the world (Kurtz, 1995). Because faith traditions can either sustain or subvert social systems, some religions attract a system's elites, whereas those on the margins may have a natural affinity with other religious beliefs or interpretations of the same traditions. Elites tend to use religious arguments to explain why they are in power, while dissidents also use religious rhetoric to legitimate their own positions. From its origins, the field of sociology has noted the centrality of religion within cultural systems. While most of the early sociologists (Marx, Durkheim and Weber) studied religion from a neo-classical perspective that tended to be subjective, in more recent years sociologists have approached the study of religion with a structural approach. Mary Douglas (1982), for instance, examined the way that, through culture, peoples' bodies become representations of the social body. Still another approach to the study of religion is the use of a dramaturgical approach through which the expressive or communicative properties of an ethno-religious culture are examined. This approach can be traced to both Durkheim and, more recently, Goffman. The most contemporary perspective to the study of religion is an institutional focus, in which people with special competencies produce and sustain culture within religious institutions. All these approaches are represented in this volume and represent an attempt to draw connections between the ways in which identity, visually manifest in dress, expresses values – religious on the one hand and cultural on the other.

In *The Elementary Forms of the Religious Life*, Durkheim (1954) argued that religion is at the base of all social and cultural behavior. He posited that simple societies were held together by homogeneity and conformity, but that as societies modernized, secularization would become increasingly important at the same time as organized religions would lose strength. His projections have come true. Well known for his distinction between the sacred and the profane, Durkheim also brought our attention to the importance of symbols and ritual in the reinforcement of cultural values. Following that line of thinking, Goffman (1967) examined social interaction; he showed how social action secularized religious morality and in doing so continued Durkheim's analysis of the shift from the prominence of organized religion to the sanctification of the individual. In essence, Goffman showed that symbolic behavior and face-to-face interaction are secularized forms of religious ritual (Chriss, 1993). Goffman stated:

> I want to explore some of the senses in which the person in our urban secular world is allotted a kind of sacredness that is displayed and confirmed by symbolic acts . . . Through these reformulations I will try to show that a version of Durkheim's social psychology can be effective in modern dress (cited in Chriss, 1993).

Dress includes both body supplements, such as clothing and accessories and behaviors, such as dieting, plastic surgery and cosmetics, leading to changes in body shape. Holistically, then, dress functions as an effective means of non-verbal communication during social interaction; it influences the establishment and projection of identity (Roach-Higgins and Eicher, 1992).

Dress is important in social interaction. For Goffman (1959, 1963) there are three important features regarding the dressed body. First, the body and dress can be used as a social resource. By dressing the part, we can manipulate social situations to our benefit. Second, when we dress the part, we locate ourselves within our social and cultural environments and we do the same for others, as we recognize symbolic meanings. In this event, dress is used as a form of non-verbal communication and forms a shared vocabulary. Third, by using dress to successfully play a role, we recognize that we have both a personal and a social identity. In every act of getting dressed, we are dealing with issues of identity, asking ourselves who we are and who we wish to be (Evenson and Trayte, 1999).

What Goffman understood was that all societies have complex social norms predicated on non-verbal and symbolic behavior. Norms are codes of behavior that indicate what acts are considered appropriate and evidence the group understanding of or appreciation for the nature of the social event or gathering (Chriss, 1993). Goffman (1967, p. 90) stated that "the rules of conduct which bind the actor and the recipient together are the bindings of society." He depicted a social action predicated on the notion of a civil religion whose outward manifestations are the tacit set of rules, customs, conventions and rituals that guide face-to-face interaction. He emphasized that individuals are driven into self-presentation and self-promotion in order to present what is considered by the group to be an appropriate expression of identity (Chriss, 1993). Nowhere is this behavior more evident than with dress as an expression of religious identity, the focus of this volume.

From Islam to Confucianism to Vodou, dress plays a pivotal role in religious expression. This book examines how dress symbolically is a part of both religious and cultural systems across a wide range of cultures, from Africa and South America to Asia, Indonesia, Malaysia and the Caribbean. Dress figures prominently in these cultures as a means of representing, sometimes concurrently, both agency and control. Members of each group actively construct their own lives and use dress symbolically to express religious beliefs. In some of the case studies presented in this volume, gender issues are paramount since the control of female sexuality is often of great importance in the world's religions. Drawing on rich case studies, this wide-ranging and interdisciplinary volume represents a major contribution to the study of both religion and dress.

The first section of the book is devoted to African and Haitian cultures where the tensions relating to accommodating Christianity leads to changes in indigenous religious systems. Cloth is an ideal medium for representing identity shifts. In the first chapter Renne shows that the presence of hand-woven Yoruba textiles in ecclesiastical dress demonstrates the ability of clothing to show a close connection between cloth and the body. In Ekiti, these textiles are used to assert the wearer's modern African identity that is simultaneously a Roman Catholic identity. In Chapter Two Hill shows how material culture and ritual performance recall well-established Bakongo religious convictions. A fusing of identities between the ritual experts and spirits is evidenced through material culture. Similarly, in Chapter Three Tselos shows Haiti's syncreticization of indigenous African and Christian elements in Vodou. Here too, the ritual practitioner is transformed from an ordinary worshipper to a divine vessel of the spirits; the body is co-opted by the spirit and the transformation is made manifest by changes in dress.

The role of Christianity in colonization of the Andes is discussed in Chapter Four. Although missionaries in the area have consistently proscribed the wearing of certain items of indigenous dress, Meisch notes that Christianization is incomplete in the Andes and this is reflected in beliefs and practices involving clothing. The dress of an order of Catholic teaching Brothers, the Marist Brothers, is examined in Chapter Five. Although this order developed a very detailed dress code during its history, social changes within the Catholic Church have resulted in dress modernization and liberalization. In doing so, Keenan shows the power of rationality to work both for ecclesiology and against spirituality.

Archeological evidence from sixteenth- and seventeenth-century grave sites in Korea is the basis for the research reported in Chapter Six. The shift from Buddhism to Confucianism led to gendered changes in dress in the Choson dynasty; these are visually manifest in Korean burial garments.

Change is also a focus of Chapter Eleven on Bali, where Crippen and Mulready discuss the changing role of a complex double *ikat* fabric called *geringsing*. This fabric is customarily used in Balinese Hindu religious ceremonies but the use of this fabric is undergoing change due to aesthetic and economic reasons.

The veil is a social enigma; it provokes controversy. To explore its meaning the remaining chapters of this volume focus on the role of the veil and head coverings in the sexual segregation of several societies. In Chapter Seven, Shirazi examines the relationship between Islam and dress codes in Iran. The practice of *hijab* (veiling) is shown to have multiple layers of symbolic meaning not easily understood from an outsider's perspective. Similarly, in Chapter Eight Daly uses an insider's perspective to shed light on the use of the *chaadaree* (whole-body veil) in Afghanistan. It is a multi-vocal symbol dependent on numerous aspects for its interpretation. The use of clothing and the veil in India, and their roles in gendered power, is presented in Chapter Nine in an excerpt from Tarlo's *Clothing Matters*. As Stimpfl shows us in Chapter Ten, Malaysian women in Singapore use a hybrid form of veiling to reject Westernization while they articulate a new identity as educated Malay women. Finally, in Chapter Twelve, the conflict over head coverings in Indonesian school uniforms was used to point out how ideologies continue to be expressed through dress. In Indonesia, the inclusion of rules allowing for Muslim head coverings and dress codes within the existing school uniform regulations points to conflict between Indonesia's two competing ideologies: a formal religion, Islam, and a civil religion, Pancasila.

In sum, dress can visually manifest the salient ideas and concepts fundamental to a culture; what dress does is to make tangible the basic categories a culture uses to define its particular conception of reality. Categories such as age, gender, caste, ethnicity and religion help to define a person's social location and are made visible when ethno-religious cultures make dress salient. Dress can be a window into the social world, as we see in this volume.

References

Chriss, J. (1993). Durkheim's cult of the individual as civil religion: its appropriation by Erving Goffman. *Sociological Spectrum*, 13, pp. 251–75.

Douglas, M. (1982). *Natural Symbols*: New York: Pantheon Books.

Durkheim, E. (1954) *The elementary forms of the religious life*. Trans. J. Swain. Glencoe: Free Press.

Evenson, S. and Trayte, D. (1999). Dress and interaction in contending cultures: Eastern Dakota and Euroamericans in Nineteenth Century Minnesota In L. B. Arthur, (Ed.) *Religion, dress and the body*. (pp. 95–116). Oxford: Berg.

Goffman, E. (1959). *The presentation of self in everyday life*. Garden City, N.J.: Doubleday.

Goffman, E. (1963). *Stigma: Notes on the management of spoiled identity*. Englewood Cliffs, N.J.: Prentice-Hall.

Goffman, E. (1967). *Interaction ritual*. Chicago: Aldine.

Goffman, E. (1971). *Relations in public*. New York: Harper and Row.

Kurtz, L. (1995). *Gods in the global village: The world's religions in sociological perspective*. Thousand Oaks, Calif.: Pine Forge Press.

Roach-Higgins, M. and Eicher, J. (1992). Dress and identity. *Clothing and Textiles Research Journal*, 10 (1), pp.1–8.

References

1

Cloth and Conversion: Yoruba Textiles and Ecclesiastical Dress

Elisha P. Renne

Do not lie to one another, seeing that you have stripped off the old self with its practices and have clothed yourself with the new self . . .

Colossians 3: 9,10

During the nineteenth and early twentieth centuries in southwestern Nigeria, part of the conversion process included the donning of new styles of dress and the taking of new names provided by European missionaries (Ajayi, 1965). For example, during the 1841 Niger Expedition, two freed women slaves were given English dresses and the names of Hannah Buxton and Elizabeth Fry (Allen and Thomson, 1967, p. 87). Nigerian-born missionaries who trained in Sierra Leone's Church Missionary Society schools also wore European dress and the Bishop Samuel A. Crowther was "always wearing European clothes" (Ayandele, 1966, p. 206; see Figure 1.1).

Local interpretations of European dress using imported materials emerged in the late 1920s as the leaders of African Christian churches such as the Cherubim and Seraphim sought to develop their own distinctive styles of worship and apparel (Omoyajowo,1982; Parrinder, 1953; Turner, 1967). This adaptation of Christianity to meet African spiritual needs may be seen more recently in the use of Yoruba narrow-strip hand-woven cloth (*aso ofi*) in traditional Christian vestments such as chasubles[1] worn by Catholic priests as well as in the *aso ofi* habits worn by nuns, associated with the implementation of Vatican II. This chapter examines the use of hand-woven Yoruba textiles in ecclesiastical dress, with specific examples from Ekiti State, Nigeria. It focuses on the process whereby locally hand-woven cloth, formerly associated with traditional Yoruba practices, including religious ritual, has been both disassociated from these beliefs and linked with a modern African identity.

Research in Southwestern Nigeria

This research project on the use of locally hand-woven cloth in church vestments began inadvertently, with a single detail noted during dissertation fieldwork in the Kabba area of southwestern Nigeria in 1987. Prior to moving

Figure 1.1 Bishop Samuel Ajayi Crowther (From E. A. Ayandele, The Missionary Impact on Modern Nigeria, London: Longman, 1966, opposite page 237; reprinted by permission of The Church Mission Society Archive.)

to the small Bunu Yoruba village of Agbede-Apaa where my dissertation research was actually conducted, I stayed with the Obasaju family in Kabba. The late Mr F.O. Obasaju, a devout Catholic and active church leader, used to attend St Augustine Catholic Church in Kabba every Sunday morning. I would often accompany his daughter, Mary, to Sunday mass. At one of these services, I noticed a priest wearing a smock-like chasuble made of brown hand-woven narrow-strips (*aso oke*), the type of cloth associated with Yoruba narrow-strip weaving (Clarke, 1997; Eicher, 1975; Lamb and Holmes, 1980; Picton and Mack, 1979). I remember being surprised and intrigued by this garment, the only such hand-woven vestment that I had seen at St Augustine's. However, once I moved to the village, there was no opportunity to pursue the subject further.

Several years later, in 1997, having completed a post-doctoral fellowship that involved research in the small Ekiti Yoruba town of Itapa-Ekiti, about 45 miles east of Kabba, I returned to Itapa to conduct follow-up research on the 1991 Nigerian census. Since there is a large Catholic population in Ekiti State, it occurred to me that I might have an opportunity to learn more about hand-woven cloth used in Catholic services there.

I began by asking Mr Kayode Owoeye, a researcher from the area, to speak with Catholic priests in Ikole-Ekiti and Itapa-Ekiti about any hand-woven vestments that they used in services. A priest in Itapa explained that at the seminary he attended, the use of hand-woven narrow-strip cloth (*aso oke*; in Ekiti referred to as *aso ofi*) in church dress was advocated. This priest recommended that we visit Cathedral Bookshop and Bishop's Court, both in Ado-Ekiti. A few weeks later we traveled to Ado-Ekiti and spoke with Anglican fathers at Bishop's Court. We found that while hand-woven cloth was used, it was primarily found in stoles. It was the next week, in July 1997, when we visited the reverend fathers at the Church of Mary Immaculate that the full range of hand-woven narrow-strip cloth (*aso ofi*) in church vestments became evident. One priest directed us to the church bookshop where several chasubles using *aso ofi* cloth were displayed. A nun working at the bookshop advised us to talk with Bishop Fagun, the Lord Bishop of Ekiti Diocese. Bishop Fagun explained the sequence of events, including the encyclical documents circulated after 1962, known as Vatican II, that encouraged the use of locally produced textiles in ecclesiastical garments worn in Catholic services. In order to understand why wearing hand-woven cloth in church is a relatively new development, background is provided in the following section on traditional Yoruba religion and the introduction of Roman Catholicism in the Ekiti area.

Elisha P. Renne

Traditional Worship and the Roman
Catholic Church in Ekiti

The first Roman Catholic Mission that opened in Ado-Ekiti in 1912 was staffed initially by Europeans who were later joined by Nigerians. According to Monsignor Oguntuyi (1979, p. 103), these early Catholic priests insisted that converts "renounce every kind of superstitious beliefs and to be clear on the nature of Christian marriage – monogamy and the inseparability of valid marriage." In referring to superstitious beliefs, Oguntuyi is referring to practices associated with traditional Yoruba religion, a polytheistic religious system that the Roman Catholic Mission hoped to supersede.

Traditional religious practice in Ekiti included worship at shrines devoted to various nature deities, known as *imole*, associated with particular geographical locations, such as streams and hilltops (Ojo, 1966). Other deities, sometimes referred to as *orisha*, were worshipped for their control over certain substances or situations. For example, the worship of the God of Iron, Ogun, was common throughout Ekiti as was that of the much-feared God of Smallpox, Soponno (Awolalu, 1979; also known locally as Baba Orisha, "Father of the Gods") and the God of Lightning, Shango (Apter, 1992). Some deities and nature spirits were worshipped by entire communities; in Itapa-Ekiti, the deity Aorogun, associated with a particular inselberg was so worshipped (Owoeye, 1999). Others were worshipped by more localized groups such as particular town quarters or families. There were also specific deities that individuals could worship, depending on their own particular preferences and situations (Barber, 1981).

The followers of some of these deities wore particular cloths during rituals such as annual festivals and special sacrifices. One woman in Ilupeju-Ekiti, who continues to worship *imole* spirits (particularly the Yoruba deity Olokun associated with the sea) described the types of cloths used by worshippers:

> People normally use white cloth called *aso ala* during the *orisha* festival Oro Omi . . . This white cloth is tied with a red cloth called *oja adodo*.[2] These are the cloths that *onimole* [worshippers of *imole*] used to celebrate. This cloth is also used at the Olokun festival.
>
> Shango worshippers will attach some cowry shells to their skirts – it has to be a big skirt and it should be red in color. Messengers of Shango [who are men dressed as women] will dye their own cloth in black or blue; they will also attach cowry shells to it. This cloth is called *apatunpa*, it is old stuff, one can hardly find it now.
>
> A female Shango worshipper will make hers red; this is because the uniform of Shango is red; male Shango worshippers make use of black cloths (Interview: Yeye Molomo, Ilupeju-Ekiti, August 1997).

All three of these cloths used in the worship of the deities Olokun or Shango could have been locally woven with handspun cotton thread on vertical broad looms used by Ekiti Yoruba women in the past (Lamb and Holmes, 1980). In the case of white cloths, these cloths could simply be used as they came off the loom while black and dark blue cloths were dyed with indigo, commonly done in Ekiti (Oguntuyi, 1979, p. 23). Red cloths presented more of a problem. It is difficult to dye cotton red although camwood may have been used. Imported red cloths were also purchased when available. The local production of these cloths coincides with the local bases of these deities.

While a small group of followers such as Yeye Molomo continue *imole* and *orisha* worship today, the majority of Ekiti residents practice some form of Christianity or Islam.[3] The shift from polytheism to monotheism, particularly Christianity, began at the very end of the nineteenth and at the beginning of the twentieth centuries in Ekiti.

The Introduction of Christianity to Ekiti

The first mission to be established in Ado-Ekiti was the Anglican mission of the Church Missionary Society in 1895. Methodist (in 1910), Catholic (in 1912) and Baptist (1915) missions soon followed (Oguntuyi, 1979, p. 100), a pattern established in many towns and villages throughout Ekiti. This introduction of Christianity to Ekiti largely coincided with the British intervention that ended inter-Yoruba warfare in the area in 1886 and its incorporation into the Protectorate of Southern Nigeria under British colonial rule in 1906. While the missions in Ado-Ekiti (which was the Ekiti District headquarters during the colonial period) had European priests and pastors, in the rural areas churches were started by local people who had worked in large towns as migrant laborers. Having converted while in Lagos or other cities in southern Nigeria, they returned to their home towns where they attempted to convert others to their new faith. Early Christians faced considerable hostility from traditionalists who saw Christianity as a threat to their own beliefs (Oguntuyi, 1979; Owoeye, 1999).

Nonetheless, these men persisted and by the 1930s many fellow towns-people and Ekiti villagers became church members. Some were attracted by the prospects of education and health care associated with church missions. New styles of dress, associated with Europeans, were also part of this attraction as one Itapa-Ekiti man explained:

Two people used to take me to the church, they were Pa Edward and Oginni. They used to put on khaki shorts called pajamas and they would wear round neck singlets.[4] These people had traveled out and were civilized, so whenever they put on their dress (of khaki and singlets), everybody in the town looked at them as miniature gods.⁵ People admired them and talked of them everywhere. This was one of the joys I inherited from these people and which attracted my interest in having education (Interview: African Church Bishop Jawolusi, Itapa-Ekiti, August 1997).⁶

While the use of European dress associated with conversion became widespread, older cloths used in traditional religious worship were rejected as relics of "pagan practices": "The types of cloth they used in worship in traditional religion were all burnt or were thrown in the bush because people didn't admire it anymore. The cloth was black and like velvet and it was the rich ones who used it" (Interview: Mr Akanle, Itapa-Ekiti, July 1997).

Catholic priests, both Europeans and Nigerians, working in Ekiti also wore primarily black garments. But these garments were tailored, made from manufactured cloth (*aso oyinbo*) in European styles, as a way of distinguishing themselves from those with superstitious beliefs and practices. For example, the Monsignor Oguntuyi of Ado-Ekiti was accustomed to wearing "black cassocks, black shoes and black socks to match, almost all of the time" (Ojo, n.d., p. 22). In church services, ecclesiastical vestments such as chasubles, stoles and miters would have been imported, European-made articles. As Peel (1978) has observed, objects from overseas, associated with *olaju* (translated as "enlightenment" or "civilization"; literally, "opening of one's eyes"), have been a powerful force for change in Yoruba social life. With such things, individuals and groups have been able to distinguish themselves from others while at the same time attracting others to them. Bishop Jawolusi, in the quotation cited above, makes reference to this association of these people with *olaju* ("these people . . . were civilized") and with new styles of dress ("khaki and singlets"), as well as the admiration felt for those who wore it ("everybody in the town looked at them as miniature gods").

Yet in the 90 years or so in which Roman Catholicism has been practiced in Ekiti, both in large towns such as Ado-Ekiti and small ones such as Itapa, there has been a shift in this exclusive association of Christianity with European dress and textiles. Currently, the Lord Bishop of Ekiti Diocese, Bishop Fagun, wears a range of European and Yoruba dress including the use of chasubles made of *aso ofi* cloth with machine-embroidery of religious themes such as that of St George slaying the dragon. He also mentioned the use of *aso ofi* cloth in albs, in censers and in altar cloths. Locally-made *aso ofi* textiles are no longer associated with "heathenism" but rather with a Nigerian identity, made manifest with the independence of the Nigerian state celebrated in 1960 and with the new vision of a diverse but universal Catholic identity supported by the implementation of Vatican II in 1962.

Church Production of *Aso ofi* Vestments in Ekiti

Attending church services in Ekiti, one is struck by the plethora of hand-woven narrow-strip cloths worn by parishioners as well as by the hand-woven *aso ofi* vestments sometimes worn by priests. What is less obvious than the actual wearing of vestments made of *aso ofi* cloth is the production of these garments by Catholic sisters. In Ado-Ekiti, this production has two parts; first, cloth is being woven by the Sisters of St Michael's the Archangel (SSMA) Generalate. There, one large room is devoted to handweaving on floor looms, some of which were brought from Emure-Ekiti. The sisters were taught to weave by local weavers and they themselves will be taking apprentices to train them to weave.[7]

Once woven, the fabric is taken to a tailoring workshop next to the bookshop on the grounds of the Church of Mary Immaculate, Ado-Ekiti, where the sisters have a tailoring center for making chasubles and other church garments using *aso ofi*. Indeed, one finished chasuble was on display in the shop, selling for N5000 (around $60 US in 1997). This particular robe would be used at weddings, celebrations, Thanksgiving and any celebratory occasion. A small album contained photographs of other examples of these sisters' work. One of the sisters said that the making and selling of these robes in Ado-Ekiti is a recent occurrence, within the past two years. While Vatican II provided a primary impetus for the use of hand-woven cloth in Catholic services in Ado, the economy has also supported this trend. Since the official devaluation of the currency in 1986, vestments obtained from overseas have become prohibitively expensive. Church leaders began to realize that they could produce appropriate vestments themselves in Nigeria. At least one chasuble owned by Bishop Fagun was made in Ado-Ekiti from cloth woven by the sisters at St Michael's (Interview: Bishop Fagun, Ado-Ekiti, July 1997).

While nuns in Ado-Ekiti weave church vestments used by bishops and priests, they themselves continue to wear blue and white habits made of manufactured cloth. There is one occasion, however, when nuns do wear hand-woven *aso ofi* dress as part of church ritual. This is during the ordination of young women as nuns, when they take their vows (the First Profession service) as brides of ChriSt At the beginning of the ceremony, they dress as Yoruba brides, wearing *aso ofi* wrappers, tops and headties, normally in blue and white. They wear this dress only once in their lives, during the First Profession service, as it vividly symbolizes their role as brides of Christ and their transition from a worldly life to a religious one.

A First Profession Service

On 7 August 1997, nine young Yoruba women took part in the First Profession service presided over by Bishop Fagun at Ado-Ekiti. Prior to the ceremony they mixed with guests, identically dressed, wearing blue and white *aso ofi* wrappers, blouses and head-tie, embroidered in white (Figure 1.2). The ceremony began with the young women and their parents entering the church along a walkway followed by sisters and a range of church dignitaries, including visiting priests and the Bishop Fagun. The service was conducted in Yoruba with prayers and singing, culminating in the young women being led down the church aisle with their parents, some of whom also wore *aso ofi* outfits, as did several visitors and family members. On taking her vows, each young woman was given a white habit, after which they all walked along the aisle to the back of the church. After a few minutes they re-emerged, wearing their blue and white habits and carrying white candles (Figure 1.3). The emotional aspect of the service was heightened by the dramatic contrast of "traditional" hand-woven Yoruba dress and "modern" manufactured foreign dress, reflecting very different ideas about religious piety and conjugality.

Figure 1.2 Catholic novitiates wearing identical *aso ofi* outfits at their First Profession, Mary Immaculate Church, Ado-Ekiti, 7 July 1997 (Photo: E. P. Renne).

Discussion

The seeming contrast between traditional African practices and modern western religious identities associated with the use of hand-woven Yoruba cloth and manufactured textiles worn in this service is actually not so clear-cut. For example, the *aso ofi* cloth (either woven in narrow-strips or on floorlooms and later cut) used by the novitiates are not traditional textiles in the Ekiti area. Rather, women wove handspun cotton thread into wide-width panels of cloth, *aso ofi*, on single-heddle vertical handlooms. These wide cloths were then sewn together and worn as wrappers. The blouse-like tops (*buba*) that they wore were also a recent innovation, introduced around 1919. Prior to that time, women wore wrappers (*iro*) and sometimes a shoulder cloth (*iponlerun*; Oguntuyi, 1979, 15). Thus while the service made references to certain African practices (the wearing of narrow-strip hand-woven cloth, the traditional Yoruba dress style of *iro* and *buba* and drumming, what

Figure 1.3 Catholic novitiates after taking vows, wearing identical blue and white habits, at their First Profession, Mary Immaculate Church, Ado-Ekiti, 7 July 1997 (Photo: E. P. Renne).

transpired was an example of "the invention of tradition" (Hobsbawm and Ranger, 1983) as their particular form was quite new in Ekiti. Indeed, older practices such as the wearing of untailored hand-woven cloth and drumming were carefully divested of associations with traditional religion (the nuns wore tailored dress and used their hands rather than a curved stick to drum). Rather than a revival of a traditional African past, what emerged was a modern invention – an amalgam of modified traditional practices (e.g., the use of new, fashionable hand-woven *aso ofi* cloth rather than old but also old-fashioned hand-woven *aso ofi* cloth) in a recently introduced ritual – that of the First Profession.

Elsewhere I have referred to this construction of a sense of continuity with past cultural traditions while simultaneously introducing new practices as "traditional modernity" (Renne, 1997). At the First Profession ceremony, it is strikingly exemplified by the dress of one visitor, Sister Monica Rowland, a nun at the Bishop Kelly Pastoral Center in Benin City (Figure 1.4). She attended the service wearing the habit of this center, made from a type of *aso ofi* cloth woven by the sisters there (Interview: Sister Monica Rowland, Ado-Ekiti, July 1997). This cloth is visually similar to the old-fashioned *kijipa* hand-woven in Ekiti and elsewhere in eastern Yorubaland. Yet the domestic production of such *aso ofi* cloth by women in Benin has not taken place there since the early part of the twentieth century (Ben-Amos, 1978). Unfortunately I did not ask Sister Monica if the cloth she wore was woven on a handloom or vertical single-heddle loom; it could have been either although I suspect it was on the former. In its old-fashioned appearance, it suggests a sort of "conspicuous archaism" (Cort, 1989), made acceptable by Vatican II with the emphasis on natural textiles that emphasize cultural distinctiveness within the universal rubric of the Church.

Vatican Council II and Natural Fabrics

The styles of dress, colors of cloth and types of textiles that have been used in religious practice in Ekiti and elsewhere in southwestern Nigeria reflect distinctive interpretations of Christianity as well as changing relations between Africans and Europeans. One of the most striking examples of a reinterpretation of these practices and relationships may be seen in the shift from an emphasis on western textiles and dress to one on local customs regarding church garments. Bishop Fagun and others attributed this shift to Vatican Council II and the conciliar and post-conciliar documents released in 1962 and thereafter.

While many non-Catholics may associate changes instituted by Vatican II with the use of vernacular languages rather than Latin in masses, this shift was part of a general move to incorporate a range of indigenous customs into Catholic worship. The adoption of vestments using local materials in church rituals was explicitly mentioned in the General Instruction on the Roman Missal:

> 304. Bishops' conferences may determine and propose to the Holy See any adaptations in the shape or style of vestments which they consider desirable by reason of local customs or needs.

Figure 1.4 Sister Monica Rowland, a nun from in Benin City, attended the First Profession, wearing habit woven at the Bishop Kelly Pastoral Centre in Benin City, Nigeria (Photo: E. P. Renne).

305. Besides the materials traditionally used for making sacred vestments, natural fabrics from each region are admissible, as also artificial fabrics which accord with the dignity of the sacred action and of those who are to wear the vestments. It is for the Bishops' conference to decide on these materials.

306. The beauty and dignity of liturgical vestments is to be sought in the excellence of their material and the elegance of their cut, rather than in an abundance of adventitious ornamentation. Any images, symbols or figures employed in decorating vestments should be sacred in character and exclude anything inappropriate (Flannery, 1992, p. 197).

This shift in church policy toward local customs or needs reflects a rethinking of earlier practices that is both open-minded and pragmatic. It is open-minded in that it suggests an acknowledgment that Western culture is not the only or highest cultural tradition of merit and beauty, an underlying subtext of colonial evangelists' insistence on converts using western dress in church services. It is pragmatic in its realization that a Catholicism revitalized by Vatican II could play a important role in supporting former colonial peoples' "efforts to create [local] institutions" that sustain their self-worth and communities (Hefner, 1993, p. 25). In so doing, the Church is better positioned to maintain the loyalty of its followers who might be tempted to defect by the influx of various Christian Pentecostal sects that have developed in Nigeria in recent years.

While Vatican II is encouraging "natural fabrics for the region" be used in ecclesiastical vestments reflecting a distinctive cultural past, Roman Catholicism continues to link local peoples with a world organization that transcends national boundaries. The Church provides opportunities for exposure to things outside, a valued attribute associated with Yoruba ideas about *olaju* (enlightenment) as mentioned earlier. Thus in the First Profession ceremony, the use of both hand-woven narrow-strip *aso ofi* cloth worn in Yoruba fashion and manufactured cloth (*aso oyinbo*) worn in Western styles may be interpreted as an attempt to bridge these two identities – as Yoruba practitioners of a Western world religion and as Roman Catholics who reside in Southwestern Nigeria.

The Habits of Nuns

The forms of dress worn by Ekiti Yoruba nuns in the First Profession ceremony express a local identity situated in the particular social, cultural, political and economic contexts of post-colonial Nigeria. The fact that the reforms of Vatican II were introduced shortly after Nigerian independence in 1960 after sixty years of colonial rule further strengthened Nigerian Catholics' resolve to integrate African cultural practices into their religious worship. As has been discussed, various modifications have taken place in Catholic masses, such as the conducting of services in Yoruba, the inclusion of drumming[8] and the use of hand-woven, narrow-strip Yoruba textiles. Nonetheless, a certain tension remains as to how, exactly, a balance between a Western-based religious identity – as Roman Catholics – and a Nigerian cultural identity – as Ekiti Yoruba – may be achieved. As A. O. Makozi and G. J. A. Ojo (1982, p. 2) have observed:

> Theoretically, there were two diametrically opposed positions in the evangelization of Nigeria. The first was that in order to found a local church and a viable Catholic Community, Nigerian socio-religious customs must supersede those of the West and her missionaries, the products of Western culture. The second position was that to found the Catholic Church in Nigeria the indigenous culture, which is repugnant to Western Christianity and Rome, the fountain-head of Catholic orthodoxy, must be suppressed and replaced by the Western expression of Christianity.

> These two approaches have not ceased to clash today, even with the newly accepted notion of indigenization of the Catholic Church in Nigeria. These positions are not always as clear-cut as they may appear to be and the conflict continues to influence the church in Nigeria today.

The continuing tension between these "two diametrically opposed positions" (cf. Comaroff and Comaroff, 1997) is evidenced in the two types of habit worn by nuns at the First Profession ceremony. The majority of nuns, both the Sisters of St Michael's the Archangel (SSMA) Generalate from Ado-Ekiti and visiting sisters from other orders, wore Western-style dress, consisting of a mid-length skirt, an overblouse and a head covering. In Nigeria, this style of habit clearly identifies its wearers as nuns who have taken vows in the Roman Catholic Church. However, the dress of one nun from the Kelly Pastoral Center expressed a somewhat different identity for its wearer. While the components of this habit are the same, the habit itself is fashioned from cloth hand-woven at the Center, suggesting that its wearer is a Nigerian who is also a Roman Catholic. In this case, a Nigerian identity seems to take precedence over a Western one.

This question of emphasis on African and Western identities is something that continues to concern Roman Catholic parishioners, priests, bishops and nuns in the Ekiti Yoruba area of southwestern Nigeria, strengthened by memories of the past. For example, in his autobiography Monsignor Oguntuyi (1984, p. 31) wrote of being snubbed by white priests on the day of his ordination in 1946. Efforts to remain Roman Catholics while reclaiming racial pride and identity in a Yoruba past were expressed in remarks of one Catholic priest in Itapa-Ekiti, "People are seriously condemning copying white people [*oyinbo*] all the time; we have to promote our own culture." The post-Vatican II solution to this "problem of dignity and self-identification" (Hefner, 1993, p. 25) among formerly colonized peoples of color consists, partly, in the use of Yoruba hand-woven textiles worn by Catholic nuns in the First Profession ceremony in Ado-Ekiti. That this solution is specific to the social historical and political context of the Ekiti Yoruba area of southwestern Nigeria may be seen by considering the differing responses of a group of American nuns to the dress reforms instituted by Vatican II discussed by Michelman (1997; 1999).

For these women, the problem of a Roman Catholic identity does not stem from the racist contradictions of a colonial past. Rather, their problem relates to the contradiction between American social ideals of secular individualism and the wearing of a habit – of whatever fashion, modified or not – and the religious uniformity it represents. For these women, the reforms of Vatican II mean the possibility of establishing a new identity as women religious (which they prefer being called) without the constraints of a habit which they view as "an impediment to individual autonomy and the ability to function in the broader secular world" (Michelman, 1997, p. 355). As in Nigeria, however, there have been a range of responses to the changes introduced by Vatican II. For example, the shift to secular dress was not followed by all orders of American nuns and has led to considerable debate among church clergy and laity alike. The vital importance of dress in expressing new identities is underscored in these debates, which reflect the continuing tensions between distinctive interpretations of Catholic faith.

Conclusion

In Ekiti, the presence of hand-woven Yoruba textiles in ecclesiastical dress demonstrates the way that cloth is used to represent a traditional Yoruba identity while at the same time being a newly invented modern one. In the first part of this century, locally hand-woven cloths associated with Yoruba religious practice were cast off as Christian converts disassociated themselves from these beliefs and identities. After Nigerian independence in 1960 and Vatican II in 1962, Roman Catholics began to reincorporate hand-woven Yoruba cloth into religious worship. While some of these cloths are woven by the Catholic nuns in Ado-Ekiti, consistent with a tradition of women weavers in this part of Nigeria, the cloths they produce are woven in an entirely new way. Using modern floorlooms, they weave cloth that is later cut into strips to produce the type of narrow-strip hand-woven *aso ofi* cloth fashions popular in Nigeria today. The wearing of hand-woven vestments in church ceremonies such as the First Profession service allows individuals to assert both a modern African identity and a Roman Catholic one.

Cloth is an ideal medium for representing these shifting interpretations of African and European identities (Kuper, 1973) not only because of the range of types, colors and styles into which it can be shaped into but also because of it proximity to the human body (Schneider and Weiner, 1986). Indeed, cloth – sometimes referred to "a second skin" – when used as tailored dress may constrain or transform the body in ways noted by Soyinka (1988, p. 14) in his description of the Vicar of St Peter's (in Abeokuta):

> His jacket was far too small, the trousers stopped some distance about his ankles and his round collar seemed about to choke him. I glanced quickly to see if he had suddenly diminished in size and was reassured by his enormous shoes. These alternations between superhuman possibilities and ordinary ill-fitting clothes unsettled me; I wished he would remain constantly in his cassock and surplice.

Because of the close connection between clothing and the human body as well as the fine distinctions that can be made through particular types of cloth and dress, these things are especially appropriate for asserting different identities and distinctions among individuals. However, they can also be used to construct a new identity that acknowledges cultural distinctiveness while at the same time emphasizing membership in a universal world church. The continually changing configurations and juxtapositions of hand-woven Yoruba (*aso ofi*) and manufactured European (*aso oyinbo*) cloths worn by Yoruba nuns in the First Profession service attest to this aspiration for linking these distinctive African and Western identities. Their attempts to find an acceptable balance of indigenous and foreign ideas and practices, of old and new ways, reflect a striving for the harmonious unity of humankind and at the same time, a need for distinctive local identities, both expressed through the particular use of cloth and dress.

Acknowledgements

An earlier version of this chapter was presented at the Eleventh ACASA Triennial, held in New Orleans in April 1998. I would like to thank Joanne Eicher for her useful comments at that time. Research support in Ekiti in 1997 was provided by the Wenner-Gren Foundation for Anthropological Research. I am grateful to Lord Bishop M. O. Fagun, the Sisters of St Michael's the

Archangel (SSMA) Generalate and Professor I.O. Orubuloye for their help and suggestions during my visits to Ado-Ekiti and to Kayode Owoeye for his excellent research assistance.

Notes

1. The various articles of ecclesiastic dress mentioned in this chapter are defined as follows (in *Webster's Ninth New Collegiate Dictionary*). A chasuble is "a sleeveless outer vestment worn by the officiating priest at mass." A cassock is "an ankle-length garment with close-fitting sleeves." An alb is "a full-length white linen ecclesiastical vestment with long sleeves that is gathered at the waist with a cincture." A miter is "a liturgical headdress worn by bishops and abbots." A surplice is "a loose white outer ecclesiastical vestment usually of knee length with large open sleeves."

2. The term, *adodo*, used in reference to the red waist-tie (*oja adodo*) mentioned by Yeye Molomo, may be related to *ododo* cloths used in Idah for masquerade costumes that were often red (Miachi, 1990).

3. In the Yoruba town of Okuku to the west, Barber (1981, p. 743) estimated that 10 percent of the population were practicing traditional worshippers.

4. According to Oguntuyi (1979, p. 14), "When singlets appeared the first time, they were called 'Ifun Oni' (the intestines of crocodile) because they were believed to have been made of the intestines of Crocodile."

5. The hero of Sarowiwa's novel, *Sozaboy* (1985, p. 53, 163), made a similar comment about joining the army because he admired the uniform.

6. Monsignor Oguntuyi (1984, p. 14) reported a similar experience on hearing of "the Boy Scouts [who] danced round Ekiti in spotless white shirts and visited towns and villages . . . I was fascinated with news about them, particularly their dress. I therefore resolved to go to school . . .)."

7. Since none of the looms were strung at the time of the interview in July 1997, the spacing of warp threads in the reed could not be ascertained. It is likely that the weavers leave gaps so that the finished fabric can be cut into strips as is common among Ekiti floor-loom weavers (Renne, 1997).

8. Monsignor Oguntuyi (1984, p. 43) described his attempt to institute drumming in a Holy Rosary procession in Ikere-Ekiti in 1952 and its subsequent prohibition by the local parish priest

References

Ajayi, J. F. A. (1965). *Christian missions in Nigeria 1841–1891*. London: Longman.
Allen, W. & Thomson, T. (1967). *A narrative of the expedition sent by Her Majesty's Government to the River Niger in 1841* (Vols. 1–2). New York: Johnson Reprint (Original work published 1848).

Apter, A. (1992). *Black kings and critics*. Chicago: University of Chicago Press.

Awolalu, J. O. (1979). *Yoruba beliefs and sacrificial rites*. London: Longman.

Ayandele, E. A. (1966). *The missionary impact of modern Nigeria 1842–1914*. London: Longman.

Barber, K. (1981). How man makes God in West Africa: Yoruba attitudes toward the Orisa. *Africa*, 51(3), 724–45.

Ben-Amos, P. (1978). *Owina N'Ido*: Royal weavers of Benin. *African Arts*, 11, 48–53, 95.

Clarke, D. (1997). *The art of African textiles*. San Diego: Thunder Bay Press.

Comaroff, J. & Comaroff, J. (1997). *Of revelation and revolution*, Vol. 2. Chicago: University of Chicago Press.

Cort, L. (1989). The changing fortunes of three archaic Japanese textiles. In A. Weiner & J. Schneider (Eds.), *Cloth in human experience*, (pp. 377–415). Washington, D.C.: Smithsonian Institution Press.

Eicher, J. (1975). *Nigerian handcrafted textiles*. Ile-Ife: University of Ife Press.

Flannery, A. (Ed.) (1992). *Vatican Council II: The Conciliar and Post Conciliar documents*. Dublin: Dominican Publications.

Hefner, R. (1993). Introduction: World building and rationality of conversion. In R. Hefner (Ed.), *Conversion to Christianity*, (pp. 3–44). Berkeley: University Of California Press.

Hobsbawn, E. & Ranger, T. (Eds.) (1983). *The invention of tradition*. Cambridge: Cambridge University Press.

Kuper, H. (1973). Costume and identity. *Comparative Studies in Society and History*, 15(3), 348–67.

Lamb, V. & Holmes, J. (1980). *Nigerian weaving*. Hertingfordbury: Roxford Books.

Makozi, A. O. & Ojo, G. J. A. (Eds.) (1982). *The history of the Catholic Church in Nigeria*. Ikeja, Ibadan: Macmillan Nigeria.

Miachi, T. (1990). *The masquerade phenomenon in Igala culture: An anthropological analysis*. PhD dissertation, University of Ibadan, Institute of African Studies, Ibadan.

Michelman, S. (1997). Changing old habits: Dress of women religious and its relationship to personal and social identity. *Sociological Inquiry* 67(3), 350–63.

Michelman, S. (1999). Fashion and identity of women religious. In Arthur, L. B. (Ed.), *Religion, Dress and the Body*. Oxford: Berg.

Oguntuyi, A. (1979). *History of Ekiti*. Ibadan: Bisi Books.

Oguntuyi, A. (1984). *My Life as a priest* Kaduna: Layon (Nig.) Ltd.

Ojo, G. A. (Ed.) (no date) *A priest forever: Biography of Monsignor Anthony Ogunleye Oguntuyi*. Ado-Ekiti.

Ojo, G. J. A. (1966). *Yoruba culture*. London: University of London.

Omoyajowo, J. A. (1982). *Cherubim and Seraphim: The history of an African independent church*. New York: Nok Publishers.

Owoeye, K. (1999). *Events and history of Itapa-Ekiti*. Ann Arbor: Kolossos Press.

Parrinder, G. (1953). *Religion in an African city*. Westport CT: Negro University Press.

Peel, J. D. Y. (1978). *Olaju*: A Yoruba concept of development. *Journal Of Development Studies,* 14(2), 139–65.

Picton, J. & Mack, J. (1979). *African textiles.* London: British Museum.

Renne, E. P. (1997). "Traditional modernity" and the economics of hand-woven cloth production in southwestern Nigeria. *Economic Development and Cultural Change,* 45(4), 773–92.

Sarowiwa, K. (1985). *Sozaboy.* Port Harcourt: Saros International.

Schneider, J. & Weiner, J. (1986). Cloth and the organization of human experience. *Current Anthropology* 27, 178–84.

Soyinka, W. (1988). *Ake: The years of childhood.* Ibadan: Spectrum.

Turner, H. W. (1967). *History of an African independent church* (Vols. 1–2). Oxford: Clarendon Press.

2

"Minkisi" Do Not Die: BaKongo Cosmology in the Christian Rituals of Simon Kimbangu and Simon Mpadi

Shannen Hill

In 1921, Simon Kimbangu (1889–1951) claimed to be the first native Christian prophet of his people, the BaKongo. His ancestors were part of a thriving kingdom on the Atlantic coast of Central Africa that fanned outward from the mouth of what is now called the Zaire River into present day Angola, Congo, Cabinda and the Democratic Republic of the Congo. It was in the last of these nations, then called the Belgian Congo, that Kimbangu's prophetic movement existed. As he gained a ready following, Belgian colonial officials became weary of his growing power and authority and imprisoned him in September 1921. He died in captivity in 1951. This chapter argues that in body, dress, gesture and word, Kimbangu recalled central elements of BaKongo cosmology in his Christian services, which contributed greatly to his massive following.[1] Thus it acknowledges Kimbangu as a critical bridge between pre- and post-colonial religious expressions wherein BaKongo cosmology is more visually pronounced. The ritual arts of Simon Mpadi, a BaKongo prophet who claims Kimbangu as a guiding predecessor, are briefly examined at the chapter's end.

Why Kimbangu? Though he preached for just one year, dozens of subsequent prophets in the region aligned themselves to him. His church, The Church of Jesus Christ on Earth Through the Prophet Simon Kimbangu (EJCSK), is considered the largest African-founded Protestant church and belongs to the World Council of Churches (MacGaffey, 1994). Why Mpadi? He is one of the better known prophets who claim a tie to Kimbangu and his church,

L'Eglise des Noirs en Afrique (ENAF), boasts a healthy membership as well. The dress, objects and performance of ENAF rituals make overt the reference to BaKongo cosmology which Kimbangu, healing at a more turbulent time, could only mask.

The argument presented here is contentious. Some scholars maintain that Kimbangu broke entirely with known BaKongo customs and that Mpadi is of another school altogether (Hastings, 1994; Isichei, 1995; Martin, 1968, 1975); others suggest that Kimbangu's popularity arose from established traditions of healing and spiritual aid (Andersson, 1958; Bockie, 1993; MacGaffey, 1983, 1994; van Wing, 1959), which Mpadi readily evokes. The former look to the catechism of Kimbangu's church as it is written today and, in Martin's case, to testimony offered by Kimbangu's assistants.[2] These sources, however, cannot clearly indicate how Kimbangu's teachings were understood by the masses of people who responded to his call in 1921. Nor do they position Kimbangu within the period, a time and place of particularly brutal colonial oppression to which Kimbangu's prophecy offered some respite. Rather, they promote the idea that the burning of *minkisi*, objects important to BaKongo religious and political rituals, indicated a complete turnabout in spiritual belief, the death of BaKongo cosmology and the wholesale acceptance of Christianity. Missionaries and explorers had witnessed this act through the centuries since Portuguese explorers arrived on the shores of the Kongo Kingdom in 1482.[3] Kimbangu's followers also burned *minkisi*, though they burned Catholic images too (MacGaffey, 1977b), a point that Andrian Hastings, Elizabeth Isichei and Mary-Louise Martin overlook. Surely the burning of *minkisi*, cloth bags containing natural substances and their figural rendition, *minkisi minkondi* (figure 2.1), must be seen as an act complexly motivated by experiences BaKongo underwent and not purely as a disavowal of established cosmological belief and practice.

To support the thesis, a cursory explanation of BaKongo cosmology is given. Visual manifestations of these ideas are then analyzed in two art forms of the Kongo Kingdom, iron-studded figural sculptures called *minkisi minkondi* (singular use is *nkisi nkondi*) and the dress and performance of people who made and used them, experts in healing called *banganga* (singular use is *nganga*). Scholars have argued elsewhere that the physical body of the ritual experts and the sculpted body of their art became, in the minds of their audience, identical in meaning (MacGaffey, 1988, 1993; Thompson, 1978; Thompson and Cornet, 1981). *Banganga* conceptually **became** *minkisi minkondi*. Through expressive coherence in ritual dress and posture, their bodies were metaphors for transformation. As such, their bodies portrayed three ideas at the very heart of BaKongo cosmology, that everything in existence undergoes change, that change is fueled by spiritual forces and that humans can alter the former by engaging with the latter.[4] The merging of identities between person and object is crucial if we are to understand Kimbangu and subsequent prophets, called *bangunza*, as living repositories of BaKongo cosmology. Such a fusion undermines the notion that BaKongo cosmology died with the burning of *minkisi*.

This research was undertaken with the conviction that customs established through centuries of practice do not simply cease. Understanding religion as

Figure 2.1 *Nkisi Nkondi.* Nineteenth century. Yombe, Kongo. Wood, metal, pigment, fiber, other materials. H. 44.5 in. (113 cm). Used by permission of the Field Museum, Chicago, Illinois. Negative #A109979-1. Photograph by Diane Alexander White.

"structures of behavior possibilities (rather) than as systems of belief" (MacGaffey, 1977b, p. 178) permits changes to ritual performance through time and external influence. Evidence of BaKongo cosmology appears to exist in the dress and performances of the prophets Simon Kimbangu and Simon Mpadi. This is not to suggest that their ritual presentations precisely enact BaKongo cosmology through dress, object, sound and motion; rather, elements of this indigenous religion seem present within their Christian churches.

Research was conducted predominately through library and museum collections in the United States. Fieldwork in Central Africa was not undertaken and certainly this is needed for a more decisive study. The considerable primary and secondary resources available in the United States enable tentative conclusions and these are presented here. While art historical and anthropological evidence inform the initial stage of this argument (Bassani, 1977; MacGaffey, 1977a, 1977b, 1988, 1991, 1993; Thompson, 1978, 1984, 1986, 1993; Thompson and Cornet, 1981; Volavkova, 1972), no visual record of Kimbangu's prophetic performances has been published. Thus the ideas regarding BaKongo cosmology within his ritual practice are drawn from written records of missionaries and colonial administrators who witnessed Kimbangu in action (in Andersson, 1958; Janzen and MacGaffey, 1974; Laman, 1936; MacGaffey, 1986a, 1986b) and from anthropologists and theologians engaged with Kimbanguism (Andersson, 1958; Laman, 1936; MacGaffey, 1983, 1994; Martin, 1968, 1975: Schoffeleers, 1994). Scholarship on Mpadi's practice is also sparse, but some description of clothing and objects used is given.

BaKongo Cosmology and its Visualization in the Ritual Arts of *Banganga*

The BaKongo cosmogram (figure 2.2) is called *dikenga*, which means to turn, to twirl, to swirl (Dawson, 1994; Fu Kiau Kia Bunseki, 1994).[5] Its abstracted reference can be found in multiple forms, from graveyards with discs pierced by tree limbs (Thompson and Cornet, 1981) to the postures of *minkisi minkondi* and the performances that involved their ritual use.[6] To fully comprehend the philosophy *dikenga* represents (Fu Kiau Kia Bunseki, 1994; Janzen and MacGaffey, 1974; Thompson and Cornet, 1981), one must note two crucial factors. First, *dikenga* is used to explain many facets of existence: elements of time, be they the origin of the cosmos, the change of seasons or the passing of a single day; elements of development, be they ideas, products or human life. According to BaKongo belief, everything in conceptual or physical existence moves in progressive stages around the cross within the sphere, which is not envisioned as a closed circle as seen in figure 2.2, but as an unending spiral in three-dimensional space. A helix illustrates the concept well. Second, *dikenga* represents **transformation**, of spirit, time and physical essence. As *banganga* called for transformation during rituals and became possessed by ancestral spirits themselves, they enacted *dikenga*. They lived it. Kimbangu, possessed by the spirit of Jesus Christ, also performed *dikenga*.

Dikenga explains evolution as a four-staged cyclical process called *dingo-dingo* (Dawson, 1994; Fu Kiau Kia Bunseki, 1994). Nothing can pass from one stage to the next without reaching its full potential within any given stage. Movement is generated by *Kalunga*, the supreme force of the universe, the energy that creates and transforms. *Kalunga* is visually manifested in our world at the water's edge, which divides the known world, *ku nseke*, the mount of the living, from the unknown world, *ku mpemba*, the mount of the dead. To explain the all-embracing nature of *dikenga* (Fu Kiau Kia Bunseki, 1974, 1980, 1994), four analogies will be used: the creation of the

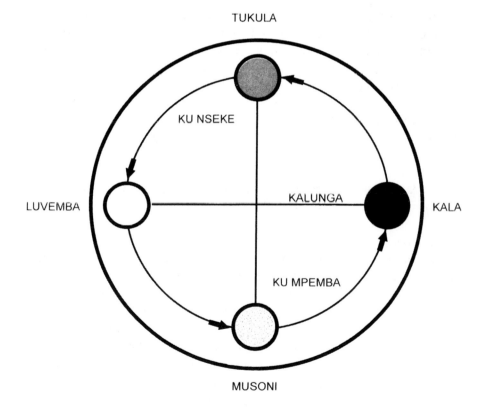

Figure 2.2 *Dikenga.* Line drawing used to illustrate BaKongo cosmological principles. The colors of the four stages of development are as follows: Musoni: yellow; Kala: black; Tukula: red; Luvemba: white.

cosmos, the passing of seasons and of lives and the process of making an object into metal.

Musoni marks the beginning of time when all things are conceived. It parallels the idea of the "big bang" which created the earth and its minerals. At this time, ironsmiths mould their product from yellowish clay, couples conceive and winter falls. *Kala* time is one of birth, that of children, plants and spring. Its symbolic color is black like charcoal before it is heated. *Tukula* is the time of one's highest creative potential. Animals filled the earth, summer has come, adults are their most energetic and iron reddens with heat. The final stage of time, *Luvemba*, marks the transition point in all existence. Iron becomes white-hot, autumn falls and humans age, finally passing from the mount of the living to the mount of the dead. In the cosmos, the first humans were created and the planet Earth reached its fullest form, thus the cosmic energy of *Kalunga* began its process of creation and transformation elsewhere in the universe.

Death in the physical world simply marks a transition in venue for the spirit (Fu Kiau Kia Bunseki, 1994; MacGaffey, 1993; Thompson, 1984, 1993; Thompson and Cornet, 1981). Upon death, one's soul migrates beneath the water. If one lived a life of goodness, his or her spirit dies a second death and returns to this world in time-resistant forms, soil, stones, leafs, twigs and the like (Jacobson-Widding, 1979; MacGaffey, 1988, 1991, 1993; Thompson, 1984, 1993; Thompson and Cornet, 1981). In this form, ancestral spirits (*bisimbi*, singular use is *simbi*) can be of benefit to the living. People who did not live a life of goodness, those who were dishonorable, deceitful or murderous die just once. These spirits (*bankuyu*, singular use is *nkuyu*) remain forever at the service of evildoers in the world of the living. *Bisimbi* must continually combat *bankuyu* (Bockie, 1993; Jacobson-Widding, 1979; Janzen and MacGaffey, 1974; MacGaffey, 1991, 1993).

As otherworldly spirits, *bisimbi* and *bankuyu* were believed to possess powers that could alter events in the world of the living. *Bisimbi* protected people from illness or misfortune or, if consulted after the fact, they cured people of these maladies by tracking and thwarting the plans of the *nkuyu* that caused them. In social agreements such as land acquisition or peace treaties, *bisimbi* helped reinforce these obligations by wreaking havoc on the lives of those who reneged. None of these actions was attainable, however, without the ritual performances of *banganga* and the objects they made and used, *minkisi*.

The ideas expressed in figure 2.2 were visualized in BaKongo society through the conceptual union of *banganga* and their most visually alluring art, *minkisi minkondi* (figures 2.1 and 2.3). Through the use of what Erving Goffman called expressive equipment (1997), person and object came to represent transformation, the principle at the heart of BaKongo cosmology. *Banganga* dressed and painted themselves like their *minkondi*, adopted the same postures, occupied the same sacred spaces and, through speech, song and action, enticed the spiritual forces within the figural sculpture to take residence in their own bodies (MacGaffey, 1988, 1991, 1993; Thompson, 1978, 1984; Thompson and Cornet, 1981).

Figure 2.3 *Nkisi Nkondi* Mawenze. Before 1914. BaKongo, Democratic Republic of the Congo. Wood, metal, pigment, other materials. H. 34.25 in. (87 cm.). Used by permission of the Africa Museum, Tervuren, Belgium. 22438.

Minkisi are objects that contain natural substances (*bilongo*) which, when combined through ritual process, generate ancestral power that can potentially effect change in the living world. *Bilongo* is commonly translated as "medicine" since *minkisi* were used to heal physical and social maladies (Janzen and MacGaffey, 1974; MacGaffey, 1977a, 1993; Thompson, 1978, 1984, 1986, 1993; Thompson and Cornet, 1981). *Banganga*, who studied and mixed hundreds of *bilongo* recipes and made the objects that contained them, were thus seen as healers, experts trained in the art of combating personal and social maladies.

Minkondi are a particular type of *minkisi*: figures studded with iron blades, pins and nails. *Banganga* carved the figures so that they are hollow within. They then inserted *bilongo*, imbued with the spirits of ancestors. These cavities were sealed with a cowrie shell or reflective glass, both of which symbolized water, the physical barrier between the living and the dead, the cosmic energy of *Kalunga* (Bassani, 1977; MacGaffey, 1988, 1991, 1993; Thompson, 1978, 1984, 1986, 1993; Thompson and Cornet, 1981; Volavkova, 1972).

Writing in 1910, a BaKongo ethnographer named Nsemi Isaki recalled the origins of *minkisi*, *banganga* and *bilongo*:

> The first one in this country to compose *minkisi* is the ancient Mukulu, but we know little about him. When Mukulu lay down and fell asleep, he dreamed a dream. "Tomorrow you will take leaves and mix them and give them to a sufferer to drink and he will be cured, for all the plants belong to me," said a voice. Then Mukulu when he opened his eyes saw that he had dreamed. He returned to sleep and was shown the medicines by God or Funza and was told to mix all things together as instructed, to help those in pain and need; and they will be charms to help you. Then he opened his eyes and did as he had seen in the dream; he mixed together the leaves and administered them to a sufferer and he was healed. Thus did the plants get their power from the one who prepared them for healing. Then Helper Mukulu, after he was taught by God or Funza, he the First Helper began to teach others in the use of *minkisi*: how they would be useful for each ailing person and how he might regain his health (Janzen and MacGaffey, 1974, p. 35).

Minkisi minkondi were used in a variety of settings, each appropriately sanctioned by ancestral power. They were used in legal proceedings and spiritual rites (Bassani, 1977; Janzen and MacGaffey, 1974; MacGaffey, 1977a, 1986b, 1988, 1993; Thompson, 1978, 1984, 1986; Thompson and Cornet, 1981; Volavkova, 1972). *Banganga* activated ancestral presence in a space that represented the cosmogram (MacGaffey, 1986b, 1991, 1993; Thompson, 1984, 1993; Thompson and Cornet, 1981). Its design was either scratched into the earth or drawn out on the ground in white chalk. *Banganga* stood at the center of the symbol, the cross point of upper and lower spheres.

Fu Kiau Kia Bunseki, a renowned BaKongo philosopher, describes its meaning: "To stand upon this sign meant that a person was fully capable of governing people, that he knew the nature of the world, that he had mastered the meaning of life and death" (Thompson, 1984, p. 109). A single *nkisi nkondi* was placed near the circle's circumference, which was encircled by three plants (MacGaffey, 1991).

Plants of all kinds, but particularly large trees, were potent ancestral symbols in BaKongo society. They pierce the earth, which was thought to be a giant *nkisi* (Dawson, 1994; MacGaffey, 1986; Thompson, 1984, 1993) and draw nourishment from the mount of the dead. Thus their bark and foliage are imbued with intense spiritual presence.

The many iron blades, pins and nails that riddle *minkisi minkondi* were not part of the original sculptures, but were added throughout time, thus transforming the compositions in a way appropriate to the ideas they represent. At the height of ritual, clients seeking ancestral aid licked the tip of an iron implement and hammered it into the wood, thereby crossing the *Kalunga* line and making contact with the spiritually charged substances contained in the sculpture's cavity (Bassani, 1977; MacGaffey, 1977a, 1986b, 1988, 1991, 1993; Thompson, 1978, 1984, 1986, 1993; Thompson and Cornet, 1981; Volavkova, 1972). In this way, a contractual agreement was formed between person and spirit, an event of enormous psychological weight. If the contract involved retributive action, a strip of cloth might be tied to the implement in order to direct the spirit in its assignment (MacGaffey, 1977a, 1988, 1991, 1993; Thompson, 1978, 1984, 1986, 1993). The greater number of iron implements, the greater the perceived power of the spirit the figure contained.

A highly programmatic system of call and response preceded the moment in which clients hammered iron into the figure. Not only did clients "hammer their oath" but they would "sing their point" (Thompson and Cornet, 1981, p. 110). In fact, all aspects of these rituals contained sequences of verbal and performative exchange. *Banganga* and their attendants activated the spirit through song, dance and insult such as spitting on the figure and making puns on its name (MacGaffey, 1977a, 1988, 1993; Thompson, 1978, 1984, 1986). By way of word, action and motion, *banganga* made their client's wishes known to the spirit within the *nkondi*. The voiced power and danced performance of *banganga* were extremely important. They were agents of transformation, a living reference to *dikenga*.

As a *nganga* moved about the figure and became entranced by its associated spirit, he or she began to shake, an action taken as a sign of the spirit's residence in the *nganga's* body (MacGaffey, 1993; Thompson, 1984). To emphasize a point, the *nganga* jabbed a staff, fitted at the end with iron, into the earth, the giant *nkisi*. Like other ritual objects, staffs (*mvwala*) were associated with the person (King or *nganga*) using them, who could also be called *mvwala* (MacGaffey, 1990). The staffs had cloth tied to their ends, as did the implements that pierced *minkisi minkondi* (MacGaffey, 1986b, 1988, 1990, 1993; Thompson, 1984, 1993). Throughout the performance, the client's attention undoubtedly vacillated between the trembling *nganga* and the static *nkisi*, between the sights and sounds that surrounded him or her. In this whirlwind of activity, the *nganga*, *nkisi* and ancestor were conceptually one. They were fused in the representation of unknown and unseen powers. They were the idea at the center of BaKongo cosmology: that ancestors have powers beyond those of the living that can be harnessed to transform the physical world.

This fusion of identities was further suggested by posture (MacGaffey, 1993; Thompson, 1984, 1993; Thompson and Cornet, 1981). During performances, *banganga* would adopt the pose of the *nkondi* they used. The vast majority of *minkisi minkondi* were carved in one of two poses, either arms akimbo (figure 2.1) or at opposing angles (figure 2.3). These poses referenced the circular rotation of the cosmogram (figure 2.2). In figure 2.1, the hands are positioned near the belly, the KiKongo word for which, *mooyo*, translates as "life" or "soul" (MacGaffey, 1993, p. 65). The relation of the arms to the body forms a cross within a circle, the center of which is the most powerful point in the cosmos (Fu Kiau Kia Bunseki, 1974, 1994; Thompson, 1984; Thompson and Cornet, 1981). In figure 2.3, the left hand emanates from the belly and extends toward the head in a counter-clockwise reading. The right hand holds a sharp object and is positioned upright, ready to thrust downward toward the belly, thereby completing the cosmic sequence.

In addition to adopting common postures, *banganga* magnified their likeness to *minkondi* by wearing similar dress and painting their faces (MacGaffey, 1988, 1990, 1993; Thompson, 1978, 1984; Thompson and Cornet, 1981). Both *banganga* and *minkondi* wore caps fitted firmly to contain specialized knowledge and often wore similar skirts, arm bands and accoutrements such as feathers, gourds, rattles, claws and skins (MacGaffey, 1990, 1993; Thompson, 1978). Some male *banganga* wore beards, as did some *minkondi*, as a sign of elderhood and the wisdom that accompanies it (MacGaffey, 1993).

The faces of *minkondi* in figures 2.1 and 2.3 were painted in the colors of the cosmogram. Designs around the eyes enhanced the ability to see what others could not, while those on the forehead marked "the seat of understanding" (MacGaffey, 1993, p. 51). Though the complexity of Kongo chromacy (Jacobson-Widding, 1979) cannot be developed in the space of this chapter, a central tenet is necessarily noted: the meaning of colors was derived from their source. All that was associated with this source was likewise identified with the color. For example, red pigment may be obtained from the bark of a coral tree, white from the clay of riverbeds. These sources were from both realms of the cosmogram, the mount of the living and that of the dead. Thus a *nganga* or *nkondi* adorned in colors derived from these sources presumably mastered the forces of their respective worlds (Jacobson-Widding, 1979; MacGaffey, 1988, 1993; Thompson, 1978, 1984).

Accoutrements attached to either person or object could similarly invest the person or object with authority (Bassani, 1977; MacGaffey, 1977a, 1988, 1990, 1993; Thompson, 1978, 1984, 1993; Thompson and Cornet, 1981; Volavkova, 1972). The cap on the *nkondi* in figure 2.3 has both feathers and a seashell, items that testify to dual dominion. Furthermore, the eyes are semi-spherical and mirrored to represent the lower, spiritual realm (Dawson, 1994; MacGaffey, 1988, 1993; Thompson, 1978, 1984, 1986, 1993; Volavkova, 1972). The *nganga* who made and performed with this much-used *nkondi* was likewise thought to possess powers in both realms of the cosmos.

Minkisi minkondi and *banganga* thus occupied the same status in BaKongo communities. As vehicles for communication with ancestors, they embodied the very concepts at the heart of BaKongo cosmology. The compositions of the objects meant to evoke fear and respect for the powers they contain (MacGaffey, 1988, 1993; Thompson, 1978, 1984, 1986, 1993). Ritual experts adopted similar gestures and dress to reinforce their essential role in accessing these powers. Words, motion and music furthered the notion that person and object were conceptually one. Together they stood at the crossroads of *dikenga*, a place where the four stages of all evolutionary processes meet, a place of great collision and extreme force. Here laid the potential for change, only realized, however, through the partnership of *minkisi minkondi* and *banganga*.

Simon Kimbangu and Simon Mpadi: *Bangunza* Who Embodied BaKongo Cosmology

Bangunza (singular use is *ngunza*) is the KiKongo word for prophets (MacGaffey, 1983). Simon Kimbangu, whose name means "true Interpreter of the hidden and obscure" (Janzen and MacGaffey, 1974, p. 125), was the first of these. On 18 March 1921, Kimbangu dreamt he was called to prophesy.

One night, (a stranger, neither white nor black) came with a Bible in its (sic) hand and said "This is a good book. You must study it and preach." Kimbangu replied "Nay . . . I am no preacher or teacher, I cannot do it." Whereupon the stranger urged him to give the Book to his mother, so that she might preach and then told him that there was a sick child in a village nearby and ordered him to go and pray for it. Still he would not obey. His mother now had a dream in which a stranger repeated his command that her son should go out and preach and heal the sick, but this summons too he ignored. It was repeated again in a tone of great authority: "There is a sick child in a certain village. You must go there, pray, lay your hands on the child and heal it. If you do not go, I shall require your soul of you." Now, as in Kinshasa,[7] Kimbangu was forced to yield. He went next day to the village in question and found the child. He laid hands on it and prayed, whereupon he was subjected to violent convulsions. The child, however, was cured of its sickness and put to its mother's breast (Andersson, 1958, p. 51).[8]

Kimbangu's dream is like that of Mukulu, the *nganga* who made the first *nkisi* on earth. Both *nganga* (ritual expert) and *ngunza* (prophet) heal sickness in their first divinely inspired assignment. Their sources are sacred instruments: Mukulu used natural substances, the *bilongo* of *minkisi*; Kimbangu used a Bible, itself considered to be a "secret *minkisi*" (Andersson, 1958, p. 44). The Bible was equated to the ancestral spirit named Ngwe Mfumu or Kipeka (Andersson, 1958), who appears to have been an attentive, traveling guardian (Laman, 1964). In this simile, a *nganga* who served Kipeka would also be considered alert and protective, as would a *ngunza* who used the Bible. Significantly, in his youth Kimbangu received training to become a *nganga*, one that served Kipeka (Andersson, 1958). In this way, he followed a profession already embraced by his family.[9]

There are many conceptual links between the roles assumed by *banganga* within the hierarchy of BaKongo cosmology and that of Kimbangu within the hierarchy of Christianity. Both *banganga* and Kimbangu were mediators between the living and spiritual realms. *Banganga* related human desires to Funza (also known as Nkambi), the Supreme Creator, through *bisimbi* (ancestors); Kimbangu was the "instrument" or "servant" of Jesus Christ, who, as the son of God, assumes a place parallel to *bisimbi* on the second tier of the spiritual hierarchy (Tambwe, 1994). The title of Kimbangu's church, The Church of Jesus Christ on Earth Through the Prophet Simon Kimbangu, suggests relationships equivalent to those in BaKongo cosmology. Kimbangu worked *through* Christ, just as *banganga* worked through *bisimbi*. Andersson (1958) reports that Kimbangu's mother dreamt of her son's call to prophesy just as *banganga* dream of spiritual intervention and the *bilongo* recipes that enable it. In this first healing, Kimbangu behaved as a *nganga* would: "(His) whole body violently (shook) during the prayer, but he also became entranced, leapt into the air, cried out and preached" (Andersson, 1958, p. 51, quoting Floden, 1933, p. 147).

The rumored success of Kimbangu's first healing spread throughout the region and thousands of people flocked to Nkamba, Kimbangu's birthplace and the site of his church (Hastings, 1994; MacGaffey, 1983; Martin, 1968,

1975). By 1921 it became known as the New Jerusalem (MacGaffey, 1983). Its natural habitat was sacred: water and soil were taken from Nkamba to be used in ritual healings and baptisms in other cities and towns (MacGaffey, 1983; Martin, 1975). The visual stimuli of baptismal ceremonies, which increased dramatically in the Lower Congo in 1922 (MacGaffey, 1983), suggested key ideas in BaKongo cosmology that were commonly understood by those undergoing this rite. The site, water, was accepted as the site of transformation. Its significance in BaKongo cosmology differs from that in Christian belief: it is not an element through which one is purified, but a boundary between worlds (the *Kalunga* line), the crossing of which fuels change. The initiates wore white (Andersson, 1958), a color that conjured associations with ancestors who had journeyed into the water's depths.

As to Kimbangu's dress and its visual coherence with that of *minkisi minkondi* and *banganga*, he did not wear shells, rattles, a cap and raffia skirts, nor did he paint his face to suggest wisdom or clairvoyance. However, a Belgian colonial administrator recorded him in red trousers and a white shirt (MacGaffey, 1983), cosmic colors in BaKongo belief. Red and white were frequently painted on the faces of *minkondi* (figure 2.1) and/or encircling the cavity entrance (figure 2.3). He is said to have preached in a long white silk robe (Martin, 1975). Kimbangu held a staff while he shook and danced and was said to repeatedly stab the earth's surface, just as *banganga* had. Though the explicit reference to BaKongo ritual is lost on Martin, she reports that both prophet and staff were called *mvwala* (1975, p. 53), the same word used for person and object in *banganga* ritual. The stabbing of the earth with staff was regarded as essential to the ritual performance, particularly when Kimbangu aimed to heal illnesses (Andersson, 1958). His staff had a red cloth tied to its end (Andersson, 1958).[10] Cloths were similarly tied to the end of *banganga*'s staffs and to nails that pierced *minkisi minkondi* (Bassani, 1977; MacGaffey, 1991, 1993; Thompson, 1978, 1984, 1986; Volavkova, 1972). They guided the spirit on its mission and, in the act of tying, bound the agreement between client and spirit.

The ritual space of Kimbangu's church reflected that of *banganga*, though the cosmogram was performed rather than drawn within this Christian enclosure.[11] Further, though he conducted services within an enclosed space (Andersson, 1958), its layout seems to have recalled the cosmogram. To partake in Kimbangu's rituals, congregations performed as they would have in *banganga* ritual. Through the course of the ceremony, they followed a counterclockwise circular path that corresponds to the four-stage cycle of *dikenga* (figure 2.2). Their walk began outside the entrance at the far end of a narrow passage flanked on either side by trees (Andersson, 1958). This starting point corresponds to *Musoni* time, the beginning. Congregations progressed toward the church entrance. Upon entering, they crossed what may be seen as *Kalunga's* energizing force at the boundary between worlds and thereby entered into *Kala*, the time of birth. This reading is derived from the changed experience of space as one moves from outside to inside, from secular to sacred, from known to unknown worlds. The sounds that accompanied this passage, Kimbangu and his singing attendants in an adjacent room (Andersson, 1958), enhanced this transition. Upon entering this second room, participants were cosmically situated in *Tukula* time, the height of transformative power and energy. This was suggested both by the congregational act of passing through *Kalunga* and by the ritual performance they witnessed once inside. Voiced power, words and song were as important to Kimbangu's performance as they had been to *banganga* ritual. Efraim Andersson reports that singers "played an important part in the healing of the sick. The prophet could not fulfill his functions in their absence" (1958, p. 53). Newly healed, people left Kimbangu via a third room to the left of the altar. From here they moved outdoors and bathed in a nearby river. In doing so, they enacted the final stage of *dikenga*, passing through *Luvemba*, beyond the physical world of *ku nseke*, for spiritual rebirth in water.

Further compelling evidence exists for the survival of BaKongo cosmology within the visual culture of Simon Mpadi's L'Eglise des Noirs en Afrique (ENAF) and the Khaki movement from which it arose. Though spatial constraints do not permit great elaboration, brief mention of this evidence seems necessary to the foregoing argument. As it exists today, the culture of EJCSK differs significantly from that of ENAF. Mpadi, however, claims to have the confidence of Kimbangu and looks to him as a guiding prophet. The visual manifestations of BaKongo cosmology within Mpadi's church thus accentuate Kimbangu's role in bridging pre- and post-colonial religious expression.

Simon Mpadi (b. 1909) claims to be the younger twin of Kimbangu, and in a speech of 1960 described the divine intervention that induced their births several decades apart (MacGaffey, 1983).[12] Kimbangu and Mpadi share at least two experiences important to their roles as prophets. Both were dismissed Baptist catechists (see note 6) who subsequently received their calling in a dream. In Mpadi's dream he received a khaki uniform, a staff, oil for blessing and a book for recording names (MacGaffey, 1983). The uniform was like those worn in the Salvation Army, which arrived in the Congo (Belgian and French) in 1934 carrying a red flag with a prominent "S" at the center. The color and initial caused people to associate the mission with the Second Coming of Simon Kimbangu (MacGaffey, 1983; Martin, 1975). Mpadi interpreted it thus and, due to the appearance of the uniform in his dream, determined that his destiny lay within the mission. By 1939 he proposed to Captain Becquet of the Salvation Army that a Mission of the Blacks be established

(Martin, 1975). Becquet rejected the idea and dismissed Mpadi, who went on to form ENAF. The rapid growth of Khakism or Mpadism, as ENAF is sometimes called (Andersson, 1958; MacGaffey, 1983; Martin, 1975), was at least partially due to the ways its visual and verbal references recalled those of Kongo cosmology. Andersson writes, "When Khaki has made any headway in a place it often spreads like a prairie fire, perhaps above all among the adherents of the native religions, who now feel at home in a way in which they had by no means felt before" (1958, p. 152). Since forming an independent church was illegal, Mpadi landed in prison in Lubumbashi, the same that held Kimbangu (Martin, 1975). Mpadi was released in 1960 and returned to ENAF.

Many objects and dress motifs in ENAF ritual recall those used by *banganga*. Foremost, the objects served protective functions, guarding their owners against evil spirits called *bankuyu*. Coiled copper wires are fastened to clothing and hung above doors as snares in which to trap such *bankuyu* (Andersson, 1958). Cloths called *muchuali* were carried and waved at patients during healing ceremonies and tied around their heads in order to fasten a cure within (Andersson, 1958). Mpadi wears such a cloth patterned with stars and fringe around his neck and his long red silk robe bears these motifs as well (see photographs in Barrett, 1968; MacGaffey, 1983). His cap is decorated with three horizontal stripes and a red cross on top. Mpadi carries a staff just as *banganga* and Kimbangu did, with patterns that are unfortunately indecipherable in the available photographs.

A flag with a crossed sun motif appears in a photograph of Mpadi and attendants taken in 1970 (in MacGaffey, 1983, plate 12). The sun is cropped from the top of the image, but the patterning within it suggests allusion to the cosmogram (figure 2.2). Furthermore, the sun itself is a reference to BaKongo cosmology, its passing regarded as four moments, or dams, of time (Fu Kiau Kia Bunseki, 1994; Thompson and Cornet, 1981). On the ENAF flag, the dividing axis, a design sewn from darker fabric, pierces the sun from beyond its circumference, dividing it into upper and lower semi-spheres. This horizontal bar is itself crossed within the sun by a two-toned line that turns at a 90-degree angle at both ends to run parallel with the dark dividing bar on either side. The form created is at once a block letter "S" and a gesture like that in figure 2.3. Words sewn in lighter fabric encircle the sun motif and stars adorn each corner.

The table used in Mpadi's rituals has a red cross painted at its center that clients sat upon while undergoing treatment (MacGaffey, 1983). Given Mpadi's dislike of the crucifix (in a speech of 1960 he described it as the key which locks Africans in prison; MacGaffey, 1983), the motif likely represents the four stages of the Kongo cosmogram. *Banganga* had similarly sat clients at the center of such crossroads during divination (Thompson, 1984, 1993; Thompson and Cornet, 1981). Mpadi's books contained recipes for "medicines", called *minkisi*, used in healing ceremonies of ENAF (Andersson, 1958; MacGaffey, 1983). Like the *bilongo* used by *banganga*, the substances were taken from the earth and indeed Wyatt MacGaffey makes the parallel explicit in stating that "medicines and their administration are like those of any *nganga*" (1983, p. 203).

This chapter has argued that the popular appeal of Simon Kimbangu and Simon Mpadi of Central Africa have been due, in significant part, to the ways their Christian performances and ritual objects recall well established BaKongo religious convictions. Like *banganga* before them, they became living repositories for BaKongo cosmology. Though this argument is more readily accepted by scholars interested in Mpadi's ENAF (Andersson, 1958; MacGaffey, 1983), it is more contentious with regard to Kimbangu. Scholars concerned with his church as it exists today (Hastings, 1994; Isichei, 1995; Martin, 1968, 1975) assume that Kimbangu's legacy stems from a break he made with established religious practice, performance and belief. With greater attention to the details of BaKongo rituals, however, it may clearly be argued that Kimbangu adopted these, in altered form, to profess for his people in a time of great need. In BaKongo cosmology, access to change was only available through a conceptual fusing of identities between ritual experts and the spirits contained in their objects. Kimbangu's identity as a mediator was already well established through the dress, objects, performance, song and space of BaKongo religious ritual. Thus the beliefs visualized through the use of *minkisi minkondi* did not die with the destruction of objects in Kimbangu's church. Rather, they took a different shape – were transformed, so to speak, in a manner appropriate to *dikenga* itself.

Notes

1. Christian elements of Kimbanguism are not addressed here, nor is an analysis of the syncretic melding of multiple belief systems. Only aspects of BaKongo cosmology are addressed, as they were expressed by Kimbangu himself. It is necessary to note that BaKongo and European-derived customs and beliefs have continuously blended in this region for at least five centuries.

2. Janzen and MacGaffey (1974) reveal that the French translation of the catechism omits a story significant to the argument presented here, suggesting that Kimbangu's history has been selectively recorded according to audience. Oddly, EJCSK explains the significance of Kimbangu's birth name as indicative of the powers he was destined to exercise, yet the church ignores any practice aligned to indigenous beliefs (MacGaffey, 1977b).

3. Congo with a "C" denotes colonial and post-colonial territory, physical and social. Kongo with a "K" distinguishes the civilization and its people, BaKongo, from colonial structures.

4. Kongo Kings also used *minkisi minkondi* in legal proceedings (MacGaffey, 1977a, 1986b, 1988, 1993; Thompson, 1978, 1984, 1986, 1993; Thompson and Cornet, 1981). Their use in such rites will not be discussed in this chapter, though MacGaffey does suggest a dependence on religion in this setting, noting that any decision would ultimately be "a function of the spirit" (1970, p. 206).

5. This rendering is based on one published in an article by A. Fu Kiau Kia Bunseki (1994), a leading BaKongo philosopher. It is now popularly referenced: I have seen it on wrist watches; Thompson (1993) illustrates its appearance on an altar in the Bronx made by an artist who identifies with the philosophy it represents.

6. *Minkisi minkondi* are no longer made for ritual purposes. Those on the art market today were made for tourists. Thus, when referring to these objects in religious context, the past tense is used. The beliefs they represent, however, are held today. Thus, when referring to beliefs, the present tense is used. MacGaffey (1993) and Songolo (1994) note that today the beliefs are given visual form in a variety of medicated objects (ink pens, sunglasses) seen throughout Central Africa.

7. Kimbangu was first called to prophesy in 1918. Refusing, he moved to Leopoldville, now called Kinshasa. His plans to teach for a Baptist missionary were not successful, so he returned to Nkamba, his birthplace, in 1921. Legend has it that misfortune befell him in Leopoldville because he refused the first call; he was destined to become the first *ngunza*.

8. This account is said to be Kimbangu's own, translated into English by a BaKongo named Budimbu.

9. Andersson (1958) reports that Kimbangu's mother was a trained *nganga;* van Wing (1959) ascribes his father this role; Bazola (1968) writes that his aunt, who oversaw much of his upbringing, was a *nganga*.

10. Martin (1975) believes this report is inaccurate. She examined the staff, which has been preserved and it has no red cloth attached to it. It is possible, however, that the cloth has been lost. She further supports her position with testimony from Kimbangu's "closest fellow workers" (p. 41). These memories contradict those of others recorded by Andersson (1958).

11. Descriptions of Kimbangu's services are found in Andersson (1958), Janzen and MacGaffey (1974) and MacGaffey (1983). Martin (1968, 1975) assumes that services she witnessed in his church in the 1960s–1970s directly reflect those practiced by Kimbangu in 1921. Suggested parallels drawn between the space of Kimbangu's original church and the space of the BaKongo cosmogram are my own, as are those that concern the performances that took place in each.

12. Twins enjoy heightened status in BaKongo society since they were believed to be children of *bisimbi*, which intervened in their conception (Jacobson-Widding, 1979; Janzen and MacGaffey, 1974).

References

Andersson, E. (1958). *Messianic popular movements in the Lower Congo*. Uppsala, Sweden: Almqvist & Wiksell.

Barrett, D. B. (1968). *Schism and renewal in Africa*. Nairobi: Oxford University Press.

Bassani, E. (1977). Kongo nail fetishes from the Chiloango River area. *African Arts* 10(3), 36–40.

Bazola, E. (1968). Le Kimbanguisme. *Cahiers des religions africaines*. Kinshasa: Louvanium.

Bockie, S. (1993). *Death and the invisible powers: The world of Kongo belief*. Bloomington: Indiana University Press.

Dawson, D. (1994). Personal communication.

Fu Kiau Kia Bunseki, A. (1974). Man in his world. In J. M. Janzen & W. MacGaffey (Eds.), *An anthology of Kongo religion* (p. 34). Lawrence: University of Kansas.

Fu Kiau Kia Bunseki, A. (1980). *The African book without title*. Privately published manuscript.

Fu Kiau Kia Bunseki, A. (1994). *Ntangu-tandu-kolo*: The Bantu-Kongo concept of time. In J. K. Adjaye (Ed.) *Time in the black experience* (pp. 17–34). Westport, CN: Greenwood.

Goffman, E. (1997). *The Goffman reader*. C. Lemert & A. Branaman (Eds.), Malden, MA: Blackwell.

Hastings, A. (1994). *The Church in Africa 1450–1950*. Oxford: Clarendon Press.

Isichei, E. (1995). *A history of Christianity in Africa*. London: Society for Promoting Christian Knowledge.

Jacobson-Widding, A. (1979). *Red-white-black as a mode of thought*. Uppsala, Sweden: Almqvist & Wiksell.

Janzen, J. M. & MacGaffey, W. (1974). *An anthology of Kongo religion*. Lawrence: University of Kansas.

Laman, K. E. (1936). *The Kongo* (Vol. 3). Uppsala, Sweden: Almqvist & Wiksell.

Laman, K. E. (1964). *Dictionnaire KiKongo-Français* (2nd ed.) Ridgewood, NJ: Gregg.

MacGaffey, W. (1970). *Custom and government in the Lower Congo*. Los Angeles: California University Press.

MacGaffey, W. (1977a). Fetishism revisited: Kongo *nkisi* in sociological perspective. *Africa* 47(2), 172–84.

MacGaffey, W. (1977b). Cultural roots of Kongo prophetism. *History of Religions* 17(1), 177–93.

MacGaffey, W. (1983). *Modern Kongo prophets*. Bloomington: Indiana University Press.

MacGaffey, W. (1986a). Ethnography and the closing of the frontier in lower Congo, 1885–1921. *Africa*. 56(3), 263–79.

MacGaffey, W. (1986b). *Religion and society in Central Africa: The BaKongo of lower Zaire*. Chicago: University of Chicago Press.

MacGaffey, W. (1988). Complexity, astonishment and power: The visual vocabulary of Kongo *minkisi*. *Journal of Southern African Studies* 14(2), 188–203.

MacGaffey, W. (1990). The personhood of Ritual Objects: Kongo *minkisi*. *Etnofoor* 3(1), 45–61.

MacGaffey, W. (1991). *Art and healing of the BaKongo commented by themselves*. Bloomington: Indiana University Press.

MacGaffey, W. (1993). The eyes of understanding: Kongo *minkisi*. In W. MacGaffey & M. D. Harris (Eds.), *Astonishment and power* (pp. 21–103). Washington, DC: Smithsonian Institution.

MacGaffey, W. (1994). Kimbanguism and the question of syncretism in Zaire. In T. D. Blakely, W. E. A. van Beek & D. L. Thomson (Eds.), *Religion in Africa* (pp. 240–56). London: James Currey.

Martin, M. L. (1968). *Prophetic Christianity in the Congo: The Church on Earth through the Prophet Simon Kimbangu*. Braamfontein: Christian Institute of Southern Africa.

Martin, M. L. (1975). *Kimbangu: An African prophet and his church*. Oxford: Basil Blackwell (D. Moore, Trans).

Schoffeleers, M. (1994). Christ in African folk theology: The *nganga* paradigm. In T. D. Blakely, W. E. A. van Beek & D. L. Thomson (Eds.), *Religion in Africa* (pp. 72–88). London: James Currey.

Songolo, A. (1994). Personal communication.

Tambwe, M. F. (1994). Personal communication.

Thompson, R. F. (1978). The grand Detroit *n"kondi*. *Bulletin of the Detroit Institute of Arts* 56(4), 207–21.

Thompson, R. F. (1984). *Flash of the spirit*. New York, Vintage Books.

Thompson, R. F. (1986). *Zinkondi*: Moral philosophy coded in blades and nails. *Bulletin du Musée Barbier-Mueller* 31(Juin), 31–5.

Thompson, R. F. (1993). *Face of the gods: Art and altars of Africa and the African Americas*. New York: Museum for African Art.

Thompson, R. F. & Cornet, J. (1981). *The four moments of the sun*. Washington, DC: National Art Gallery.

van Wing, J. (1959) *Etudes Bakongo*, 2nd ed. Brussels: Desclée de Brouwer.

Volavkova, Z. (1972). *Nkisi* figures of the lower Congo. *African Arts* 5(2), 52–9.

3

Dressing the Divine Horsemen: Dress as Spirit Identification in Haitian Vodou

Susan Tselos

Ceremony and Dress: Introduction

Haitian Vodou *seremoni* (ceremonies) are a colorful, exuberant, vociferous way of honoring and worshipping the *lwa*, a pantheon of ancestral spirits who govern the well-being of the living. The *lwa* are intermediaries between the living and *Gran Met* (God). The *lwa* are responsible for all aspects of life. They provide for the success or failure of crops, good or bad business fortunes, financial riches or poverty, the life or death of a loved one and the abundance or dearth of one's personal love life. Throughout each *seremoni*, the religious and cultural history of Haiti is visibly retold: elements of African religious beliefs and art forms, specifically from Benin (formerly Dahomey) and Kongo, seventeenth- and eighteenth- century French Catholicism, references to *commedia dell'arte* and Freemasonry, as well as the French nobility. These disparate elements combined in the calaloo that was colonial Haiti. The result is a stunning, visually arresting method of worship, born of cultural appropriation and bricolage. Within this ritual atmosphere, the collective memories and understanding of the participants provide a setting within which direct communication with the *lwa* is encouraged and expected.[1]

The *lwa* are called into the *ounfo* (temple) by a combination of *veve* (sacred line drawings), song, sacrifice and ritual drumming. These elements work together to create a high-energy, spiritually charged environment into which the *lwa* ascend to the world of the living and directly manifest themselves by inhabiting the body of the initiated. The host body is most often the *oungan* or *manbo* (Vodou priest or priestess) but may sometimes be another initiate.

The human host is commonly referred to as the "horse" and the *lwa* as the "divine horseman". Each *lwa* is initially recognized by his or her body language and speech. Once the divine possession has taken place and the *lwa* is firmly within the body of the host, sacred garments, which have been consecrated for use by the *lwa*, are brought forward from the *baji* (altar room). The "horse" is then dressed in these garments for the duration of the possession, during which the *lwa* gives council as well as blessings or admonishments to its *serviteurs*. The garments worn by each *lwa* are specific to him or her alone and every *ounfo* is careful to have the garments freshly cleaned and waiting for the divine manifestation.

The purpose of this chapter is to discuss the ceremonial context of Vodou in which the social and religious history of Haiti is recreated. The roles of the various participants will be identified through their status within the *sosyete* (the Vodou religious community), their use of ceremonial garments and how these garments serve to control or free them during the ceremonial roles played. Incorporated into the discussion will be references to the work of Erving Goffman and Mary Douglas, whose writings suggest that religious groups who perform ceremonies of transition not only express a social solidarity but also possess a shared vocabulary of body idiom which provides commonly understood information.

The discussion of the Vodou *seremoni* will focus primarily on the sacred garments worn by the *lwa* during manifestation. The garments worn by the *ounsi* (initiates) and *oungan* prior to manifestation will also be discussed, since they act to bind the group together as a unit and are considered non-verbal identification of their status within the religious community. Upon possession by the *lwa*, the change of garments simultaneously separates the chosen "horse" from the other participants in the *seremoni* and signifies the dramatic spiritual change that has occurred. Using the *seremoni* as a context, I will also discuss the historical religious and cultural appropriations that shaped Haitian Vodou, laying the groundwork for the use of dress within the current religion. Economic considerations of the use of these ritual garments will also be addressed, since in a country as poor as Haiti, financial outlay for the garments and other ceremonial materials is enormous, often creating a burden in the process.

Divine Horsemen

Like the spiritual pantheons of the ancient Greeks and Romans, the Vodou *lwa* may number into the hundreds, but for the purpose of this chapter, only a few will be chosen for discussion. The *lwa* are divided into *nachons* (nations) determined primarily by their African or New World origins. The two groups for which most *seremoni* are performed today are the Rada – recognized as cool, sweet and benevolent – whose origins in Alladah in the ancient Kingdom of Dahomey (which encompasses parts of today's Western Nigeria, Benin and Togo), and the Petro, with origins in the New World: born of slavery and revolt, they are recognized as hot, bitter and violent. Together, the *lwa* symbolize the natural values of humans (love, jealousy, fidelity, benevolence, kindness, anger and rage), as well as elements of nature: wind, fire, vegetation, thunder, rain and water). Within these roles, the *lwa* are recognized and honored as the foundations and cohesion of the cultural social group.

Cultural Antecedents

African Roots

Africa provided the basic structural elements of Vodou. Under French rule, during the eighteenth century, over one million slaves were brought from the Slave Coast of Africa to the New World. The slaves who arrived in San Domingue (Haiti) were primarily Fon and Yoruba from Benin, Togo and Nigeria. Later during the eighteenth century, slaves from the Central African kingdom of Kongo also survived the Middle Passage to San Domingue. The art, liturgy and theology seen in Haitian Vodou today are a mix of common denominators from these areas. Many of the Fon artistic forms are created from the predisposition to borrow and the pairing of disparate elements.

In addition, belief in a pantheon of intermediary spirits who manifest directly through spirit possession, along with liturgical efficacy of music and dance, are common elements of both West and Central African religious practices. The Fon provided many of the elements of Haitian Vodou: the word *vodun* is Fon for "sacred" and *ounsi* means "wife of the spirit". According to Blier (1995), many of the Haitian *lwa* have counterparts in Benin and Togo. The most widely recognized of these are *Danbala* and *Ayida Wedo*, *Ogou*, *Guede*, *Legba* and *Agwe*.

Kongo art forms are also seen within Vodou culture. *Minkisi*, Kongo medicinal packets which contain elements believed to embody and direct spiritual energy, have been transformed into *Pake* Kongo in Haiti. They have retained their shape and powers of divine attraction, but have undergone the process of creolization into much more elegant packaging through the use of satin and sequins. According to Thompson (1983), the use of *veve* on the ground during ceremonies also has antecedents in both Fon and Kongo culture.

Blier (1995) has documented the use of textiles and costume within *vodun* ritual in Benin: "Hats, draped cloths and skirts bearing applique motifs also were a principal part of the attire of local *vodun* priests and devotees (p. 68)."

She points out, however, that there are also many distinctions in the way Vodou in the Americas is different today than in Africa. She bases her evaluation on the change in material goods available and the use of textiles which it has been possible to embellish with various sequins, buttons and other decorative elements not widely available in Africa (Blier, 1995).

The Yoruba culture offers color-coding as a connection to Haitian Vodou. Among the Yoruba, three chromatic groups are recognized: *funfun* which includes white, silver and gray is a group that evokes coolness and is associated with age and wisdom; *pupa* includes warm/hot colors of red, orange, deep yellow and pink and is associated with heat, passion and aggression; *dudu* bridges the hot/warm and cold/cool colors and includes dark colors such as black, blue, purple and green, as well as dark brown, dark red and dark gray (Drewal, 1998).

These chromatic divisions are important not only in recognizing Yoruba-based colors for the Haitian *lwa*, but also in identifying the nature of their temperament. Each *lwa* has colors and personality specific to it; for example, red represents *Ogou*, the fierce warrior, sword drawn in the heat of battle, while white represents *Danbala*, the ancient, venerable, wise, benevolent serpent spirit.

The colors that represent the *lwa* are seen not only in the garments worn during possession, but also in the garments known as *rad penitans*, worn by serviteurs to protect themselves from evil and to attract good energy to themselves. Men wear shirts of multicolored strips; women wear dresses of the same. These garments are in abundant evidence at the Vodou pilgrimage sites of *Sodo* and *Trou Sen Jak*. According to Thompson (1995), this form of Vodou ritual dress structurally aligns itself "with sub-Saharan narrow-strip textile traditions. They are edge-sewn in Haiti, not unlike certain textiles in Abomey or Mbanza Kongo" (p. 92).

The French Connection

The African religious elements discussed above made their way to Haiti (San Domingue) on the shoulders and in the heads of the slaves who were imported by the French. At the time of colonization, Haiti was considered the "Pearl of the Antilles", the wealthiest colony in France's possession. In order to keep up the exportation of sugar and other goods, France imported thousands of new slaves on a continuous basis. Due to relentless, unspeakable cruelty on the part of the French, slaves were worked to death in several years and new Africans brought to replace them. A result of this is that the African traditions were constantly being reinforced throughout the years of colonization.

Catholicism was already well known in many of the areas of Africa from which the slaves originated. The Portuguese had begun to establish outposts along the West Coast of Africa by the middle of the fifteenth century. In 1491, one year before Columbus ever set foot in the New World, the king of Kongo was baptized as a Catholic. In 1685, France developed the "Code Noir", which declared that all slaves in their colonies would be baptized and the practice of any religion except Catholicism would be forbidden. To satisfy this decree, the Catholic priests introduced the slaves to images of the saints, alongside stories of their lives, in hopes of educating and converting the Africans. However, the groups of slaves shipped from West Africa were already used to borrowing and appropriating imagery and theology from their neighbors. In the New World, they continued to do the same with this new pantheon offered to them. Within the images of the saints were symbols that they could identify with their own loved and familiar spirits and ancestors.

Syncretization

Sen Jak

The appropriation of iconography as well as other aspects of European cultural influences is understood by the term "syncretism". An example of this is the image of St. James the Elder (the patron saint of Spain), also known as Santiago, who is recognized among the Vodouists as *Sen Jak* (Saint Jacques). The ubiquitous image of *Sen Jak* seen today in Haiti is that of a powerful and strong warrior on horseback, trampling on the body of a Moor. In his right hand is a sword pointed upward in victory. An obvious and mighty hero, this image held the symbols of *Ogou*, known as *Ogun* to the Yoruba and Fon. We already know the African *Ogun* as a warrior spirit, the patron of iron and other metal workers. In Haiti he was recognized not only as such, but also as the senior member of a spiritual military family which included heroes of Haitian history and their successful independence from the French. In addition, his annual *fête* takes place on July 26th, the Catholic feast day of St. James. As noted before, in Africa, *Ogun's* color is red; in Haitian Vodou, *Ogou/Sen Jak* is represented by red and blue, the original African red evolving into the red and blue borrowed from the Haitian national flag. During possession by the *lwa*, often the horse will be dressed in red military uniform or other red or blue garments. A sword or machete is part of the ensemble as well.

Gede

A second example of the syncretization of the image of a Catholic saint with African spirits is that of St. Gerard, who represents the family of Haitian Vodou *lwa* known as *Gede*. The Catholic St. Gerard is a somber-looking young priest, standing in front of a table upon which rests a skull. The colors in the chromolithographs of him are predominantly mauve, black and white (the funeral colors of the Catholic Church). According to Blier (1995), the origins of *gede* are in Benin, near the Fon capital of Abomey, where *gede* have ritual control over the land and those buried in it.

In Haiti, the *Gede* are recognized as a family of spirits of the ancestral dead. They are graveyard *lwa*, whose patriarch is *Bawon Samedi*. They are the masters of healing and the keepers of small children. They are guardians of the past, the masters of death and simultaneously, the future of life. They are the keeper of mortals after life and the ones to whom we all eventually go. As such, they make a mockery of human endeavors, laugh at our sexuality and poke fun at our self-importance. Their annual *seremoni* are November 1st and 2nd, coinciding with Catholic All Saints' and All Souls' Days.

Ezili

The name of *Ezili Freda Daome*, the *lwa* of love, feminine beauty and wealth reflects her African origins as *Ezili* of Ouidah, Dahomey. Within Nigeria is a river *Azili* and according to Alfred Metraux, today in Benin, Nigeria and Togo there are still shrines dedicated to *Ezili* (1959). In Haiti she became syncretized with the Catholic Virgin of Sorrows (Mater Dolorosa). *Ezili* adopts the accoutrements of Mater Dolorosa, who is depicted as a beautiful, young, weeping Madonna wearing garments of satin, surrounded by jewels and gold hearts. In addition, because of the river *Azili* in Nigeria, *Ezili* is recognized as having an aquatic incarnation as *Lasirenn*, a mermaid who, if captured by a human man, has the ability to make him rich.

Zaka

The last *lwa* that I will discuss in detail is *Zaka*, the Vodou *lwa* of agriculture (Figure 3.1). *Zaka's* origins are somewhat obscure. According to Desmangles (1992) the name *Zaka* probably derives from the Taino Indian word *zada*, meaning corn. In addition, in Northern Haiti he is recognized as *Mazaka*, also derived from the Taino word *maza*, or maize in English. This would connect him to Haiti's pre-Columbian Amerindian culture. However, his characterizations within Haitian Vodou relate him to *Yalode*, the Fon diety of agriculture, who is identified with yams instead of corn.

More important for this discussion, however, is *Zaka's* syncretism with the Catholic image of St. Isidore (Figure 3.2). St. Isidore is pictured as a poor peasant kneeling in prayer in the fields. He wears rough, homespun garments and often carries a straw bag over his shoulder. The *lwa Zaka* is regarded as a poor country bumpkin, lacking in manners. He is also referred to as *Kouzen Zaka*, indicating that he is the cousin, or brother of a common person.

Additional Appropriations

According to Cosentino, there is evidence of colonial Haiti within each Vodou *seremoni*. "Echoes of the *ancien régime* reverberate in the curtsy of the *ounsi*, the handshake of the *oungan*, the martial feints of the *laplas* during the ceremonial presentation of the *drapo* whose sequined surfaces mime both military flags and the glittering iconography of a Catholic chasuble" (1995). There is no doubt that the nightmare of colonial life provided the props hungrily appropriated by the African slaves. Historical accounts provide a glimpse of civil society at that time: absentee French plantation owners, pampered French wives, uneducated overseers, lower-class shopkeepers, free

Figure 3.1 *Kouzin Zaka,* the *lwa* of agriculture; his image is painted on the wall in an *oumfo* in Port-au-Prince. Foods are offered to him during his annual ceremony in May. Photo by Susan E. Tselos.

people of color who were the offspring of slave owners and their black or mulatto mistresses. In addition, the colonized slaves and the slaves just off the ships from Africa led to group jealousy and suspicion.

Cosentino continues that all strata of this grotesque society experienced the daily offerings of the Jesuit churches, Masonic lodges and *commedia dell'arte* presented in theaters such as the one at Cap Haitien, as well as the numerous *soirées* where the minuet was danced in ballgowns and gold epaulettes. None of this escaped notice and eventual appropriation by the Africans. All was for the taking and all provided a rich treasure house of customs and costumes

Figure 3.2 Chromolithograph of St. Isidore, who is visually syncretized with Voodou *Iwa Kouzin Zaka*. Kneeling in the fields, he wears garments of rough cloth to identify him as a poor agricultural peasant. Photo by Susan E. Tselos.

eventually incorporated into the Vodou *seremoni*. Even the names of the *lwa* reflect colonial social roles: *General Ogou, Admiral Agwe, Bawon Samedi, Kouzin Zaka and Maitress Ezili*. These ancient titles are further borne out within the *seremoni* through body language and use of the sacred garments worn during manifestation (1995).

The Ceremonial as Performed

Setting the Stage

Each *seremoni* includes numerous practices which vary from *ounfo* to *ounfo* and which complement as well as complicate the basic rituals. In addition, there are endless subtleties in etiquette, taught at initiation, which are loaded with symbolic meaning. However, the description which I will provide is that of the basic rituals included within many *seremoni* in the area of Port-au-Prince with which I am the most familiar.

Seremoni

The *seremoni* commences with an invocation of song and prayer, in which a long list of *lwa* are called by name. In order to reach the world of the *lwa*, *Legba* the gatekeeper must be called to open the gates so that the mortals may invite the designated *lwa* into the *ounfo* and subsequently into the body of the devotee. The *oungan* is assisted in this by his *laplas*, or second-in-command and a choir of *ounsi*. During this time a sacred *veve*, incorporating the symbols of the *lwa* for whom the *seremoni* is being given, is drawn on the ground at the base of the *poteau mitan*. There are salutations between the *oungan* and visiting dignitaries from other *ounfo*, as well as important invited guests. The *oungan* and *manbo* greet each other with a series of hand-shakes and pirouettes, kneeling and kissing the ground before the one of higher rank. A battery of drummers helps to *"fe cho"* (heat up) the *seremoni* as the pace of the songs and invocation quickens.

A series of libations are performed in front of sacred objects as a way of salutation. The cardinal points are anointed, as well as the sacred drums, the *poteau mitan* and the doorway from the *badji*, or altar room.

Following this, the *lwa* is beckoned with the spectacular presentation of the *drapo* (ceremonial flags) representing the *sosyete* (society). The *drapo* are paraded around the *poteau mitan* by two *drapo reine* (flag queens), who are chased by the *laplas* in a mock battle. During this time the energy in the *ounfo* is rising. The singing, urged by the furious drumming, rises to a level of cacophony.

Simultaneously, sacrificial offerings, appropriate to the *lwa* for whom the *seremoni* is being performed, are given at the base of the *poteau mitan*. In addition to the prayer, drumming, dancing and flag parade, each sacrifice acts to reinforce the bond between the mortals and the *lwa*.

By this time the spiritual environment in the *ounfo* has reached a peak and the *lwa* enters the world of the mortals through the body of the *oungan*. The possession is usually rocky and rough. The body of the "horse" shudders and convulses as the *lwa* enters. The transformation takes only a minute or so, as the "horse" succumbs to divine and the *lwa* is identified by body language and speech.

Immediately following the transference, several high-ranking initiates help the possessed "horse" into the *badji*, to cloth him or her in the garments which serve to honor and further identify the divine. The consecrated garments are "host-specific", meaning that they have been made specifically to fit the body of the *oungan* or *manbo* within whom the divine manifestation has taken place. A few minutes later, the *lwa* enters the main part of the *ounfo* once more, ready to be saluted and fed. In turn, the *lwa* then proceeds with counsel, admonishments and further words of wisdom for the group.

When the *seremoni* is complete, the *lwa* leaves. The "horse's" body again goes through convulsions as the divine departs. Exhausted and usually confused, the "horse", having regained its own mortal self, is helped to a chair for rest and recovery. The ritual objects are retired to the places they occupy when not in use. The *drapo* are rolled around their standards and placed against the altar to renew their sacred strength. The costumes worn by the *lwa* are cleaned and also placed at the altar awaiting the next arrival of the divine.

The Ceremonial as Dressed

Top Hats, Lace and Epaulettes

Although the colors associated with many of the *lwa* may have their origins in Africa, the style of garments worn by them during manifestation is based on the cultural and religious history of colonial Haiti. For further understanding of their ceremonial use, a closer examination of these garments is now required.

The general's uniform worn by *Ogou* during manifestation reflects the power of Napoleon's forces, the pomp and posturing of the French military officers sent to quell the Haitian slave revolt which, successful in the end, provided the African slaves with independence. Following upon the heels of the revolution, the grandeur of the French military uniform became the property of the Haitian revolutionary heroes and finally evolved into the wardrobe of *Ogou*. During manifestation, *Ogou* swaggers and bolts around the *oumfo*, brandishing his machete in the air.

Maitress Ezili, in her role as the *lwa* of love and feminine beauty, is the spiritual incarnation of the beautiful mulatto mistresses of colonization. During possession by *Ezili*, the "horse" is dressed in fine lace, satin, gold jewels, pearls and perfumes. She flirts her way through the *oumfo*, playing the young coquette. However, according to Dayan (1995), she subverts the role she plays. In colonial Haiti, the mulatto mistress received her jewels and finery through submission to a dominant slavemaster. In this role, the sentiments attached to her were of lust and debauchery, rather than love. As played out within the *seremoni*, *Ezili*, as the pale, privileged mulatress enters the body of a black devotee, thereby recreating a history of dominance and submission.

According to tradition, *Bawon Samedi*, the leader of the *Gede* (both a singular *lwa* as well as a group of *lwa*), prefers to dress as a dandy in top hat and tails during his manifestation. The colors of his costume are those of the funerary colors of the Catholic Church: black, white and mauve. But the outfit is equally influenced by Catholicism's nemesis, Freemasonry. Although there were numerous secret societies thriving in Africa at the time of the slave trade, Freemasonry constitutes the largest secret brotherhood of the western world. During colonial times (and still existing today), there were numerous Masonic Lodges in Haiti. Initiation into Masonic temples involves costumes and role-playing. One of the initiation characters is a Baron von Altendorf, whose outfit includes a top hat, mourning coat, as well as coffins and gravedigger's tools (Cosentino, 1995).

I passed a funeral gathering outside a large Catholic Church on Delmas Road in May 1998 in Port-au-Prince. The funeral evidently was for an important member of the Masons, who may also have been an important *oungan*, since many *oungan* are also Masons. Milling around outside the church were up to a dozen men, dressed in black hats and cutaway jackets, black and white striped pants, with white shirts and mauve handkerchiefs in their pockets. It was a sunny, late afternoon and some of the men were wearing sunglasses. It could have been a gathering of *Gede*, had it not been for the circumstance and the location.

During possession, the *Bawon Samedi* and *Gede* also wear sunglasses (they live with the dead, the light of the earth blinds them) and their faces are powdered white (they are, after all, *lwa* of the dead). They carry *zozos* (carved wooden penises) with which they make obscene gestures and poke fun at the participants in the *seremoni*. This further identifies their role as not only the *lwa* of the dead but that of sexuality as well.

During manifestation *Kouzen Zaka* is initially identified as a country peasant by his body language and lack of refined manners. He hungrily approaches the sacrificial food prepared for him (Figure 3.3). With his hands he stuffs food into his mouth, spilling some down the front of his blue denim shirt. After his meal, he smokes a rough-hewn pipe. As depicted in the image of the Catholic Saint Isidore and further identifying *Zaka* as a country peasant, the clothes worn during manifestation are of rough, denim fabric; often of the type made in Haiti known as *karabel*. Traditionally, the outfit worn by agrarian Haitian peasants was made up of pants and shirt of this fabric, a

Figure 3.3 *Oungan* E.P., wearing the rough woven garments that identify him as being possessed by *Kouzin Zaka*. Note the straw bag with tassels and the lattice work designs on the denim shirt. Photo by Susan E. Tselos.

straw hat and a straw shoulder bag called a *makout*. The denim outfit worn by *Zaka* recalls the blue pants and cape in the image of St. Isidore (Figure 3.4). The *makout* carried during manifestation has ties to the early Spanish ownership of the island. According to Thompson (1995) the makout is derived from an Iberian straw knapsack known as an *alforja*, which, like the bag worn by *Zaka*, has red trim and tassels at the bottom corners. In addition to the Iberian influence, the name "*makout*" is derived from the Ki-Kongo word *nkutu* that describes a "small cotton bag carried on the shoulder".

Figure 3.4 During the annual ceremony for *Kousin Zaka*, the *oungan* becomes possessed by the *lwa*, during which time he acts like *Zaka* and wears clothes reserved for him as well. Photo by Susan E. Tselos.

The Haitian bag is covered with a latticework design also seen in the sacred *veve* ground-drawing done during *seremoni* for *Zaka*. According to Thompson, McGaffey (1993) has described this design as similar to knotted-cord designs around some *nkisi* bags from Kongo. However, according to LeGrace Benson (1996) the latticework design has probable Muslim influences, resembling mystical square diagrams found on Islamic amulets. Muslim influence was pervasive in West Africa since 900 CE and ships' manifests show that during the early eighteenth century there were large groups of Islamic Mende slaves brought to Hispaniola.

Symbols of Unity

The garments worn by participants during the *seremoni* are visual markers of the unity of the group. In most *seremoni*, the *ounsi*, as well as the *oungan* or *manbo*, wear white garments, symbols of purity, at the commencement of the *servis*. The men wear white shirts and trousers, usually made of cotton. Often, but not always, the shirt will be the guyabera style, which is worn over the pants like a tunic. Not only is this style of shirt common in everyday use in tropical Haiti, but unlike a western-style shirt that is tucked into trousers, it allows for more freedom in movement during the salutations and possession by the *lwa*.

The women wear white dresses of varying individual designs. They usually have full skirts and wide sleeves, which again make for ease in the movements required during the *seremoni*. Although sleeveless dresses would perhaps provide even more comfort to the moving body, they are worn less frequently. In addition, the length of the dress always falls below the knees, usually down to the calf. Their heads are covered by white *mouchoir*, wrapped around the head in the fashion worn by many of the African diaspora, especially within religious communities (see Foster, 1997).

Sometimes, if the *seremoni* is being made to honor and pay respect to a *lwa* to whom the *ounfo* is dedicated, the *ounsi* will commence the *seremoni* already wearing the colors sacred to the *lwa*. As an example, for *Ogou*, the women might wear blue dresses and red *mouchoirs* and the men will wear blue guyaberas and trousers and have a red *mouchoir* around their necks. However, the style of the clothes remains consistent to those seen in the white garments.

The clothes worn by the initiates are made specifically for them, to be worn only during *seremoni* or other religious events, such as the annual pilgrimages to sites sacred to the *lwa*. If they know how to sew, the initiates may make the garments themselves. If not, another initiate may make the garments for them. On one occasion, having arrived early for a *seremoni*, I witnessed one poor *ounsi* sewing furiously, desperately trying to finish all the dresses that would be worn that afternoon. At another *seremoni* I attended, the officiating *manbo*, who had come to Haiti from New York, had brought the fabric for all the initiates' garments. She had purchased several white Battenberg lace tablecloths and napkins that the *ounsi* could sew into their individually designed garments. *Manbo* Gladys M., one of my informants, had made her dress of overlapping napkins sewn together at the waist. The bodice was a portion of the body of the tablecloth and the sleeves were again fashioned from two of the napkins.

The men's shirts were also made from the tablecloths and napkins. Designed in the guyabera style, the shirts used the lace edging for collars and the napkins were sewn on the front as pockets. In this instance, by providing the fabric for the *ounsi*'s garments, the *manbo* had enabled the *ounsi* to individualize themselves, while simultaneously identifying them as belonging to a specific group.

Although the style of the white dresses worn by the *ounsi* changes to a certain extent to reflect the current fashion, the wearing of these white garments has been documented numerous times by various photographers. Some of the earliest documentation appears in photos that accompany an otherwise shockingly racist book by an early white visitor to the island (Seabrook, 1929). In addition, other photos from throughout the decades of the twentieth century support this continuity of style remaining consistent with the current fashion of the times (Courlander, 1960; Deren, 1970; Metraux, 1959).

A Matter of Money

Money and gift exchanges play important roles within the structure of the *seremoni*. All of the ritual objects used to show honor and pay respect to the *lwa* must either be purchased, or received as gifts to be used in a ceremonial context. Great effort is made by the Vodou *sosyete* to provide appropriate materials with which to serve the *lwa*.

The idea of money and gift exchange within the Vodou community is discussed in detail by Karen McCarthy Brown. She describes the *seremoni* as a series of interpersonal exchanges of gifts and counter-gifts between man and man and man and the gods (1976). The gift exchange includes the not only the songs and prayers offered to the *lwa* for the receipt of blessings and counsel, but the food which is offered from *serviteur* to *lwa* and then in return from *lwa* to its *serviteurs* (1976). The first she describes as "metonymic" gifts, those that are gifts of time and effort. The gifts of ceremonial food and garments are "metaphoric" in nature, since they merge with the specific personality of each *lwa*.

Haiti is the poorest country in the Western Hemisphere. Eighty percent of the population is illiterate, infant mortality is high and the per capita income is around $300 per year. In this context, the money spent to provide material goods for the Vodou *seremoni* reflects a more than serious desire to serve the *lwa* by the best possible means. If the *lwa* requires a meat sacrifice, such as chickens, goats or bulls, the costs can be prohibitive. The *oungan* is required to obtain all the items for sacrificial use prior to the commencement of the *seremoni*. Often, a member of the *sosyete* may provide the money for purchasing the items, especially if he or she has requested the specific *seremoni*. Otherwise, the *oungan* may receive some of the sacrificial items from initiates for whom the *oungan* has provided help in the past. As the wife of an *oungan*, Gladys M., who is a *manbo* herself, positions herself within the hierarchy of the *ounfo* through various acts of devotion which include doing special favors for the *oungan*, as well as providing various necessities for the day-to-day running of the *ounfo*. Since she is an excellent seamstress, she designs and creates the garments worn by the *oungan* during possession by the *lwa*. She made the blue shirt worn by *Zaka* during manifestation within a *seremoni* performed for him in May, 1998. Note the blue denim fabric of the shirt, as well as the square, latticework designs and symbols specific to *Zaka*, which are discussed earlier in this chapter (Figure 3.4).

Some *oungan* make a pretense of showing off their *konesans* (spiritual knowledge) by producing a *seremoni* laden with material goods. Invited guests will be given the most expensive whiskeys, soft drinks and beer. The altars groan with an abundance of food and the garments provided for the *lwa* are spectacular. (Much time and attention is paid to making the garments worn by the *met tet*, the *lwa* specific to the *oungan* performing the ritual. It is not uncommon for the other, less personally important *lwa* to be dressed in simpler attire, sometimes only a scarf or hat in the appropriate color.) Although the *lwa* expect the best gifts that the *oungan* can provide, human ego and greed may also play a role in what is provided. According to *oungan* Edner P., some *oungan* like to present themselves as being spiritually superior to the other *oungan* with whom they are associated. They do this through an ostentatious display of material goods and food prepared for a specific *seremoni*. However, according to Edner, this can backfire upon the *oungan* by alienating him so much from his peers that they will not participate in his *seremoni* when he needs their additional spiritual strength. An unspoken recognition of checks and balances usually works to keep the members of the greater spiritual community in balance with each other. Too much ego on the part of an *oungan* may be interpreted as offensive to the *lwa* and may pave the way to human misfortune.

Finishing the Ends

Returning to the ideas posed by Goffman, I have attempted to demonstrate that the ritual setting that supports the act of divine possession within Vodou displays a vocabulary of knowledge and memory shared by the participants. The ceremonial space becomes the "setting" which involves the décor, scenery and props for the human action to be played out (1959, p. 22). The preferred choice of *oungan* as "horse" who, at just the right time, becomes the vessel for the divine, supports his role as leader of the group. As such, he commands a specific idiom, exercised continuously without conscious calculation. Prior to divine manifestation, the garments worn by the *manbo* or *oungan* connect them visually to the other participants. They belong together as a social unit. However, because of the prior years of participation as an initiate and recognition by the group as having superior *konesans*, the *oungan* is able to separate himself within the act of ritual obligation. In so doing, the garments used to clothe the *lwa* visually mark the transfer of role of the *oungan* from group member to divine vessel. The result is the balance necessary to human life.

The material presented here also supports the research of Mary Douglas (1973) who states that religious movements that take this form are expressing social solidarity without differentiation and that the possibilities of abandoning conscious control are available only to the extent that the social system relaxes control of the individual. She believes that as such, religion is not compensation, but a fair representation of the social reality experienced by the participants. Douglas' (1973) work also contains reference to Van Gennep (1960), who first discerned the common form in all ceremonies of transition, in which transfer from one social status to another is to be expressed. Gennep noted that material symbols of transition were inevitably used and that the rite itself takes the form of preliminary separation from and reintegration into the community.

Reinforcing the work of both Douglas and Goffman, Haitian scholar Laennec Hurbon believes that within the Haitian Vodou *sosyete*, the *lwa* represent a mode of articulation of the real and the social and the self within the real and the social. Through this the Vodouist experiences his or her identity. Through the act of ritual remembering and living history, the *sosyete* is responsible for the ongoing identification and well-being of the divine. In turn, the divine performs a continual dialogue with the living, insuring the health of the *serviteurs*. To be deprived of dialogue with them is to be deprived of dialogue with the community and in turn, deprived of a way of coping with life's misfortunes (1995).

Note

1. The discussion of clothing as identification of spirit possession within Vodou ceremonies is based primarily on my own personal documentation within the Vodou community around the Marché Solomon, in Port-au-Prince, the capital of Haiti. All visuals, personal communications and the description of *seremoni* come from *ounfo* within that area. Historical information and other documentation by scholars are cited in support of the material. In addition, I have chosen to use the Haitian *Kreyol* (Creole) spelling of the terms used within the Vodou vocabulary in an attempt to be consistent with the *Kreyol* spellings used in *Sacred Arts of Haitian Vodou*. Within Kreyol grammar, plurals are not identified with an additional letter s.

References

Benson, L. (1996). Some Breton and Muslim antecedents of Vodou drapo. In *sacred and ceremonial textiles*. Textile Society of America Proceedings, 1997.

Blier, S. P. (1995). Vodun: West African roots of Vodou. In D. J. Cosentino (Ed.), *Sacred Arts of Haitian Vodou* (pp. 61–87). Los Angeles: UCLA Fowler Museum of Cultural History.

Brown, K. M. (1976). *The veve of Haitian Vodou: a structural analysis of visual imagery*. PhD dissertation, Temple University.

Cosentino, D. J. (1995). Imagine heaven. In D. J. Cosentino (Ed.), *Sacred Arts of Haitian Voodoo* (pp.25-55). Los Angeles: UCLA Fowler Museum of Cultural History.

Courlander, H. (1960). *The drum and the hoe*. Berkeley: The University of California Press.

Dayan, J. (1995). *Haiti, history and the gods*. Berkeley: The University of California Press.

Deren, M. (1970). *Divine horsemen: Voodoo gods of Haiti*. New York: Chelsea House Publishers.

Desmangles, L. G. (1992). *The faces of the gods*. Chapel Hill & London: The University of North Carolina Press.

Douglas, M. (1973). *Natural symbols*. New York: Routledge.

Drewel, J. and Mason, J. (1998). *Beads body and soul: Art and light in the Yoruba universe*. Los Angeles: UCLA Fowler Museum of Cultural History.

Goffman, E. (1959). *Presentation of self in everyday life*. New York: Doubleday.

Hurbon, L. (1995). *Voodoo: the search for the spirit*. New York: Harry N. Abrams.

Metraux, A. (1959).*Voodoo in Haiti*. New York: Oxford University Press.

Seabrook, W. (1929). *The magic island*. New York: Harcourt, Brace and Company, Inc.

Thompson, R. F. (1983). *Flash of the spirit: African and Afro-American art and philosophy*. New York: Random House.

Thompson, R. F. (1995). Interleaf D, Azaka (Zaka): In D. J. Cosentino (Ed.), *Sacred Arts of Haitian Voodoo* (pp.120–1). Los Angeles: UCLA Fowler Museum of Cultural History.

Van Gannep, A. (1960). *The rites of passage*. London: Routledge & Kegan Paul.

Personal Communications

Conversations with *manbo* Gladys M. and *oungan* Edner P. about the use of clothing and *konesans* within Haitian Vodou, over several visits between 1993 and 1999.

4

Christianity, Cloth and Dress in the Andes

Lynn A. Meisch

When the Spanish arrived in the Andes of South America in A. D. 1532–3 they encountered cultures with concepts of the cosmos, spirit world, human body, cloth and dress that they considered abhorrent and pagan. This resulted in a series of well-documented campaigns through the mid-seventeenth century to "extirpate idolatry." Because Christianity accompanied geopolitical conquest, religion and political control were the interwoven warp and weft of colonial rule and Spanish prohibitions on the use of certain kinds of clothing had political as well as theological implications. This chapter examines the effect of Christianity on the use of cloth and dress in the Andes and includes contemporary survivals of ancient practices.

As an anthropologist I have found it impossible to study contemporary societies without understanding their past. In writing this chapter, therefore I relied on primary and secondary historical sources as well as extensive fieldwork in the Andes over the past 25 years.

Cloth in the Andes

The territory that constituted the Inca Empire (much of Peru, Bolivia and Ecuador and part of northern Argentina and Chile) contained societies that were among the most textile-oriented in the world. The collections of pre-Hispanic textiles in museums worldwide, including cloth from such pre-Inca cultures as Paracas, Nazca, Moche and Chimu, offer stunning visual testimony to the skills of ancient spinners and weavers and of the primacy of cloth in the Andean world.

We can construct interpretations of the meaning of cloth for ancient South Americans from the abundant archaeological record including intact burials, written colonial accounts by Spaniards and native Andeans and current ethno-graphic practices. I have used cloth and clothing synonymously because except for blankets, food-storage sacks and occasionally what appear to be temple wall hangings on the coast, the two were basically synonymous. Almost every-thing woven was somehow attached to or wrapped around the human body: tunics, breech cloths, belts, carrying cloths of all sizes, coca leaf bags, full-body wraps for females, mantles for both sexes, headdresses of various kinds and even slings. Such non-textile adornment as hairstyles, headgear, footwear and jewelry also fall under the rubric of dress and are included in my discussion.

Pre-Hispanic Cloth and Dress

Pre-Hispanic cloth was made from two main fibers, cotton and camelid (llama, alpaca and vicuña), handspun with stick spindles usually by females but sometimes by males depending on community practice. Weaving was also gendered, but varied by community or ethnic group. Females predominated as weavers in central and southern Peru and Bolivia, males in northern Peru and Ecuador, which is also true today. Cloth was woven on stick looms with different kinds of tensioning systems including backstraps, frames or being staked to four posts in the ground (the latter most common in the high, treeless regions of Peru and Bolivia). Cloth made on such stick looms was not tailored, but woven to the desired size with four uncut selvedges, or joined to make larger pieces.

In the Andes, ancient weavers utilized virtually every technique known to us with the exception of card weaving and they invested time and energy in textiles that far surpassed what is necessary to produce utilitarian cloth. Colors, stripes, the placement of motifs within areas of plain weave and the motifs themselves carried heavy symbolic weight, much of which we are unable to decipher, although current ethnographic practices offer clues. Textiles, metallurgy, ceramics and monumental architecture were the high art forms of the Andean region and there is a large body of literature (too voluminous to cite here) on pre-Hispanic textiles, particularly those of the Peruvian coast where desert conditions facilitate their preservation.

The textile bounty found in many coastal Peruvian mummy bundles includes not only layers of clothing but also sumptuous mortuary wraps, leading one researcher to call these textiles "clothes for the dead" (Vreeland, 1977, p. 167). Judging from the archaeological record, some funeral practices involving clothing in the Andes today have pre-Hispanic antecedents.

The Incas were merely the last in a series of great civilizations and we know more about them than about their predecessors because of the written records left by the Spanish and by literate native Andeans. Virtually all the Conquistadors commented favorably and sometimes at length, on the quantity and quality of cloth worn by Inca nobility or encountered in Inca storehouses.

The Incas believed "that the highest form of weaving was made expressly for the sun (*inti*), which they considered the greatest of the celestial powers" (Stone-Miller, 1992, p. 11). Chosen women lived in separate housing in Inca centers. Some were virgins and devoted their lives to the service of the Inca and the Sun. They made corn beer for ritual use and spun and wove fine cloth *(qumpi)* for the Inca himself (the son of the Sun), for state gifts and for sacrifices. Some chosen women also served as concubines and were given as wives to those who served the Inca well. Occasionally, women were sacrificed. Certain males, residing in their own homes, wove fine cloth and peasants paid their labor tax in dyestuffs, yarn and textiles. As Murra pointed out in a landmark article on the function of cloth in the Inca state, for common people and indigenous nobility alike, no life-course event was complete without gifts, exchanges or sacrifices of cloth (1989 [1962]). One of the early Spanish missionaries observed that in Peru among native Andeans: "Fine clothing was just as common as that of the most frequent offerings. It was part of nearly every major sacrifice . . . Sometimes they burned the clothing alone and other times they set fire to statues of men and women made of carved wood, dressed in this clothing and in this way they burned them" (Cobo, 1990 [1653], p. 117).

The Clash of Cultures and Religions

Although there were correspondences between Andean religions and Christianity, the early Spanish clergy in the Andes eventually decided that the two belief systems were fundamentally incompatible, hence the many Spanish campaigns to "extirpate idolatry." To list just a few glaring theological differences, Andeans were pantheistic and the Spanish were monotheistic Roman Catholics. Women as well as men officiated at religious rites in the Andes. (Under the Incas, females had a separate cult devoted to the Moon.) Andeans believed in non-Christian conceptions of the soul and the afterlife and worshipped what the Spanish called "idols" including the mummified bodies of their ancestors and other *waka* (also spelled *guaca*, which means "sacred things"). Andeans believed their divinities could speak to them through oracles, which the Spanish saw as apparitions of the devil. The Andeans, in fact, did not have a dualistic notion of an absolutely benign God and an equally evil Devil; their gods could help or harm and therefore needed to be propitiated.

An Inca origin myth, recounted by one of the earliest Spanish arrivals in Peru, Juan de Betanzos, who married a former wife of the Inca Atahualpa, offers insight into Andean thinking about the relationship between humanity and dress. According to the story, the different peoples of the world were created by the god Viracocha who called out to them to come forth from caves, rivers and high mountains (Betanzos, 1996 [1557]). This association of land forms with the ancestors made virtually the entire landscape sacred. In short, "the relationships Andeans perceived between life and death and between humanity and the natural environment were profoundly different from their Spanish and Christian equivalents" (MacCormack, 1991, p. 97).

As for the ancestors of the Inca rulers themselves, they emerged from a cave in town near Cuzco called Pacarictambo:

> The men came out dressed in garments of fine wool woven with gold. On their necks they brought out some bags, also of elaborately woven wool; in these bags they carried sinewed sashes that they call *chumbis* well woven with gold and with fine gold fasteners, large pins about two palms long, which they call *tupos* (Betanzos, 1996 [1557], pp. 13–14).

In other words, the Incas' ancestors emerged fully clothed in elaborate and beautiful dress, a symbol of their civilized status. Because Andeans believed that different ethnic groups sprang from their separate places of origin fully clothed in distinct dress, they found utterly ludicrous the idea that all humans were descended from one naked couple, Adam and Eve (Classen, 1993). Father Cobo observed that, "Thus, each province started to worship their place [of origin] as a major *guaca* because their lineage originated there . . . [T]hey held their earliest ancestors to be gods and they put images of them in the places mentioned above. Thus each nation dressed in the clothing that they painted on their *guaca*" (1990 [1653], p. 13). The Andean concept of clothing as an essential signifier of humanness cannot be overemphasized; it is a "social skin," a cultural medium specialized in the shaping and communication of personal and social identity (Turner, 1980, p. 114). Today, Quechua-speakers[1] in Peru call whites and *mestizos* "*q'ara*," which translates as "naked, uncultured, or uncivilized," because they do not wear traditional indigenous clothing (Mannheim, 1991, p. 19).

As the Spanish soon learned Andeans believed that clothing literally embodied the essence of a person or thing. In the Coricancha in Cuzco, the Incas' main temple, a statue of the creator god Viracocha was made entirely of mantles and three statues of the Sun in the same temple were also made from mantles in such a way that they stood up. Each statue had a *llauto* (the Inca-style headband) around its head and large earplugs like the ones worn by Inca nobles (Cobo, 1990 [1653]).

After they were dethroned by the Spanish, the Inca fought among themselves and during their civil wars "Andean troops believed that their enemy could be harmed or killed by getting hold of his clothes and using them to dress an effigy which was hanged and spat upon" (Murra, (1989 [1962]), p. 289).

Domesticated animals, especially llamas, alpacas and guinea pigs, were esteemed second only to humans as sacrifices. This is not surprising given the importance of camelid fibers in the Andean textile economy. Because clothing represented or embodied humanness, in some instances when llamas were sacrificed they were dressed in red garments and gold ear ornaments or with vests and ear decorations (Cobo, 1990 [1653]), thus representing and substituting for humans.

The Augustinians, during their "persecution of the demon" in northern Peru in the mid-1500s, described indigenous religious practices, including those involving dress:

> They made a little pillow very elaborately worked for their principal holy object (*guaca*) and for those that were not so important they made a little basket of white gold or silver wire woven with wool, wide at the bottom and narrower at the top . . . and in the concavity they put their *guaca and* this basket they dress like a person with very beautiful and rich tunics of fine cloth, which are woven from wool, with mantles and cords for dressing the head richly in diverse manners with silver or with gold or silver discs and with elegant feathers and they put on their coca leaf bags filled with coca and they put on slings for throwing things and on some they put helmets of silver or copper and shields and many other things and the devil (*el demonyo*) came here and he entered into the little dressed basket and there he spoke with the male witches . . . (San Pedro, 1992 [1560], pp. 169–79; my translation).

Note that the above *waka* was "dressed like a person." *Wakas*, which the Spanish called the *indígenas'* (natives') "idols" could be a holy place, or something as simple as a stone, piece of wood or cadaver, which represented a descent group's ancestor or a god or the spirit of a particular place (Figure 4.1). *Wakas*, including the mummified bodies of the dead, dressed in their finest clothes with other garments folded beside them, were often kept in caves (Cobo, 1990 [1653]). These mummies were dressed in new clothes annually and offered sacrifices of blood, food and *chicha* (corn beer) (Duviols, 1986 cited in MacCormack, 1991).

When the Incas moved populations around their empire either as colonists or a punishment for rebellion, the transferred people could not always take their *wakas*, but: "Of great importance and kept most hidden are those of a piece of clothing taken from their *waka paqarisqa* of their homeland . . ." If their *waka* is a stone, they put the piece of clothing they have brought over another stone . . ." (Albornóz, 1989 quoted in Abercrombie, 1998, pp. 187–8).

Figure 4.1 Andeans offer a black llama and bundles of coca leaves to a *waka*, dressed in dress similar to theirs. Drawing of Inca-era customs by Felipe Guaman Poma de Ayala, *c*. 1615.

When the Spanish discovered *wakas* they destroyed them and thought their job was done. But as Father Arriaga discovered during his anti-idolatry campaigns, smashing the *waka* made no difference to the *indígenas* because the essence of holiness resided in the cloth. They simply found another stone and re-dressed it, so Father Arriaga insisted that extirpators had to burn or otherwise completely destroy the associated cloth (Arriaga, 1968 [1621]). Albornóz, another extirpator, agreed:

> It must be known that the majority of *wakas*, apart from their properties, have clothing of fine cloth that they call *capac huchas* . . . And the first thing one must do so that no relic of the *waka* remains is to procure these *capac huchas* because if they remain in their power, they will dress any stone they like with it" (Albornóz, 1989 quoted in Abercrombie, 1998, pp. 188).

In other words, the "little basket" described above was not in itself sacred, but merely a framework for sacred clothing.

Because clothing so intimately represented a person, funeral rituals in the Inca empire included washing the deceased's clothing and blankets. For five days after death the deceased made a long, difficult journey to return to his ancestors' place of origin (*paqarina*) in the other world. After five days the family washed the deceased's good clothes for reuse and burned the older ones, or burned all the clothes for the deceased's own use in the afterlife (Duviols, 1986 cited in MacCormack, 1991). A "true noble" was buried dressed in his finest garments and jewelry. Next to him were placed other new garments that were folded, as well as food, drink, weapons, tools of his craft and other valuables (Cobo, 1990 [1653]) for his use (Figure 4.2).

The Spanish attempts to Christianize indigenous Andeans moved from persuasion to force, partly because the Spanish came to believe that "the demons held an almost invincible command over the Indians, a command that could ultimately be broken only by religious coercion" (MacCormack, 1985, p. 452). In 1560, the Augustinian missionaries in Guamachuco still considered using Andean textiles to decorate Catholic buildings and images, but by the end of the 1500s they rejected such adaptations of Christianity to Andean lifeways (MacCormack, 1985).

Andean female dress also offended the Spanish because the side opening in the body wrap (*ak'su* or *anaku*) revealed the leg and thigh. Father Cobo wrote approvingly that "for this reason, now that the women are Christians and profess more decency, they are in the habit of sewing up the side in order to avoid that immodesty" (1990 [1653], p. 188).

Cobo also disapproved of the Andean practice of head deformation: The Collas of the Peruvian and Bolivian altiplano flattened and elongated the heads of their babies, "since they were not satisfied with the heads given them by God . . .". Not only was the head deformation an affront to God (in Catholic thought), but there were pagan rituals surrounding the making of the child's first hat: "And they made the children's first hat with many ceremonies and superstitious acts, both in spinning the wool and in weaving it" (1990 [1653], p. 201).

Religious, Political and Cultural Resistance

Colonial economic, political, cultural and religious coercion by the Spanish met passive and violent resistance from Andeans, culminating in several major pan-Andean uprisings. Not surprisingly, both the resistance to the Spanish and the subsequent suppression of the revolts involved both cloth and dress. In 1564, an area from La Paz, Bolivia, to central Peru experienced a revolt called *Taqui Onqoy* (dancing sickness, i.e., ecstatic dancing). The essence of this

Figure 4.2 A burial during Inca times. Cadaver dressed in elaborate traditional dress and headgear. Drawing of Inca-era customs by Felipe Guaman Poma de Ayala, *c.* 1615.

movement was a rejection of all things Christian and Spanish including Spanish dress and a return to the old ways including wearing traditional dress and worshipping the *wakas*. Choosing Andean religion meant choosing Andean culture and returning to a life uncontaminated by the Spanish invaders (MacCormack, 1991). *Taqui Onkoy* took several years to suppress and was followed in 1571 by the destruction of the hold-out Inca rebel government in Vilcabamba, Peru.

Another major revolt engulfed the Andean heartland in 1780–82. The leaders of this revolt appropriated Inca titles and some wore a mixture of Spanish colonial and Inca-style clothing. As with previous uprisings, this revolt was ultimately suppressed and the bishop of Cuzco and the colonial government prohibited the use of Inca-style clothing. The bishop was particularly incensed that *indígenas* traditionally wore Inca dress and insignia during the fiesta of Corpus Christi in Cuzco, including jewelry "engraved with the image of the Inca or the Sun, their adored deity" (Manuel, 1980 [1781], p. 633; my translation).

The *visitador* José Antonio de Areche, in his sentence against the main rebel leader José Gabriel de Tupac-Amaru, noted that Tupac-Amaru wore the Inca-style tunic (*unco*) with royal Inca insignia and the Inca headband (*mascapaicha*). Areche announced abolition of the use of tunics, mantles (*yacollas*) and headbands: "Indians are prohibited from wearing the dress of their ancestors, especially that of the nobility, . . . that which was used by the ancient Incas, . . ." Just to make sure indígenas got the point, he repeated, "And so that these Indians withdraw their hatred of Spaniards and dress according to the laws, they must dress according to Spanish customs and speak the Castillian language . . ." (Areche, 1836 [1781], p. 50; my translation). This was certainly one of the more concerted attempts to control indigenous dress and it was partially successful, especially in the Cuzco heartland. Indígenas in more distant regions still wear tunics (e.g. Q'ero, Peru, Saraguro, Ecuador) but, currently, no one wears the male's mantle or Inca-style headgear.

Religion and Clothing Today

Were the Spanish successful in their campaigns to Christianize Andeans and control their dress and uses of cloth? Many formal, public pre-Hispanic religious practices were forcibly abolished or disappeared in the chaos following the dissolution of the Inca empire and the suppression of colonial revolts. Most contemporary indigenous Andeans consider themselves to be good Christians, but pre-Hispanic observances remain, usually those practiced by households in private. Pre-Inca and Inca conceptions of the cosmos and society survive today, including the importance of traditional cloth and dress in defining identity and ethnicity.

Throughout the Andes, gifts of traditional dress still accompany significant events in the life-cycle, from the first haircut or baptism to marriage. But not surprisingly, death is the one event where pre-Hispanic religious concepts involving cloth survive. The ethnographic evidence from my own and others' fieldwork is abundant. As Allen has pointed out with respect to Sonqo, Cuzco, Peru, there are fundamental incompatibilities between current indigenous Andean and Christian beliefs about the nature of the soul and its fate after death. "The Andean worldview does not accommodate the Western dualism of body and soul, for Andeans, all matter is in some sense alive and conversely, all life has a materialist base" (Allen, 1988, pp. 61–2). This concept finds expression in funeral rites.

In Otavalo, Ecuador, for example, *indígenas* believe that a person's *alma* (soul) or *espíritu* (spirit) lingers after death and can cause others in the family to become ill or even die. Someone outside the family, either a volunteer or a paid person, must ritually wash (*rupa takshay*) all the deceased's clothing and blankets in boiling water and *Agave americana* (century plant cactus) leaves or nettles. The clothes must be washed within two or three days because the body, bathed and always dressed in white clothing so the person "will be clean before God", is buried on the fourth. All the person's clothes, including a female's jewelry, are put in the coffin and buried with him or her (Juana Arrayán, Breenan and Marta Conterón, Cornelio Cabascango, José Luis Cotacachi, Daniel De La Torre, personal communication). There is an obvious link between this custom and the Inca practice of washing the deceased's clothing after five days, as well as with that of burying a person's clothing with him or her to use in the afterlife.

The ritual clothes-washing (*p'acha t'aqsay*) in Abancay, Apurimac, Peru, is similar but not identical. The clothes and bedding are washed in the river the day following the burial (instead of before) by ritual kin rather than by immediate family. The underlying concept is similar to that in Otavalo: the odor of the dead is believed to spread to his or her clothing where it can contaminate the living. After the clothes have dried, the best of each kind is chosen and laid out with great care on a poncho or woman's mantle, to reproduce faithfully the figure of the deceased. Those attending the ritual, who may include relatives from distant villages who were unable to get to the funeral, "embrace the bundle of clothes shaped as a living person and talk to it as if it were alive." This is the last farewell. Clothes are also laid out in a similar manner at masses for the souls of the dead. In these instances and in witchcraft and healing rituals, "clothing replaces the person" (Ackerman, 1991, pp. 241–5).

74

A third example (and undoubtedly there are many more) comes from Huaquirca, Apurimac, Peru. The main object of funeral rituals is to break the link between the body and *alma* and send the *alma* to the afterlife. As in Inca times, the wake continues for five days before burial. On the day of the interment, the ritual clothes-washing takes place. The ethnographic details of the clothes-washing differ; here it occurs the day of the burial and is done in a local creek by the male affines of the deceased (for fear females will be polluted). The most ragged clothes are burned unwashed by the deceased's son-in-law and the washed clothes are taken to the cemetery and given to the deceased's family for the vigils that take place on the eve of All Saints' Day. Both burial and clothes-washing serve to dispatch the *alma* to the afterlife (Gose, 1994).

Perhaps the most tragic example of the continuity of the pre-Christian concept of clothing representing the essence of a person comes from Ayacucho, Peru, where during the war between the Shining Path guerrilla group and the Peruvian government from 1980 to 1992, thousands of civilians were "disappeared" by both sides. "Disappear" became a transitive verb and "to disappear someone" became an instrument of political repression. Tortured and mutilated cadavers sometimes turned up in local dumping grounds, but in many instances no trace of the missing person was ever found. The relatives of the disappeared held funerals with clothing laid out in lieu of a corpse. A heart-rending photograph of such a wake appeared on the cover of the *1984 Peru Briefing*, published by Amnesty International (Meisch, 1997).

Even though the early Christian missionaries forced Andeans to inter their dead in Christian graveyards rather than their customary caves, in many parts of the Andes mountains, natural features such as caves are still considered the true abode of the dead (Abercrombie, 1998; Allen, 1988; Bastien, 1985; Gose, 1994).

Another area where pre-Hispanic practices concerning clothing survive is in the shearing or sacrifice of camelids. The explicit connection between humans and camelids is found in many places. In the Aymara-speaking community of Qaqachka, Oruro, Bolivia, when camelids are sheared the men say to male animals "Take off your poncho, I shall put on a poncho, too" and the women say "Take off your mantle, I shall put on a mantle, too". The animals are not only addressed in gendered terms usually reserved for humans, but "Alpacas are left with special clumps of wool dangling from their coats, which are called the 'coca-cloths' (*inkuña*) if they are females or 'coca-bags' (*wallqipu*) if they are male" (Arnold, 1997, pp. 108–9).

Among the Aymara-speaking K'ulta of Santa Bárbara de Culta, Oruro, Bolivia, men become authorities within their community by being equated with the lead llamas of a domesticated herd. During certain fiestas, the lead llamas are dressed in mature men's garments (taken from the sponsor and his followers) including long scarves, coca bags (*ch'uspas*), charm bundles and battle helmets (*monteros*) that resemble those of the conquistadors (Abercrombie, 1998).

In other rituals, humans don the skins of sacrificed llamas, illustrating the interchangeability of humans and llamas as sacrifices and reconfirming the central importance of clothing in making this identification. Abercrombie goes further, arguing that "focusing exclusively on llama sacrifices, however, is to miss the point, for herd animals and herding metaphors serve to express sacrifices of persons, saints and, yes, of *Jesucristo*. Llama sacrifice grants *K'ultas* access to the power of the Eucharist" (1998, p. 196).

Yet another survival of pre-Hispanic clothing conventions concerns dressing the crucifix or statues of a parish's patron saint in traditional indigenous dress. For example, in Cañar, Ecuador, the statue of Saint Anthony (patron saint of the town) is dressed in miniature Cañari dress, while the statue of the Virgin Mary in San Juan, Chimborazo, Ecuador, is dressed in traditional women's dress (Figure 4.3) and holds a distaff and spindle in the local style. Visitors to Andean churches are sometimes amused to see a statue of the Virgin or saint dressed in full-size or miniature local, traditional dress, but resonance goes deeper than mere folklore. I am not arguing that *indígenas* remember the Inca myth describing the birth of the ancestors fully clothed in each ethnic group's distinctive dress, or the custom of clothing a group's *wakas* in traditional dress. Rather, I argue that the link between dress, humanness and group identity was never severed.

Among the K'ulta, the miniature image of the saint Guadalupe is kept in a box, which is wrapped in multiple layers of adult-sized ponchos and women's mantles. Inside the box is the saint's image and miniature garments patterned on local traditional dress. In a ceremony called *isa turka* (changing or exchanging of clothes), the image is unwrapped and undressed. The male and female sponsors of the *fiesta* (celebration) make offerings to the image, then touch a corner of their outerwear (poncho for the man, mantle for the woman) to the saint. This is repeated by their followers. The miniature clothes are replaced, then the box is wrapped in ponchos and mantles provided by the followers. The sponsors sort out the full-sized garments in which the box had been wrapped and drape them over their shoulders and the shoulders of their followers who had loaned garments (Abercrombie, 1998). As Abercrombie notes:

> Remember that the llama herd comes to the ritual-center town dressed in the clothes of men; the sponsor's human herd . . . dresses in the clothing of llamas; the sponsors (like the saint image) dress in the transformed pelts (weavings) . . . All are iconic

indexes of the raising of the clothes givers to the honored status of sacrificial victim and an appropriation of certain of their substances and/or qualities by the wearers (1998, p. 399).

As in pre-Hispanic times, clothing continues to play an essential role in representing humans and in connecting and mediating between the human and the divine.

Although Christianity originally meant Roman Catholicism, in the twentieth century Protestantism became increasingly influential in Latin America with growing numbers of converts (Stoll, 1990). In Ecuador, Evangelical Protestant missionizing activities affected traditional dress. One concerns bead necklaces, which are an essential element of indigenous female dress. Throughout my research in Ecuador I encountered in the markets glass-bead necklaces with small silver charms, coins, or Catholic medals and sometimes a crucifix attached. Many had dirty ties and bore other signs of use. Some people referred to them as simply necklaces, others called them *rosarios* (rosaries), a Roman Catholic device for meditating on religious mysteries and counting

Figure 4.3 Young *indígenas* from Chimborazo, in traditional dress. In this region, statues are dressed in miniature versions of this dress, with rosaries replaced by bead necklaces. Photo by Lynn Meisch.

prayers that was introduced to the Andes in the early colonial era. The problem, however, was that I never actually saw such a necklace worn until a visit to the Guamote, Chimborazo, market in 1988.

Chimborazo province has been a locus for Evangelical Protestant missionizing for several decades. Two Evangelical indígenas in El Troje explained that rosaries and multi-strand coin and bead necklaces were worn through the 1970s. After this time, evangelical missionaries forbade converts to use rosaries because of their Roman Catholic associations and they also prohibited the use of coin and bead necklaces because of their resemblance to rosaries. Thousands of converts stopped using coin and bead necklaces, wearing just beads instead. Many sold their old necklaces, hence the plethora of such necklaces in the markets and others kept them *"guardado"* (guarded, put away) (Meisch, 1998). This dramatic change was a result of Christian missionaries proscribing an item of traditional dress because of its association with an older religion in the region, only now, ironically, the missionaries were Evangelical Protestants and the traditional religion had become Roman Catholicism.

Summary

The colonial prohibitions against wearing certain kinds of indigenous dress had political, cultural and religious ramifications and given the intimate associations between cloth and human identity in the present and the afterlife, such prohibitions were in a very real sense a battle for *indigenas'* bodies and souls. In many ways the Christianization of the Andes is incomplete and this is reflected in beliefs and practices involving clothing. As Ambercrombie (1998, p. 400) noted, for the K'ulta:

> the ancestral *wak'as* and mountain gods that were once "created" by clothing them in precious cloth and the sacrificial pilgrimages construing social memory still exist . . . but the visible, tangible and portable manifestations of the mountain gods and ceque paths of the pilgrimages have been taken over by the saint images and pathways to churches and chapels.

Concerted fieldwork in the Andes usually offers similar glimpses of the persistence of pre-Hispanic beliefs beneath a veneer of Christianity (Figure 4.4). A powerful example of such persistence is found in Coroma, Potosí, Bolivia. Beginning around 1983, sacred textiles, consisting of clothing of considerable antiquity (some dating to the fifteenth or sixteenth centuries) began disappearing from the sacred bundles owned by the *ayllus* (lineages) of the people of Coroma. The textiles were stolen at the behest of North American ethnic art dealers, who sold them on the international art market in violation of Bolivian law. An international legal effort led by Bolivian anthropologist Cristina Bubba Zamora resulted in the eventual return of around a hundred pieces to Coroma in 1992.

Why are these garments so important? On *Todos Santos* (All Saints' Day, November 2) each year the textiles are taken from their bundles, which are held on behalf of the *ayllu* by its elected authorities. The *ayllu* authorities wear the textiles (tunics, headdresses, coca bags, mantles women's skirts) and dance. The most cogent explanation of the textiles' importance comes from the Coromans themselves. According to the legal testimony of Sebastiana Aviza de Pérez of Ayllu Achuma, "The textiles which the authorities wear are from the time of our ancestors. They are only used for worship, they are sacred and ceremonial, we hold an all night vigil before them and we adore them all the time" (1988, p. 5). Even more significant, however "[W]e pray with the sacristan and then we dance with the textiles as if they were our grandparents because Todos Santos is the festival in which the souls of our ancestors arrive on this date and dance" (Aviza de Pérez, 1988, p. 3).

The manner in which clothing literally embodies the ancestors is made even more explicit in the testimony of Primitivo Pérez Beltrán of Ayllu Achuma:

Figure 4.4 Aymara women dancing during a fiesta in La Paz, Bolivia. Photo by Lynn Meisch.

[E]ach year we make offerings to grandparents as well as to our ancestors . . . [F]irst we adore the textiles in an all-night vigil, then we pray with the sacristan and then we make the textiles dance as if they were our grandparents. Because *Todos Santos* is the festival of the souls, the grandparents arrive on this date and dance (1988, p. 13).

As with many traditional uses of clothing and cloth in the Andes, the overt celebration is Christian (*Todos Santos*), but the underlying logic is distinctly Andean.

Note

1. Quechua is family of languages indigenous to the Andean countries. The Quechua of Cuzco spoken by the Incas was spread throughout their empire as a language of conquest and later used by the Spanish as a lingua franca to Christianize the *indígenas*. Today there are approximately 12 million speakers of the various Quechua languages. Aymara is also an indigenous Andean language spoken by approximately 2 million persons, primarily in the *altiplano* (high plains) around Lake Titicaca in Peru and Bolivia. Because Quechua and Aymara were not written languages when the Spanish arrived, they were first written with sixteenth-century Spanish orthography and there is still considerable disagreement about spelling. All quotes are in the original spelling.

References

Abercrombie, T. (1998). *Pathways of memory and power: Ethnography and history among an Andean people*. Madison, Wis. and London: The University of Wisconsin Press.

Ackerman, R. (1991). Clothes and identity in the central Andes: Province of Abancay, Peru. In M. Schevill, J. Berlo and E. Dwyer (Eds.). *Textile Traditions of Mesoamerica and the Andes: An Anthology*. (pp. 231–60). Austin: University of Texas Press.

Albornóz, C. de (1989). Instrucción para descubrir todas las huacas del piru y sus camayos y haziendas (1581/1585). In C. de Molina and C. de Albornóz, *Fábulas y mitos de los incas*. (pp. 16, 135-198). H. Urbano y P. Duviols (Eds.) Crónicas de América, vol. 48. Madrid: Historia.

Allen, C. (1988). *The hold life has: Coca and cultural identity in an Andean community*. Washington, D.C.: Smithsonian Institution Press.

Areche, D. J. de (1836 [1781]). Sentencia pronunciada en el Cuzco por el visitador D. José Antonio de Areche, contra José Gabriel Tupac-Amaru, su muger, hijos, y demas reos principales de la sublevación," *Documentos para la historia de la sublevación de José Gabriel de Tupac-Amaru, Cacique de la Provincia de Tinta, en el Perú*. (pp. 44–52). Primera Edición. Buenos-Aires: Imprenta del Estado.

Arnold, D. (1997). Making men in her own image: Gender, text and textile in Qaqchaka. In R. Howard-Malverde (Ed.) *Creating Context in Andean Cultures* (pp. 99–131). Oxford: Oxford University Press.

Arriaga, P. J. de (1968 [1621]). *The extirpation of idolatry in Peru*. Trans. and Ed. L. Clark Keating, Lexington: University of Kentucky Press.

Aviza de Pérez, S. (1988). *Statement of accusation before the Judge of Minima Cuantia, Coroma, Potosí, Bolivia* (ms.), November 29.

Bastien, J. W. (1985 [1978]). *The mountain of the condor: Metaphor and ritual in an Andean ayllu*. Prospect Heights, Illinois: Waveland Press.

Beltrán, P. P. (1988). *Statement of accusation before the Judge of Minima Cuantia, Coroma, Potosí, Bolivia* (ms.), November 29.

Betanzos, J. de (1996 [1557]). *Narrative of the Incas*. Trans. and Eds. R. Hamilton and D. Buchanan. Austin: University of Texas Press.

Classen, C. (1993). *Inca cosmology and the human body*. Salt Lake City: University of Utah Press.

Cobo, B. (1979 [1653]). *History of the Inca empire*. Trans. and Ed. Roland Hamilton, Austin: University of Texas Press.

Cobo, B. (1990 [1653]). *Inca religion and customs*. Trans. and Ed. R. Hamilton, Austin: University of Texas Press.

Duviols, P. (1986). *Cultura andina y represión. Procesos y visitas de idolatrías y hechicerías, Cajatambo siglo XVII*. Cuzco.

Gose, P. (1994). *Deathly waters and hungry mountains: Agrarian ritual and class formation in an Andean town*. Toronto: University of Toronto Press.

MacCormack, S. (1985). The heart has its reasons: Predicaments of missionary Christianity in early colonial Peru, *Hispanic American Historical Review*, vol. 65, no. 3, 443–6.

MacCormack, S. (1991). *Religion in the Andes: Vision and imagination in early Colonial Peru*. Princeton: Princeton University Press.

Mannheim, B. (1991).*The Language of the Inka since the European invasion*. Austin: University of Texas Press.

Manuel J. (1980 [1781]). "Documento 81," *Colección documental del bicentenario de la revolución emancipadora de Tupac Amaru. Tomo II, Descargos del Obispo del Cuzco Juan Manuel Moscoso*. Lima: Comisión Nacional del Bicentenario de la rebelion emancipadora de Tupac Amaru.

Meisch, L. (1997). To honor the ancestors: Life and cloth in the Andes". In L. Meisch (Ed.), *Textile traditions of the Andes: Life and cloth in the Highlands* (pp. 8–15). New York and San Francisco: Thames and Hudson and the Fine Arts Museums of San Francisco.

Meisch, L. (1998). Why do they like red? Beads, ethnicity and gender in Ecuador. In J. Eicher and L. Sciama (Eds.), *Beads and bead makers: Gender, material culture and meaning* (pp. 147-75). Oxford and New York: Berg.

Murra, J. (1989 [1962]). *Cloth and its function in the Inka state*. In Weiner, A. and Schneider, J., (Eds.) Cloth and human experience. Washington DC; Smithsonian Press.

San Pedro, Juan de (1992 [1560]). *La persecución del demonio. Crónica de los primeros agustinos en el norte de Perú (1560).* Manuscrito del Archivo de Indias transcrito por Eric E. Deeds. Málaga-México: Algarza-C.A.M.E.I.

Stoll, D. (1990). *Is Latin America turning Protestant: The politics of evangelical growth.* Berkeley: University of California Press.

Stone-Miller, R. (1992). To weave for the sun: An introduction to the fiber arts of the ancient Andes. In *To weave for the sun: Ancient Andean textiles in the Museum of Fine Arts, Boston* (pp. 11–24). Rebecca Stone-Miller with contributions by Anne Paul, Susan A. Niles, Margaret Young-Sánchez. New York: Thames and Hudson.

Turner, T. (1980). The social skin. In: *Not work alone: A cross-cultural view of activities superfluous to survival* (pp. 112–40). Jeremy Cherfas and Roger, Lewin (Eds.). Beverly Hills: Sage Publications.

Vreeland, J. (1977). Ancient Andean textiles: Clothes for the dead. *Archaeology,* vol. 30, 166–78.

5

Clothed with Authority: The Rationalization of Marist Dress-Culture

William J. F. Keenan

This chapter provides a neo-Weberian account of the rationalization of the dress culture of body regulation of a Roman Catholic religious order, the Marist Brothers' Institute. The Marist case of dress "uniformization" serves to refine sociological discourse on the march of modernity by drawing attention to "counter-modern" modes of "rational" cultural intervention (Schluchter, 1981) upon the religious body (individual and corporate). The "disciplining" of the Marist body through ecclesiastical dress controls has the paradoxical quality of being, at one and the same moment, an expression of "the limits of rationality" (Brubacker, 1984, pp. 82–6) and its "triumph" (Habermas, 1981, pp. 143–5) as the Church subjects its "men of the cloth" to the most pervasive and invasive system of body control through dress codes. The incorporation of the Marist dress code within the regime of uniform-dress body control of the Tridentine Church represents just such a case of, in Max Weber's terms (1968, p. 1173), "substantive rational" or "technical rational" resistance to the modern idea or ideology of individual dress choice and bodily self-expression. Research involved close inspection of the internal archives of the Marist Brothers in order to understand the process of Marist dress rationalization. The detailed formal codification of dress prescriptions is documented in this chapter; first, as a contribution to understanding ways in which religious dress cultures and traditions of body control are shaped by "power" (charismatic and bureaucratic); and, second, as background to enhanced insight into just how momentous Vatican II's religious dress reforms proved to be in collapsing a many-centuries-old regime of body-dress control.

In nineteenth-century Europe, at the time of the Marist foundation in 1817, the Catholic Church embarked upon what Lamennais was to call the project of post-French Revolution "recatholicization" (Loome, 1979). Scores of new "active" religious congregations were founded as part of a drive to claw back territory lost to atheistic modernism (Zind, 1969). The Marist Brothers were among these new "apostolic" religious foundations which, like others of their ilk before and since, adopted a special mode of dress as a means of confirming their status as religious virtuosi (Hill, 1973). Unlike the majority of their co-foundations (Hostie, 1972), the Marist Brothers have survived and remain active throughout the world mainly, though not exclusively, as a teaching congregation. They comprise today some five and a half thousand members operating in some sixty different countries of the globe. What follows is an account of the Marist dress story paying special heed to the routinization of Marist "dressways" as the Marist Brothers evolved from being in mid-nineteenth century an obscure, rural *Gemeinschaft* to becoming, a century later, among the most prominent cosmopolitan religious *Gesellschaften* within the Roman Catholic Church. Wellmer (1985, pp. 40–1) provides a useful starting-point to an application of a Weberian approach to the methodization of the sartorial economy of a religious community:

> "rationalisation" signifies a transition from "communal" to "associative" forms of social action. While communal socialisation is oriented towards traditional norms and personal characteristics, associative social action is oriented towards impersonal, enacted, and general norms, and dominated by instrumental or strategic considerations . . . in the context of bureaucratic organisations . . .

Roach and Eicher (1965, p. 61) comment: "In a basically secular world, a religious influence on dress and adornment is likely to be incidental for the general population and coercive only for the dedicated who join religious orders or the priesthood." Nevertheless, as the Marist case study below serves to illustrate, the religious influence on the sacred dress option comes in a variety of forms even within the same religious order. Moreover, the coercion itself takes a number of forms from the charismatic and patrimonial to the bureaucratic and legal-rational, to employ the familiar categories of Max Weber. Throughout its century of cross-cultural diasporization and global reach (1862–1963), the Marist religious uniform served as a key symbol (Ortner, 1973) of church identity and belonging, a somewhat different dress sense, as we shall outline, from that attached to the "Livery of Mary" of the founding generation. Becoming a sponsored organization of the Roman Church traditionally entailed normative compliance with the detailed regulative framework governing dress instituted by the Vatican's Sacred Congregation for Religious. In dress terms, this was tantamount to voluntary entry into the iron cage, Weber's celebrated metaphor for bureaucratic domination (Tiriyakian, 1981).

Albeit the origins of the ancient institution of ecclesiastical dress lie deep within the histories of early monasticism (Mayo, 1984) and medieval clericalism (Mayer-Thurman, 1975), the charter of Tridentine Roman Catholic religious dress rules derives from the prescriptions of the sixteenth-century Council of Trent regarding the Counter-Reformation "night battle" (Lash, 1977) of the Church. The religious orders served as "the pope's battalions" in what was to prove something of a counter-modern rearguard offensive against the increasingly liberal currents of the democratic age. The religious habit became an arch symbol of the otherness of religious life "in but not of" the modern world. It was *the* corporeal sign of contradiction, a highly visible, portable, "in-your-face" statement of faith in belonging to the Church in its most defiant triumphalist incarnation. As put by Arthur (1999, p. 1): "Dress is the most obvious of the many symbolic boundary markers used by conservative religious groups." With the Marist Brothers, "the garments of God" (Roach and Eicher, 1979, p.18), having initially been re-contextualized as the veritable "garments of Mary", are subsequently reconstituted for a century in the role of a uniform in Roman Catholic warfare against, as apocalyptic Marian lore and language have it (Coste, 1982), "the worldly snares of the devil".

A Developmental Perspective on Marist Dress Tradition

While in recent years there has been an accumulation of studies of religious-life communities (mainly of women) where the liberalization of dress codes has been a point of focus, it would appear that in-depth historical sociological investigations of the longer-term development processes of sacred-dress traditions has been largely neglected. Comprehensive dress histories of Roman Catholic religious congregations (male religious orders especially) are largely virgin soil for research workers and the present study offers what is, perhaps, the first strike in cultivating a potentially very rich field of empirical enquiry into the construction of the religious dress traditions through history. There is a need for what might be called mezo-level studies of religious-life sacred-dress traditions falling in that vastly undercultivated tract between the micro-level studies emphasizing attitudes to dress changes within the contemporary Church (Campbell-Jones, 1979; Fuchs-Ebaugh, 1977; Sullivan, 1988; Michelman, 1999) on the one side, and the broadbrush macro-level sweeps over the *"longue durée"* of ecclesiastical dress history as such (Mayer-Thurman, 1975; Mayo, 1984) on the other side. Peel's comment (1973, p. 303) is apt in this context: "The serious task for sociology, and especially for the sociology of development, is to set about the analysis of cultural traditions, not as disembodied emanations of original ideals, but as definitions that shape and are modified by each new context." According to Mayo (1984, p. 9): "One of the problems of the study of ecclesiastical dress is that the development is so slow that contemporary writers do not feel the need to describe it." An underlying contention here is that it is necessary take the longer view to grasp the full strength of the "iron cage" of Tridentine dress controls. To get some measure of the anomie set in train within religious-life dress-culture as the post-conciliar liberal reforms projected members of religious institutes into the permissive dress ways of late-modern consumer culture, historically-informed "thick descriptions" of the old dress order of the Church are much needed. While the main problem of the contemporary paradigm of religious-life dress study centers on "the great transition" from pre-conciliar dress un-freedom to the taboric light of post-conciliar dress liberty, the full import and impact of Vatican II's seismic shift within the longer-term developmental processes of Catholic sacred-dress culture are occluded from view by this preoccupation with the most recent decades. By contrast, the encyclopediacal view of a thousand years and more of ecclesiastical-dress history leaves unslaked the thirst for detailed knowledge of the dress careers of specific religious orders and religious congregations.

How did the dress culture of this or that religious community – Benedictine, Ursuline, Dominican, Franciscan, Cistercian, Daughters of Charity, Servite and so on – actually originate and develop over considerable periods of time and, in cases, many centuries? What were the resources within the tradition that enabled it to survive within and against "the world"? How did it fare under Tridentine "counter-modern" and, later, Vatican II "liberal modern" conditions? Only by setting the dramatic impact of the Second Vatican Council in the perspective of a fuller, more detailed picture of particular Catholic dress histories and traditions will it be possible, perhaps, to fully understand exactly what is at stake in the complex story of body, dress and the Church as it reaches its late-modern moment of crisis or renewal. For that to happen, it is suggested, we need to examine the sacred dress of religious communities over a significant span of history. Marshall and Swift (1993, p. 147) make a seminal point, doubly important, one might aver, in the context of sacred-dress traditions: "Respect for cultural particularity requires attention to the ways in which a community understands its goods." Different Marist generations, as we shall see, understood and valued their dress "goods" in different ways, according to quite different fundamental assumptions about the meaning and purpose of the religious habit.

In a sense, comprehending and respecting the quiddity of the Marist Brothers as a distinctive religious society means understanding the diverse and seemingly contradictory modalities of their sacred-dress sense. Does the Marist dress culture and tradition remain coherent despite discernible shifts in religious-dress sensibility as the Brothers passed through radically different circumstances within the Church and the modern world? A main aim of this present exploration of the Marist dress tradition over its full historical trajectory is to illuminate ways in which Catholic sacred-dress traditions are constructed out of intricate and changeful relationships between personality, Church and the world. If the Marist dress story told here serves to highlight some of the concrete dynamics and transitional episodes whereby religious-dress symbolic cultures within the Church and the modern world are created, consolidated and transformed, it will have served its purpose.

The Livery of Mary: Foundation Garments, 1817–1863

If "by their dress shall ye know them", then members of religious orders and congregations signalled through the adoption of the dress of the Church that they belonged to a separate other-worldly and even anti-worldly kingdom. As a concrete expression of their religious apartness, the habit represented self-renunciation of the will and the flesh. Its silent language spoke eloquently of a consecrated life in and under orders, a vowed life of Poverty, Chastity and Obedience even down to the very clothes on one's back. In the Marist case this theology of the religious habit took on a Marian inflection.

The Marist Founder, Father Marcellin Champagnat (1789–1840), wove a distinctly Marian thread into what can be termed his sacred-dress spirituality. He was born in the fateful year of 1789 and brought up in the context of the "Terror" within a smallholder household that sheltered two exclaustrated sisters and, on occasion, recusant priests. His father was a deputy mayor of Marlhes and reluctant spokesman of the Revolution while his mother (of ten children, four of whom died in infancy) was a devout woman deeply suffused with Marian piety (Furet, 1856/1989; Chastel, 1948).

Champagnat was socialized in Catholic Marian devotionalism (Gibson, 1971). He was especially given to the idea of the Virgin Mother as "Comforter", "Refuge", "Intercessor", "Safeguard", "Help of Christians" and "Mediatrix" (Laveille, 1921; Sester, 1991–2), as prayers dedicated to Mary's spiritual titles put it. As a village priest, entirely steeped in the Catholic cult of Mary, Mother of God, a devotion then especially rife within the Lyonnais hinterland (McMahon, 1988), Champagnat received his priestly training in Lyons and served his entire ministry in the mountainous villages around St. Etienne and Marlhes. During his seminary years he was an active founding member of The Society of Mary and took on the task of establishing a community of catechists who would assist in the evangelization and schooling of children, notably in rural districts outside the urban educational reaches of the established Jesuit and De La Salle teaching congregations (Farrell, 1983). Dress differentation was one modality open to any new founder in the struggle to make his mark as the spiritual pantocrator of a new band of religious devotees.

Following a struggle with a rival founder, Father Jean-Claude Courveille, who had proposed a somewhat worldly costume for the "Blue Brothers" consisting of a sky blue frock coat, top hat and brass-knobbed cane (Zind, 1969, p. 416; Farrell, 1983, p. 6), Father Champagnat succeeded in rigging out his small band of followers, mainly peasant youths, in a less flamboyant outfit made up of "a sort of blue coat which reached just below the knee, black trousers, a small cloak and a round hat" (Furet, 1989 ed., p. 67). The favored dress of the charismatic Founder had prevailed. What was untypical, however, was the emphasis Champagnat placed on the Marian dimension of the religious habit of his new catechetical community. He referred to it as "the Livery of Mary" and taught his devotees, whom he called "The Little Brothers of Mary", to honour their religious costume as they would clothing gifts conferred upon them by their Divine Mother, the Queen of Heaven. He went so far as instilling in his recruits the belief that their sacred livery of Mary would afford them special protection against both spiritual and practical dangers. Two examples of the Marist Founder's talismanic (Wilson, 1965, p. 56) conception of "the dress of sanctity" (Crawley, 1965, p. 141) suffice here. First, his quasi-animistic reactions to the anticlerical outbursts of the 1830 July Revolution are recorded by his first biographer, the eyewitness Brother Jean-Baptiste Furet (loc. cit., pp. 173–4):

> Some Brothers asked him if it would not be well to be prepared, in case of a surprise, and be provided with secular clothes; the Father answered: "The precautions that you ought to take are to fear nothing . . . Your religious habit is your best safeguard. Let alone the livery of the world; it can no more preserve you from danger than a cobweb can . . . Do not forget that you have Mary for your protectress and that she is terrible as an army set in array."

Second, later in his hagiographic account (ibid., pp. 356–7), Furet underscores the "Marian dress magic" (cf. Binder, 1986, p. 95) of the Marist Founder:

> (H)e was convinced that all the Brothers who have the happiness of dying in the Society, will be saved. Many a time he was heard to say: "I firmly believe that Mary will not permit to be lost anyone of those who persevere till death in their vocation, and will leave this world clothed in her livery. All the Brothers wear this holy habit, and if the Blessed Virgin preserves from eternal damnation those who simply wear her scapular, how much more will she preserve from such a fate those who, together with the scapular, bear her name, wear her costume, live in her House, offer her daily a tribute of homage, etc."

Champagnat's patrimonial authority within the fledgling Marist community was reinforced by this spiritual, even sacramental definition of the religious habit as an outward and visible sign of an interior Marian faith. Viewed thus, their dress (Bogatyrev, 1937/1971) became an integral element within the sacred cosmos of an emerging quasi-sect (Stark, 1969, p. 253). It provided a totem around which a vulnerable religious family could unite and a conduit through which the *mana* (Lurie, 1981, p. 30) of Mary could be dispensed from heaven to earth. It resonated with the supernaturalistic and highly Marianized mind of the Church at this time (McSweeney, 1987) and struck sympathetic chords especially among devout and impressionable young followers largely steeped in the same cult of the Virgin of their charismatic countryman and Founder. With little else to call their own, these poor, long-suffering toilers in the divine vineyard in the rugged alpine terrain around Mt. Pilat would have found the magical gift of their unique Livery of Mary something attractive to cling to particularly amid the vicissitudes of religious life at the point in mid-century when society around them was traversing the fiery brook of secular modernity.

After Champagnat's demise in 1840 and the retirement of Brother Francis (his chosen successor) in 1860, the principal objective of Marist General Superiors became not so much to carry on the tradition of Marist dress-spirituality inaugurated by their "father in faith" as to ensure the adoption by the Roman Church authorities of the Institute as a fully fledged religious order within the Church (Coste and Lessard, 1960–7). The days of a largely informal and implicit dress-spirituality congenial to a face-to-face *Gemeinschaft* gathered around a charismatic founder and his direct spiritual heir were numbered. The time of an ecclesial uniform – rationally codified in every detail from top to toe, befitting a highly dispersed international organization or *Gesellschaft* diffused throughout the modern world – was decidedly at hand. Joseph (1986, p.131) puts his finger right on the button:

> The change to a Gesellschaft society, and from a patrimonial to a bureaucratic system of organisation, entailed corresponding changes in underlying values, perhaps the most essential of which was an increased emphasis on rationality. These trends were accompanied by changes in clothing, especially in the emergence of uniforms and quasi-uniforms.

Entering the Tridentine "Iron Cage"

Come adoption in 1863 as a fully-fledged religious order of the Roman Catholic Church by the anti-modernist pontiff, Pope Pius IX, significant shifts of emphasis within Marist dress-culture were in the offing. By this time, the scale and complexity of Marist corporate operations in the educational systems of diverse countries and cultures had grown immeasurably, in stark contrast to the primarily French rural and small-town setting of Marist activities hitherto. The halcyon days of "the Livery of Mary" were over. The relative freedom of the Brothers from external dress restraints and scope for corporate dress self-determination ended with the subjugation of the Marist Brothers Institute to the governmental system of the Church hierarchy. And, as Tom Paine reputedly remarked: "Government, like dress, is the badge of lost innocence." Thereafter, at least for the duration of its Tridentine "uniform" century, men of Marist cloth would wear the regulation religious dress of the embattled Church.

As a teaching congregation proven in the cauldron of French educational politics, the Marists became absorbed into the global missionary strategy of "fortress Catholicism" and, thus, were entangled in the tentacles of Vatican officialdom. The "Livery of Mary" was woven into the "iron cage" of ecclesiastical dress controls. The time of Marist dress-legal-rationalization was at hand. For a century during which the Marist Brothers Institute expanded as a globalized teaching congregation operating on all five continents, until the liberalization set in train by the Second Vatican Council (1962–65), the dress culture of the Marist Brothers, in common with that of every other religious order within the Church, was subjected to bureaucratic control in the most minute particulars by administrators of the Tridentine dress *normae* of the hierarchical Roman Church. According to Langer (1965, pp. 124–5), "authority is generally indicated by clothing . . . uniforms distinguish the limbs of authority from the common herd and secure immediate obedience". Langer has military dress in mind as the sartorial foundations and manifestations of government, but his insights here can be extended profitably to the sphere of ecclesiastical dress. If the primary referent of "the Livery of Mary" was the transcendent vertical realm, with incorporation the emphasis switches to the horizontal Church as the concrete, visible "body of Christ". The Marian dimension of Marist dress-culture becomes sublimated, drowned, as we shall see below, in a welter of detailed dress regulations and controls which function to demonstrate to members of religious congregations and the world alike that the bodies of religious virtuosi belong to Mother Church.

Religious superiors, acting as agents of papal power, must ensure that the official code books – Rule, Constitutions, Directory – of their religious communities set out in formal detail the dress rules of the religious order. The act of approbation of a religious community gives official endorsement to the rule books incorporating the dress-code provisions of the new religious "family". The initial act of Vatican sponsorship sanctions use of the official dress of the Church – the sacred habit – and opens the floodgates thereafter, as it transpires, to a deluge of minute religious-dress regulations that are incorporated into the rules and regulations of particular religious communities. How did this process of incremental drift in the body-control of religious virtuosi through uniform dress pan out historically in the Marist case in the century before the Second Vatican Council challenged and radically changed what, following Weber, we can call the hierocratic or bureaucratic-centralist dress regime of the Tridentine Church?

The Uniform Century, 1863–1962

Joseph (1986, p. 131) considers that "the modern uniform is closely linked to the central tendency of our age – an increasingly pervasive bureaucratization." If we look closely at Marist official documents, we find ample evidence that the dress culture of religious life had also become deeply penetrated by the bureaucratic spirit. One would be hard pressed to find a more uniformed body of men than Roman Catholic religious during the century in question here – 1863–1962 – when the centralist predilections of the Vatican authorities were at their most active (within the modern period). Take, for example, the following extract from Chapter V (The Clothing, the Food, and the Residence of the Brothers) of the first main Vatican-approved version of the Marist Constitutions of 1881:

Article 40: The Brothers' clothes shall be plain, modest, and conformable to evangelical poverty. They shall wear a triangular hat, a white rabat, a soutane of black cloth, closing in front with hooks and eyes in the middle, then sewn to the bottom (of the soutane); a mantle of the same cloth as the soutane, and long enough to cover the arms stretched out; cloth or linen stockings, not knitted but sewn; shoes with laces; those who have made the Vow of Obedience shall wear, besides, a woollen cord, and the Professed Brothers a cross.

Article 41: There must be entire uniformity in the whole costume of the little Brothers of Mary, both in the form of the clothes, and the quality of their material, as well as in the manner of wearing them.

Article 42: The Procurator-General and all those under him, whose duty it is to supply and procure the Brothers' clothing, are bound to follow exactly all that the Constitutions prescribe on this subject.

Against a background of civil disaffection with the religious teaching congregations in their mother country of France (Ozouf, 1963; Mayeur, 1966) and the pressures to contribute to the world-wide expansion of the Catholic educational system (Thurion, 1903), the Marists were drawn further and further, as the century wore on, into the conservative religious and clerical dress hegemony of the Vatican. The Marist historian, Brother André Lanfrey commented (personal correspondence): "In my detailed researches between 1850 and 1903, I never found one single document indicating any changes in Marist costume." Lurie (1981, pp. 18 and 20) suggests that conformity to externally imposed uniform regulations, is:

> in terms of speech to be partially or wholly censored . . . To wear a uniform is to give up your right to free speech in the language of clothes; instead you are forced to repeat dialogue composed by someone else. In the extreme case, you become part of a mass of identical persons, all of whom are, as it were, shouting the same words at the same time.

The dress tradition of the Brothers had become sclerotic, frozen in the icy grip of bureaucratic regulation, the spiritual eloquence of its unique "Marian" voice rendered silent; or perhaps it was repressed. By the time of Vatican approval of the new 1908 Marist Directory, the uniformization of Marist dress-culture was virtually complete. Established now throughout the European mainland, Britain and Ireland, Latin America, North America, Asia, Africa and Australia, the Marist Brothers' Institute had become the quintessential religious "uniformed organization" (see Fig.5.1). The following extracts from the twenty-five separate articles of Chapter VII of the 1908 Marist Directory (Marist Archives, Rome) devoted to "The Marist Costume" (pp. 176–80) provide strong evidence of the overwhelming "rationalization" of the Marist uniform dress code:

Article 606: The Brothers shall wear a soutane the hem of which shall reach the ankle. This soutane shall be lined with calico from the collar to the waist, shall have the upper half fastened in front by means of iron hooks and eyes, and the lower half sewn. They shall be made of common black cloth.

Article 608: The Brothers shall wear the cloak fastened every time they go to church, or that they pay a visit. When out for a walk, or when travelling, they may carry it on their arm, with the collar turned towards their body; or it may be carried suspended from their arm.

Article 609: Their stockings shall be of the same material as the soutane, and consequently, not knitted, but sewn.

Article 612: They shall wear a white rabat, about five and a half inches long, five inches broad, with a slit of an inch and five-eighths from the middle of the bottom upwards.

Article 614: The pocket handkerchiefs used by the Brothers shall be made of cotton.

Article 618: The Brothers' shoes shall be made of cowhide leather, shall cover the whole foot, be fastened with mohair or cotton shoelaces, and have round toes regardless of fashions, times or places.

Article 626: The Brothers' wearing apparel and all other objects belonging to them shall bear their admission number.

Article 627: A Brother may have a new soutane every eighteen months, A Cloak every five years, three pairs of Stockings every year, two pairs of Breeches (one for summer and one for winter wear), and a hat every three years.

Article 629: The Brothers shall have their hair cut every two months. The Brother Director shall see that they all have it cut alike.

Nothing here is left to chance. Everything is calculated, counted and numbered. Provisions include a prohibition on wearing gloves "unless some ailment of the hands obliges them to do so" (Article 615), the issue of a standard religious umbrella "when necessary . . . and all alike" (Article 617), and, perhaps unique to any total institution, an allocation of "eight cotton night caps" (Article 624). Every eventuality is covered. The Church had impressed herself from

Figure 5.1 Marist regulation uniform c. 1886

top to toe on the corporate body and individual bodies of Champagnat's descendants, a disciplined body of churchmen now who had somehow outgrown "the Livery of Mary". Now dressed by the book, the Brothers had succumbed to the purposive rationality of the Church bent on close corporeal control of its religious agents operating within and against the modern force field dominated by secular reason (Whimster and Lash, 1987). This technicalization of Marist dress culture signified the imposition of a coherent and systematic regime of body discipline and surveillance upon the increasingly complex manifold of a by this time highly differentiated – in terms of geography, national cultures, political and economic circumstances, social conditions – professional educational corporation.

To all intents and purposes, barring some refinements such as the toleration of a white or tropical habit in particularly hot climes and the Roman "dog collar" as an alternative to the rabat, The Marist dress code remained fixed within this Tridentine prison. State interdictions (for example, in France from 1903 or Mexico in 1922) against religious dress in public (Ignace, 1956; Lanfrey, 1979; Bellone, 1980) made it necessary for Brothers to wear "a costume different from that prescribed by the Constitutions" (1930 edition of the Marist "Rules of Government", Article 84). But other than in times of persecution and state prohibition, the highly rationalized Tridentine religious habit prevailed until Vatican II permissiveness exploded onto the religious life *habitus* in the mid-1960s.

The Eclipse of Marist Dress Magic

Members of approved religious orders and religious congregations are first and foremost servants of the Church. It is her uniform, the most palpable sign of their role as "representative church(wo)men", that marks them out as the religious other of both the laity within the Church and those outside "the household of faith". Joseph (1986, p. 206) makes a telling point in relation to quasi-uniforms which expresses almost exactly the predicament of the Marist religious-dress tradition at its point of transition from a charismatic to a legal-rational stage of development: "Costumes attempt to express the inexpressible and to rationalise the unrational. From a social point of view, costume wearers strive to institutionalise and routinise the paradoxical." Arguably, however, any sustained self-conscious effort to employ the religious habit as a major vehicle of a supernaturalistic, other-worldly, "Marian" orientation to the material goods of religious life had long since been eclipsed within the Marist Brothers' Institute.

In the Marist case, and perhaps in the case of the majority of members of religious-life institutes within the Church during this era, the processes of institutionalization and routinization dominated their dress beliefs and practices to the exclusion of any sense of the sublime and ineffable, let alone the magico-sacramental, that may have bubbled up within their dress culture. Certainly, in the Marist case, it is during the foundation era, when, in Maffesoli's words (1996, p. x), "a new culture, in its nascent state, is brimming over with effervescence", that the Marist dress culture is at its most "spirit-intoxicated" or, in Weber's phrase, "religiously musical". Henceforth, the sacred-dress sense becomes much less uplifted and esoteric. It begins to strike a more prosaic note, concentrating on the moral aspects of dress discipline and good order and emphasizing, above all, conformity and compliance with the dress law of the Church. Of the original "Livery of Mary", a Foucauldian "carceral institution" had been designed in the guise of a dress uniform of the Church.

The Marist dress-story serves to illuminate just exactly how the "squeezing of the transcendent" (Berger, 1970) from religious dress-culture can occur. What the Marist case serves to show is the power of rationality at work as it were, against spirituality, yet for ecclesiology. In other words, in the nineteenth-century evolution of Marist dress-culture, we see one mode of Reason – reasons of Vatican state – in the form of bureaucratic or instrumental rationality set to capture another mode of rationality – value rationality – in the form of primitive dress beliefs which had been worked into the ritual life of an emergent religious community. The intricate and pervasive regulatory framework of the Vatican with regard to religious dress descended as an imperious moral and legal regime on the Marist body, both individual and corporate. This drove the Founder's original totemic understanding of "the Livery of Mary" into the recesses of Marist folk memory and the cold historical documents lodged in the archives of the Institute.

Conclusion: The End of Marist Dress History?

The Second Vatican Council helped dissolve the "polar night of icy darkness", to use Weber's haunting words (Weber, 1958, p. 182) of the over-rationalized Tridentine system. Among its other significant effects, the conciliar "second spring" thawed the frozen dress norms of the old Church order. The Marist Brothers' Institute, in concert with other religious orders, were experiencing a crisis of vocations, and were in a state of decline (Cada *et al.*, 1979) through attrition (Hostie, 1972), aging (Nebrada, 1975) and de-Europeanization

(Hornsby, 1986). While in the 1960s there were almost ten thousand members, by the 1990s the population would fall by some fifty per cent. Marists met the threat of "demaristization" (Benvanides, 1970) with dress modernization, the response à la mode among many religious communities at this time. The Brothers gave symbolic expression to the "renewal" mandate to adapt to and adopt the signs of the times by introducing a radical simplification of their dress code. The 1968 Marist Directory has the following highly truncated observations (Article 40) to make on the subject:

> The costume of the Brothers is the soutane and cord, with rabat and collar, and for those who are perpetually professed, the cross. Provided it has the endorsement of the General Council, the Provincial Chapter may authorise clerical or lay attire, as well as the details of its use.

The principles of subsidiarity and tolerance evident here relative to the previous Tridentine dress regime were the entrée for the informalization and de-clericalization, if not secularization, of Marist dress-culture (Fig. 5.2). The revised Constitutions of the same year all but dispense with a century and a half or so of Marist dress tradition under both its patrimonial and regimental incarnations at a stroke in the interests of modernization: "The Brothers will dress in a simple and modest manner, conformable to the poverty of the Gospel". By 1985, the Draft Constitutions and Statutes (Section 55, "Our Dwellings and Our Dress") had evacuated Marist dress-culture of most of its historic detail and defining ethos, reducing a complex, many-stranded religious dress tradition to a lapel-badge: "Our dress, whatever it be, should be a sign of our consecration, and should be characterised by Marist simplicity. We wear a distinctive badge of the Institute." This probably represents the high point of Marist dress latitudinarianism. The official version of the Marist Statutes of 1985 (Chapter 6, Section 41), while still very pluralistic, open and committed to the modern "voluntaristic" principle when contrasted with previous stages of Marist-dress development, reinstated an overtly hierarchical dimension. This may have reflected a discernible mood in Vatican circles that "de-traditionalization" within the Church had gone too far:

> We dress as is becoming to a Religious member of a lay institute. The Provincial Chapter is to fix the details. We should avoid both negligence and worldly vanity. If the directives of the local Church or the Statutes of the Province require it, our religious habit consists of a soutane, with a rabat or Roman collar, a cord, and, for those perpetually professed, a crucifix.

In 1987 renewed Constitutions and Statutes were published. Since that point in Marist dress history, there have been no alterations to the dualistic, holding position it (Article 61) represents – symptomatic, perhaps, of the ambivalent condition of the "renewed" religious-life communities in the modern world:

> Our habit is a type of attire, such as a suit, which is appropriate for a member of a lay Institute. Alternatively, it may be a soutane, with a Roman collar or Rabat, a cord or for the permanently professed, a crucifix . . . The norms of the Province fix the details of dress . . .

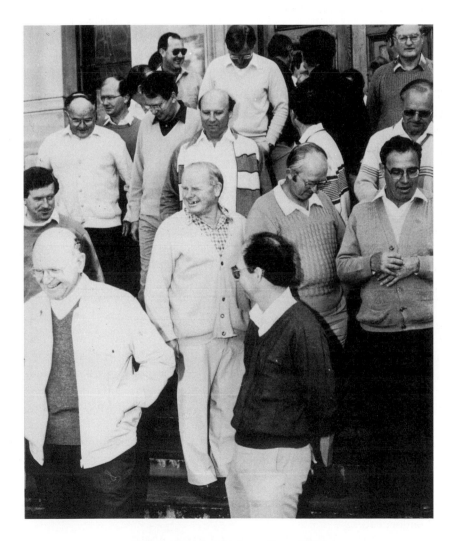

Figure 5.2 Marist informality c. 1996

Whether Champagnat's Marian sacred-dress sensibility will ever be renewed or regenerated within this more permissive and flexible Vatican II-inspired religious-dress sense remains an open historical question. Becoming "clothed with authority" in ecclesiastical terms has been a mixed blessing for the "Little Brothers of Mary". Can religious virtuosi, released from the straitjacket of ecclesiastical body control through uniform-dress regulation, somehow manage to retain the prophetic element of their dress as a sign of religious alterity within a global climate where commodified bodies are increasingly dominated by the lure of the market place and the snares of "consuming fashion" (Brydon and Niessen, 1998)?

Acknowledgements

I wish to express thanks to the Marist Brothers Institute and to the European Union Social Sciences Information Research Fund (EUSSIRF) for a grant that allowed me to visit the European University Institute, Florence, Italy in March 1999.

References

Arthur, L. B. (1999). Introduction: Dress and the sociology of the body. In L. B. Arthur (Ed.) *Religion, dress and the body* (pp.1–7). Oxford & New York: Berg.

Bellone, G. B. (1980). Un Itinerario Di Gloria: Il Fratello Maristi e il suo calvario, 1830–1980. Geneva: Edizioni I.T.I.

Benvanides, L. B. (1970). A predicament to consider: "demaristization". *Marist Bulletin*, 29 (211), 109–28.

Berger, P. L. (1970). *A rumour of angels: modern society and the rediscovery of the supernatural*. London: Allen Lane.

Binder, P. (1986). *Dressing up, dressing down*. London: Allen and Unwin.

Bogatyrev, P. (1937/1971). *The functions of folk costume in Moravian Slovakia*. Trans. R. G. Crum. The Hague, Paris: Mouton.

Brubacker, R. (1984). *The limits of rationality: An essay on the social and moral thought of Max Weber*. London: Allen & Unwin.

Brydon, A. & Niessen, S. (Eds.) (1998). *Consuming fashion: Adorning the transnational body*. Oxford & New York: Berg.

Cada, L. J., Fitz, R. L., Foley, G., Giardino, T. & Lichtenberg, C. (1979). *Shaping the coming age of religious life*. New York: The Seabury Press.

Campbell-Jones, S. (1979). *In habit: an anthropological study of working nuns*. London: Faber.

Chastel, G. (1948). *Marcellin Champagnat*. Paris: E. Alsatia.

Coste, J. (1982). Maristes et eschatologie. *Recherche et Documents du Centre Thomas More*, 36 (Dec.), 25–37.

Coste, J. & Lessard, G. (1960–7). *Origines Maristes* (4 vols.). Rome: Via Poerio 63.

Crawley, E. (1931). Sacred dress. In T. Besterman (Ed.), *Dress, drink and drums* (pp.159–64). London: Methuen.

Crawley, E. (1965). Nudity and dress. In: Roach, M.E. and Eicher, J.B. *Dress, adornment and the social order*. New York: John Wiley and Sons.

Farrell, K. B. (1983). *Achievement from the depths: A critical historical survey of the life of Marcellin Champagnat (1789–1840)*. PhD Thesis. Australia: University of New England.

Fuchs-Ebaugh, H. R. (1977). *Out of the cloister: A study of organizational dilemmas*. Austin: University of Texas Press.

Furet, J.-B. (1856/1989). *Life of Joseph Benedict Marcellin Champagnat*. Rome: Marist Generalate.

Gibson, R. (1971). *Father Champagnat: The man and his spirituality*. Rome: Marist Generalate.

Habermas, J. (1981). *Theory of communicative action: Vol. 1: Reason and the rationalization of society*. Trans. T. McCarthy. Boston: Beacon Press.

Hill, M. (1973). *The religious order: A study of virtuosi religious life and its legitimation in the nineteenth-century Church of England*. London: Heinemann.

Hornsby, D. (1986). Marist third world future. *Marist Newsletter*, 18(2), March.

Hostie, R. (1972). *Vie et mort des ordres religieux*. Paris: Desclée de Brouwer.

Ignace, Fr. (1956). *La passion des Frères en Chine*. Genval, Belgium: Marie-Médiatrice.

Joseph, N. (1986). *Uniforms and non-uniforms: Communication through clothing*. New York and London: Greenwood Press.

Lanfrey, A. (1979). *Une congrégation enseignante: Les Frères Maristes de 1850 à 1904*. Lyon: Université de Lyon II, U.E.R. des Sciences de l'Homme et son Environment.

Langer, L. (1965). Clothes and government. In M. E. Roach & J. B. Eicher (Eds.), *Dress, adornment and the social order* (pp.125–7). New York: John Wiley & Sons.

Lash, N. (1977). Modernism, aggiornamento and the night-battle. In A. Hastings (Ed.), *Bishops and writers: Aspects of the evolution of modern British Catholicism* (pp. 51–79). London: Wheathampsted.

Laveille, Mgr. (1921). *Marcellin Champagnat, Prêtre Mariste*. Paris: Tequi.

Loome, T. M. (1979). *Liberal Catholicism, reform Catholicism, and modernism*. Tübingen.

Lurie, A. (1981). *The language of clothes*. New York: Random House.

Maffesoli, M. (1996). *The contemplation of the world: Figures of community style*. Translated by S. Emanuel. Minneapolis: University of Minnesota Press.

Marshall, S. & Swift, A. (1993). *Liberals and communitarians*. New York and London: Blackwell.

Mayer-Thurman, C. C. (1975). *Raiments for the Lord's service: A thousand years of western vestments*. Chicago: The Art Institute.

Mayeur, J. M. (1966). *La séparation de l'église et de l'état*. Paris: Juillard.

Mayo, J. (1984). *A history of ecclesiastical dress*. London: B.T. Batsford.

McMahon, F. (1988). *Strong mind, gentle heart: A life of Blessed Marcellin Champagnat*. Drummoyne, New South Wales: Marist Brothers.

McSweeney, B. (1987). Catholic piety in the nineteenth century. *Social Compass* XXXIV (2–3).

Michelman, S. O. (1999). Fashion and identity of women religious. In L. Arthur (Ed.), *Religion, dress and the body* (pp. 135–46). Oxford & New York: Berg.

Nebreda, J. (1975). La crisis vocacional de Instituto Marista. *Cuadernos de Realidades Sociales, 6*, 59–107.

Ortner, S. B. (1973). On key symbols. *American Anthropologist*, 75, 1338–46.

Ozouf, M. (1963). *L'Ecole, l'église et la république*. Paris: Armand Colin.

Peel, J. D. Y. (1973). Cultural factors in the contemporary theory of development. *Archives Européennes de Sociologie*, 14, 17–32.

Roach, M. E. and Eicher, J. B. (1965). *Dress, adornment and the social order*. New York: John Wiley and Sons.

Roach, M. E. & Eicher, J. B. (1979). The language of personal adornment. In J. M. Cordwell & R. A. Schwarz (Eds.), *The fabrics of culture: The anthropology of clothing and adornment* (pp.7-21). New York, Paris, The Hague: Mouton Publishers.

Schluchter, W. (1981). *The rise of western rationalism: Max Weber's developmental history*. Berkeley: University of California Press.

Sester, P. & Borne, R. (1991-2). *Letters of Marcellin J. B. Champagnat*. (2 vols.) Trans. L. Voegtle. Rome: Marist Generalate.

Stark, W. (1969).*The sociology of religion: A study of Christendom*. London: Routledge and Kegan Paul.

Sullivan, R. (1988). Breaking habits: Gender, class and the sacred in the dress of women religious. In A. Brydon & S. Niessen (Eds.) *Consuming fashion. Adorning the transnational body* (pp.109–28). Oxford & New York: Berg.

Thurion, J. (1903). *En exil: les congrégations françaises hors de France*. Paris: Guillard.

Tiryakian, E. A. (1981). The sociological import of metaphor: Tracing the sources of Max Weber's Iron Cage. *Sociological Inquiry*, Vol. 51, No.1.

Weber, M. (1958 ed.). *The Protestant ethic and the spirit of capitalism*. Trans. T. Parsons. New York: Charles Scribner.

Weber, M. (1968 ed.). *Economy and society: an outline of interpretive sociology*. In G. Roth & C. W. Mills, (Eds.) New York: Bedminster Press.

Wellmer, A. (1985). Reason, utopia and enlightenment. In J. Bernstein (Ed.), *Habermas and modernity* (pp. 35–66). Cambridge, Mass.: M.I.T. Press and Polity Press.

Whimster, S. & Lash, S. (Eds.) (1987). *Max Weber: Rationality and modernity*. London: Allen & Unwin.

Wilson, E. (1965). *Adorned in dreams: fashion and modernity*. London: Virago Press.

Zind, P. (1969). *Les nouvelles congrégations enseignantes en France de 1800 à 1830*. (3 vols.). St. Genis Laval, Lyon: Le Montet.

6

Confucianism Manifested in Korean Dress from the Sixteenth to Seventeenth Centuries

Inwoo Chang and Haekyung L. Yu

In spite of limited availability, actual garments from the past are the most precious information source for costume historians. The history of monarchial Korea is often described in three periods: Three-Kingdoms period (*c.* AD 200–918), Koryo dynasty (918–1392), and Choson dynasty (1392–1919). Garments from the Three-Kingdoms period are virtually non-existent, while a few garments from the Koryo dynasty have been discovered inside the middle cavity of Buddha statues. In comparison, a good quantity of garments from the Choson dynasty has survived. Some have been kept in families, and others have been excavated from old tombs.

While the garments retrieved from inside Buddha statues reflect the supremacy of Buddhism in the Koryo dynasty as the national religion, the excavated garments from Choson dynasty resulted from burial rites performed according to Confucian doctrine, the dominant philosophy during that period. Since the 1970s, wide-scale construction of highways has led to the discovery of many old tombs and a large number of garments buried within the tombs. Garments retrieved from these archeological sites include dress worn by the deceased as well as textile pieces used to stuff the coffins. Prominent families could put many garments in a coffin as tribute to the dead, while some families had to use paper as a substitute. The dates of the tombs can be often identified using extensive family records which contain records of birth and death dates of most family members.

Substantial numbers of garments from the Choson dynasty have been already retrieved in different parts of Korea and more tombs from that period are currently being excavated, providing direct information on the costume of that time period. Therefore, for this study, information has been gathered about more than 400 excavated garment pieces from the Choson dynasty, and approximately 100 pieces from the late sixteenth to early seventeenth centuries have been examined, as this was the time period when most of the excavated garments were buried. The results of the study showed the influences of folk religion as well as Confucianism which peaked at that time and accompanying social changes in Korean society.

The Korean peninsula lies in the northeast portion of the Asian continent; it neighbors China and is separated by a narrow strait from Japan. During the Three-Kingdoms period, people believed in an immortal universe where one's spirit lives an eternal life, and the kings had divine authority over their people. In comparison, during the Koryo period, the country was Buddhist and governed by a small group of aristocratic families. Confucianism was the official national religion in the Choson dynasty and commoners with education and training formed the ruling classes. Consequently, commoner's dress was important during that era.

The founder of the Choson dynasty, King Taejong, adopted Confucianism as the national religion and ruling philosophy in order to maintain strict social order and to justify his revolt against the Koryo dynasty. In 1447 and 1453, two major books based on Confucius' teachings were completed in order to specify the codes and the rules for the government organizations and official ceremonies (Ko, 1992; Lee, 1991). Later in the Choson dynasty, numerous family ritual manuals and etiquette guides were published by common families. Rituals and etiquette were more than socially desirable conduct in the Choson dynasty. They were the embodiment of Confucianism itself, and thus it was extremely important that all rituals, ceremonies and even everyday lives would follow the right Confucian procedures (Ko, 1992). Additionally, the ruling class of the Choson dynasty, particularly at the beginning, believed that inculcating Confucian customs would help to bring stability to local society and establish the firm ruling of the central government.

Background on Korean Clothing

The basic garments in Korean traditional dress consist of two pieces, a top and a bottom. The top is a caftan-style jacket or blouse called *jogori*. Both men and women wear *jogori* regardless of age and socio-economic status. With *jogori* men wear pants called *baji*, and women wear skirts called *chima*.

On top of these basic garments, people can wear a variety of *po* (coat or robe-type outer wear) depending on the weather and occasion. In addition to these basic garments, there are several important ceremonial garments worn on specific occasions including *jaebok* for memorial services, *honraebok* for a wedding and *jobok*, the uniforms that government officials wear at work (Ko, 1986). Because there are four distinctive seasons, diverse materials and construction techniques including quilting have been used in the construction of Korean garments.

Up till the middle Choson dynasty, *jogori* and *po* were almost identical garments except for the length. *Jogori* was short, looking more like a jacket, and *po* was of coat-length. Even though the five components of *jogori* and *po* – *git* (collar), *gil* (bodice), *somae* (sleeve), *sup* (front gusset) and *moo* (side gusset) – have remained (see figure 6.1), the shapes of five components in *jogori* and *po* were diverted, and *jogori* and *po* have become two distinctively different garments. Compared to the changes in *jogori* and *po*, *chima* and *baji* went through little change. Therefore, it is easier to identify the influences of Confucianism and the social changes by examining *po* and *jogori* among the excavated garments. In particular, *po* as optional outerwear seemed then to be a more sensitive mirror of Choson society.

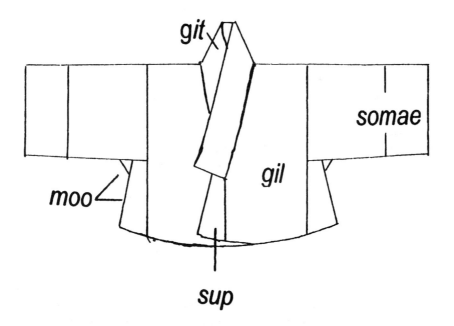

Figure 6.1 Construction of an old *jogori*

Excavated Garments and Confucian Rites

While garments from the past have been recovered in many regions of the world including Egypt, Sweden and China, the garments excavated in Korea differ in some ways from those retrieved in other regions. First, in other areas of the world excavated garments usually belonged to royal families and the aristocratic class. However, in Korea, the excavated garments were found in the tombs of many commoners as well as those of royalty and aristocrats. Secondly, while almost all excavated garments from Egypt and other regions date back to the prehistoric era, the excavated garments in Korea were mostly buried just 400 to 500 years ago, showing the relatively recent changes in the history of Korean costume. Finally and most importantly in this chapter, the physical surroundings of the burial sites are different. In other areas, the natural environment, e.g. dry weather or icy field, has kept the garments from decay. But in Korea it is the burial ritual itself that resulted in preservation of the excavated garments.

The Confucian rituals and etiquette reinforced in the Choson dynasty were mostly drawn from *Chuja-kareh* (The Book of Family Rituals), a book of the neo-Confucian school (Ko, 1991). *Chuja-kareh* became widely disseminated toward the end of the Koryo dynasty and the beginning of the Choson dynasty. However, in spite of the efforts to instill Confucian order in Chosun society, Buddhist and Shamanist influences persisted among ordinary Koreans and even some in the ruling class. The influence of Buddhism in royal families was officially abolished at the time of King *Sejong*. By the middle of the Choson dynasty, funeral rites based on the *Chuja-kareh* were well rooted among the upper class and were gradually gaining acceptance among the common people (Chung, 1994).

As the Confucian funeral rituals became established, burial ceremonies also had changed. In Koryo, royal members were buried in *suksilmyo*, tombs with stone chambers. But from the early Choson dynasty, *hwaegwakmyo*, tombs with lime layers as prescribed in *Chuja-kareh,* were constructed for the kings. These royal customs were disseminated to the ordinary Koreans by the middle of the Choson dynasty (Chung, 1994).

In *hwaegwakmyo*, the body of the deceased was contained in three tiers of coffins before soil was hauled in to make a mound. The dressed corpse was first laid in a wooden coffin and the coffin was put inside another wooden coffin. A mortar of lime powder was poured into the digging to form the bottom of the third coffin. Then, the wooden coffin was lowered onto the mortar bed and additional mortar was poured outside the four sides and the top of the outer wooden coffin. The lime layers were usually one meter thick on the top and the bottom, and 40 to 50 centimeters on the sides. When the mortar became solidified to a high density, it sealed the coffin from the penetration of air, water and bacteria and thus the garments as well as other artifacts were often protected from decay. The density of a lime layer and its closeness to the wooden coffin determined whether artifacts and corpses would remain preserved or not (Jang, 1998). Excavated garments in Korea have been retrieved only from these *hwaegwakmyo* (Chung, 1994). Supporting the relationship between excavated garments and Confucianism, most of the excavated garments date from the sixteenth to the seventeenth centuries when Confucianism was dominant in Korea. (Chang, 1996; Kim, Kim & Chang, 1993; Kim, 1993; Kim & Ko, 1978a, 1978b; Kim & Lee, 1983; Kim & Yu, 1980a, 1980b, 1980c, 1980d; Yoo & Kim, 1991).

Geographical origins of the excavated garments also confirm their relationship with Confucianism. Almost all of the excavated garments showing Confucian influences were retrieved from *Kyonggi, Ch'ungchong* and *Kyungsang* provinces where two dominant Confucian schools (*Kiho* and *Youngnam*) started and prospered. The names of schools themselves indicate that *Kiho* scholars resided mainly in *Kyonggi* and *Ch'ungchong* provinces, and *Youngnam* in *Kyongsang* province. It is notable that garments from the early Choson dynasty (the fifteenth to early sixteenth centuries) were excavated only in *Kyonggi* province, which included Seoul (the capital city) and the surrounding area. Other areas seem to have followed later the Confucian burial rites carried out in *Kyonggi* province. This suggests that Confucian beliefs initiated in Seoul and *Kyonggi* province gained wider support in later periods and dispersed to other areas.

Even though the Confucian rites resulted in preservation of burial clothing, the garments themselves also show the influences of folk religion. The excavated garments have traces of previous wear indicating that used garments, not new ones, were buried with the owner. This seems to reflect folk beliefs of Koreans concerning the world after death. In folk religion, people live through two worlds – the world now and the afterworld (Chong,1988; Kim,1966, 1991). These two worlds cannot coexist in one temporal or spatial sphere, but they circulate around one axle like a wheel. The circulation of human life is embedded in the changes of nature such as night after day, and a crescent moon followed by a full moon (Chong, 1988; Kim, 1966). Naturally the dead would need the same clothes that they wore when they were living in this world, not any special clothes. The excavated garments from sixteenth- to seventeenth-century Korea reflect simultaneous influences of Confucianism and folk beliefs of the circulatory world.

Changes in *Po* due to Confucian Influence

The *po* is an optional outfit needed for protection from cold or for showing courtesy in ceremonial and formal occasions. On ceremonial occasions, people wore three *po* on top of each other. The top *po* was naturally more important and formal than the other *po* worn under the top *po* (*Karaewonru, c.*1700; Kim, 1599; *Kukchooraeui,* 1474). The top *po* was always made of a single layer of fabric without a lining and worn throughout the year, but the middle and under *po* varied according to season. In summer, they were often made of a single layer of ramie fabric, but winter ones were made of two layers of fabric and sometimes were quilted with cotton padding (Chang, 1996).

As a style of *po,* the *dopo* was one of the most important styles during the Choson dynasty and is still the symbol of Confucian scholars and worn at Confucian memorial services to ancestors (see figure 6.2). It is not clear exactly when people started to wear *dopo,* but the name *dopo* first appeared in 1607 on *Sejong-sillok* (1607). The *dopo* dating from the sixteenth to the seventeenth centuries were excavated mostly outside of Seoul. They are made of cotton varying in styles. The lack of uniform style, material and geographic origins of excavated *dopo* all suggest that they are the earliest *dopo* which were worn by local scholars, not by government officials for whom the regulations were in effect.

Figure 6.2 *Dopo.* Courtesy of the Museum of Ch'ungbuk National University.

At the beginning of the Choson dynasty, nobility in the central government were the dominant power and hindered the influx of local officers and scholars who were forming a new social class, *Sarim*. These Confucian scholars, residing outside of the capital area, were usually from small local noble families. They were highly educated and trained, but opportunities to involve themselves in the central government were restricted due to the limited number of positions. Therefore, *Sarim* justified their existence and importance in Choson society through a philosophy of group ruling, *Bung-dang* in Confucianism. *Bung-dang* was a concept similar to a political party, but it was organized mainly through the networks of scholars who studied together in one school. Only a few from one school might be able to work in the central government, but they could exert their influence on the central government as a group through those officials from their *Bung-dang*. The number and power of *Sarim* greatly expanded and by the eighteenth century they became one of the most powerful social classes in Choson society (Lee, 1991). Consequently, the *dopo,* the symbolic garment of *Sarim*, was elevated to the foremost of formal wear as their patrons became politically prominent. The excavated *dopo* from this period were often made not of cotton, but of more expensive materials such as silk brocade. As the public domain strictly belonged to men, *dopo* were worn only by men.

Changes in other *po* styles, the *danryong* and *jikryong,* also reflect the transformation of Choson society into a Confucian nation. *Danryong* literally means a circular *git* forming a round neckline, while *jikryong* means that it has a straight *git*. Excavated *danryong* dating from before the fifteenth century through the seventeenth century are made of undyed fabric without linings. The single layer of excavated *danryong* indicates that they were worn as top *po*. This is consistent with what has been written in several pieces of literature. According to *Karaewonryu* (*c.* 1700s) and Kim (1599*),* in the fifteenth century, commoners as well as kings and aristocrats wore *danryong* on formal occasions and *danryong* was the utmost formal wear for Koreans except for the kings. However, from the seventeenth century *danryong* became uniforms for government officials and thus ordinary citizens had to wear *jikryong* and *simoui* instead of *danryong* as formal wear (Sin, 1621; *Saraepyongram, c.* 1700s). Therefore, in the seventeenth century a *danryong* was a clear indicator of social roles in Korean society. The importance of *danryong* as formal wear for commoners can be found in modern Korea; grooms wear *danryong* in a Korean traditional wedding.

As *danryong* became uniforms for government officials, the importance of *jikryong* as formal wear increased in the middle Choson dynasty. *Jikryong* dating from the early sixteenth century were excavated and they are made of brown silk brocade with a cloud pattern. The *jikryong* was not just a substitute for a *danryong* which could be worn when a *danryong* was not readily available (Sin,1621; *Karaekojung*,1624), but was considered as important as a *danryong*

(Sin,1621). In summary, expansion of public domains for men must have necessitated diversification in men's wear and this trend is well reflected in *danryong* and *jikryong*.

Gender-specification of Garments and Confucian Teachings

Some *po* seemed to have changed as the strict prescription of Confucianism on gender segregation trickled into all levels of Choson society. Korean women enjoyed relatively equal partnership during the Buddhist Koryo dynasty, which did not adhere to a strict patriarchal system. Confucianism, which views the universe consisting of and running in the yin–yang principle, emphasized gender differences and their accompanying gender roles. Furthermore, Confucian family rituals were aimed at consolidating patriarchal authority. As Confucian teachings were practiced even in commoners' households, women were stripped of their property rights, and the rights to serve and lead memorial services, which signified full membership in a family and Choson society, were also taken away from women. Accordingly, some unisex garments became gender-specific and new-style *po* appeared to be worn for either men only or women only.

The case of *jangoui* shows an interesting path of gender-specification in garments (See figure 6.3). *Jangoui* are the most commonly excavated *po* found in all regions of Korea. The excavated *jangoui* dating from the fifteenth to seventeenth centuries have one style, but in two sizes. This indicates both men and women wore identical *jangoui*. However, from the eighteenth century, women used *jangoui* to cover their heads like long veils when they were going outside of the home. On the other hand, men wore other *po* far more frequently, and over a period of more than one hundred years *jangoui* were rarely worn by men.

Chupri (*po* having two parts) show another case of gender-specification. The excavated *chupri* have two styles depending on the ratio between the lengths of the upper and lower part of the *po* and the width of the pleats. *Chupri* which had the upper part as long as the lower part with small pleats were found in both men's and women's tombs. They were made of single or double layers of fabric depending on the season, and some of them were quilted. The materials suggest that these *chupri* were probably worn under other *po*. On the other hand, other styles of *chupri* with wider pleats and a longer lower part were made of silk fabric, which indicates they were top *po*. They came in only men's sizes showing that only men wore this style *chupri*, called *chul-lik* (see figure 6.4). They were worn sometimes as soldiers' uniforms.

Figure 6.3 *Jangoui* for men. Courtesy of the Museum of Ch'ungbuk National University.

Figure 6.4 *Chu-lik.* Courtesy of the Museum of Ch'ungbuk National University.

A basic item worn by both sexes, *jogori* have same styles regardless of gender, but *jogori* with *dangko git* were found only in women's tombs from the middle of the Choson dynasty. In addition, more elaborate styles and constructions were observed in women's *jogori*, which seems to indicate the increasing emphasis on *jogori* for women. In contrast, *po* had become more important in men's wear; a new *po*, *dopo*, emerged as one of the most important *po* styles; diverse styles became available and widely worn as more men had to take expanded roles and occupations in society.

Excavated garments in Korea are the consequences of Confucian burial rites. They show the influences of Confucianism and lingering folk religion as well as the social changes brought in as Confucianism became widely accepted in the Choson society. Confucianism was more than a religion during the Choson dynasty. It was a philosophy with sets of rules to be practiced in order to maintain social order. Confucian principles became the basis in all areas and aspects of Choson society including government organization, official and private ceremonies, different social roles and even everyday etiquette. The excavated garments from sixteenth- to seventeenth-century Korea reflect more than personal tastes and circumstances of individuals who lived in the past. They manifest the religious and social environments as well as philosophical and cultural changes in Korea during that period.

References

Chang, I. W. (1996). 중요민속자료 조사보고서 [A study on the daily costumes among excavated costumes in the middle Choson dynasty]. Unpublished Doctoral dissertation, Dongkuk University, Seoul, Korea.

Chong, J. H. (1988). 韓國宗敎文化의 展開 [Development of religious culture of Korea] Seoul: *Chipmuntang*.

Chung, J. S. (1994). 조선초기 상장의례 연구 [A Study on Funeral Customs in the Early Chosun Dynasty]. Unpublished doctoral dissertation, Choong-ang University, Seoul, Korea, pp. 246–57.

Jang, Y. Z. (1998). 다큐멘타리 역사스페셜 [History special of KBS documentary]. Seoul: Korean Broadcasting Service.

Karaekojung, (1624). 家禮考證 [Book on the Confucian rites], *Kyu-chang-kak* Library No.717.

Karaewonru. (*c.* 1700s). [家禮原流 , Book on Confucian rites]. *Kyu-chang-kak* (Library of Old Books in Seoul National University). Library No. 1633.

Kim, J. S. (1599). 家禮便覽 [*Karaepyonram*: Book on Confucian rites]. *Kyu-chang-kak*. Library No. 6913 & 1685.

Kim, M. S. (1993). 홍우협묘 출토 17세기 복식논고 [Excavated costumes of Hong Woo-Hyup]. Korea: Chungbuk University Museum.

Kim, T. K. (1966). 무가연구 [Study on shamans]. Seoul : *Chahgusa*.

Kim, T. K. (1991). 韓國巫俗硏究 [Study on shamans of Korea]. Seoul: *Chipmuntang*.

Kim, D. U. & Ko, B. N. (1978a). 중요민속자료 조사보고서 [Designated report of important folk materials. No. 63]. Seoul : Korea Department of Cultural Properties.

Kim, D. U. & Ko, B. N. (1978b). 출토조선시대유의의 복식사적 연구 [A study on excavated costumes of Choson dynasty]. *Journal of Costume, 2*, 9–21.

Kim, D. U. & Lee, S. B. (1983). 임란전후출토복식 및 상례 [Excavated costume of around 7-Year War]. Report. No.8. Ch'ungjoo, Korea: Museum of Ch'ungbuk National University.

Kim, D. U. & Yu, S. O. (1980a). 광주이씨 의복유물 [Excavated costume of Lady Lee]. Designated report of important folk materials. No. 80. Seoul: Korea Department Of Cultural Properties.

Kim, D. U. & Yu, S. O. (1980b). 충북청원군 구례손씨묘 출토유물 [Excavated costume of Lady Ku]. Designated Report of Important Folk Materials. No. 82. Seoul: Korea Department of Cultural Properties.

Kim, D. U. & Yu, S. O. (1980c). 충북청원군전박장군묘출토유물 [Excavated costume of General Park]. Designated Report of Important Folk Materials, No. 83. Seoul: Korea Department of Cultural Properties.

Kim, D. U. & Yu, S. O. (1980d). 충북괴산군김위묘출토유물 [Excavated costumes of Kim Wi]. Designated report of important folk materials. No. 84. Seoul: Korea Department of Cultural Properties.

Kim, D. U., Kim, Y. J. & Chang, I. W. (1993). 출토유의 및 근대복식논고 [Report of excavated costume No.20]. Ch'ungjoo: Museum of Ch'ungbuk National University.

Ko, B. N. (1986). 한국전통복식연구 [Study on traditional costumes of Korea]. Seoul: *Il-cho-kak*.

Ko, Y. J. (1991). 16세기말 사례서의 성립과 예학의 발달 [Development of ritualism and completion of ritual book in the late sixteenth century], *Journal of Korean Culture, 12*, 456.

Ko, Y. J. (1992). 조선중기 예설과 예서 [Confucian ritual book in the middle Choson dynasty]. Unpublished doctoral dissertation, Seoul National University, Korea.

Kukchooraeui. (1474). 國朝五禮儀 [Book on Confucian rites]. *Kyu-chang-kak*.

Lee, K. K. (around the 1700s) 五洲衍文長箋散稿 [Book on folk customs of the Choson Dynasty].

Lee, P. J. (1991). 조선중세예사상연구 [The Study of Confucian ritual thought in the middle Choson dynasty]. Seoul: *Il-cho-kak*.

Saraepyonram. (around 1700). [四禮便覽 : Book on the Confucian rites].

Sejong-shillok. (1607). 世宗實錄 [Record of King Sejong, 31st year].

Sin, U. K. (1621). 喪禮備要 [*Sangraepiyo*: Book on the Confucian Rites]. *Kyu-chang-kak*. Library No. 1258.

Yoo, H. K. & Kim, M. J. (1991). 진주하씨묘 출토문헌과 복식조사보고서 [Excavated costumes of Lady Ha]. Chinjoo: *Gondle Baru* Museum.

7

Islamic Religion and Women's Dress Code: The Islamic Republic of Iran

Faegheh Shirazi

The Iran Air carrier departed from London for its destination, Tehran's Mehrabad airport. I thought to myself, "by the time I arrive, I would actually be veiled for almost a day and a half." It is commonly understood that by choosing Iran Air from any destination in the world, women passengers are obliged to obey the same rule that is applied to women in Iran: compulsory veiling in the public. There are no exceptions, even for foreign women traveling to and from Iran. I already knew the rule first hand through my personal experiences from extensive trips to Iran over the past 20 years. Every time I visited home, I chafed at the necessity of wearing this cumbersome attire, but I always complied with the dress code in order to avoid being harassed or imprisoned.

Because Iran Air is the official airline of the Islamic Republic of Iran, people should realize that they are in "Iranian territory" controlled by the government of Iran once in the departure lounge for any Iran Air operation outside of Iran. Thus seeing female passengers of all religions and nationalities sitting in the Iran Air lobby in any foreign country donning the veil is not an unusual scene.

It was long past midnight on the trip from London to Tehran when the crew announced that we were arriving in Iranian air space, and the law of *hijab* (the Arabic term for the veil) was enforced. The crew cautioned the passengers that use of alcoholic beverages, illegal drugs, gambling devices, publications or audio and video tapes that may violate the legal principles of Islam or any guidelines set by the Islamic Republic of Iran was to be avoided. I thought to myself, "who would risk smuggling anything illegal? Or, who would be brave enough to challenge the law of *hijab*, and remove the veil in

113

public?" The punishment would be great. All the women had donned the veils from the lobby of Iran Air in London, England and they kept it on in the aircraft at all times throughout the trip. Although veiling was observed during the trip, the aircrew had the responsibility of giving such information to the passengers upon landing. The same rule applies to any other foreign carrier flying to Iran in order to be able to operate in the country.

My initial interest in the issue of veiling began since the Islamic Revolution swept through Iran, my native country. I came to realize the importance of veiling as an interesting topic when I began to teach courses on Middle Eastern cultures at The University of Texas at Austin. My vast collection of visual and printed material that depict veiled women points to the increasing significance of the veil over the years. This unassuming piece of cloth has a history that antedates the Islamic Republic of Iran by thousands of years, and predates the culture of Arabia even before the lifetime of Muhammad, the Prophet of Islam.

The first known reference to veiling was made in an Assyrian legal text of the thirteenth century BCE. In this text, veiling is a sign of nobility reserved for respectable women and prohibited for prostitutes (Driver and Miles,1952). The Middle-Assyrian Laws (750–612 BCE) mention a harlot or slave girl found improperly wearing a veil in public. She was ordered to be brought to the palace for punishment. In Book IV of *Metamorphoses*, Ovid (43 BCE– 17 CE) mentions the significance of a white veil to a story of the Bablonians Pyramus and Thisbe who fall in love and decide to meet at the tomb of King Ninus. Thisbe, who arrives early, sees a lioness and flees into a cave, dropping her white veil behind. The lioness, whose muzzle is dripping with the blood of a fresh kill, rips the white veil. When Pyramus finds the torn bloodied veil, he concludes that his lover has been killed by the lioness and he commits suicide with his sword. Eventually, Thisbe finds Pyramus' dead body and she kills herself as well. All such misfortunes are caused by a piece of cloth, the veil (Innes, 1955). These are just two of many examples of how veiling is not a recent phenomenon or an invention of Islam, but rather an ancient and cultural practice with a specific function and purpose.

In this chapter, I discuss several issues: 1) the importance of the veil or the Islamic *hijab* as a significant marker in the lives of the Iranian women; 2) how this single article of clothing has created a range of meanings and religious and political concepts in the life of Iranians at home and abroad; and 3) how the veil, which began as a symbol of piety and later was prescribed to women, gave birth to endless debate, discussion and interpretation that will continue for years to come.

Hijab Defined

The issue of *hijab* has become a fascinating topic not only in academia, but also in popular culture. The veil as an article of clothing or a garment carries multiple meanings and interpretations. The *hijab* no longer means a piece of cloth draped on a woman's head. Now, the *hijab* is pregnant with meanings acquired during the most recent history of contemporary Islamic societies (Shirazi, in press).[1] A specific style of *hijab* that a woman may adopt can be interpreted in numerous ways. It might serve as an indication of her degree of religiosity or affiliation with or protest against a political party; a cue of her progressiveness; a silent communicator of her strong belief in the feminist movement; a symbol of her struggle against colonial regime; or it might indicate nothing more than her adherence to traditional cultural values.

The morphology of word *hijab* in the Arabic language is from *hajaba*, meaning to veil, cover, screen, shelter, seclude (from); to hide, obscure (from sight); to eclipse, outshine, overshadow; to make imperceptible, invisible; to conceal (from); to make or form a separation (between). As evident from the wealth of meanings of the term *hijab*, we can conclude that the word *hijab* can be understood in numerous ways depending on a given situation based on culture. Generally in popular Islamic culture, *hijab* is understood in two specific forms: 1) concealment donned by women as a religious obligation mentioned in the holy *Qur'an* with its various stylistic interpretations, and 2) as practiced or understood by Muslim women in various Islamic societies. In this regard, one finds variations in styles of veils adopted by women within the same culture. Thus, we can not claim that there is a "uniform" style of *hijab* that is common among women in Islamic cultures.

Hijab, a Significant Marker

In the field of clothing and textiles, the concept of Symbolic Interaction is known as a "perspective that pursues the study of social actions and social objects" (Kaiser 1990, p. 39). In this regard, symbolic interaction emphasizes a two-way interaction: appearance management and appearance perception. This perspective emphasizes the fact that the intended messages are not meaningful if the sender of the message (the wearer of an article of clothing) and the receiver of the message (the observer) do not process the message in the same way. The objects themselves – in this case, clothing – acquire meanings, and the ways that people use and relate to the clothing as material culture becomes meaningful (Shirazi-Mahajan, 1993).

I will argue that if one applies the symbolic-interaction perspective to the issue of *hijab* in the Islamic Republic of Iran, it becomes evident that symbolic interaction relies upon social objects and social actions. For example, a particular style of *hijab* can explain how an ideal image can be created to project impressions that are part of the message conveyed to others through outward appearance. In this respect, we can assume that meanings assigned to clothing and appearance are open to interpretation, manipulation and modification that can result in a new set of meanings.

Clothing can be used as an experiment to study trends that reflect social and political attitudes, and it is therefore of common interest among a large number of social scientists. Further, a common theme is the relationship between power and political influence on clothing. In contemporary Iranian society *hijab* has acquired a political power and has been constantly promoted by the Islamic government since the victory of the Islamic regime over the monarchy of the Shah.

The fall of the monarchy in 1979 awakened and politicized the women of Iran. During the late 1970s and early 1980s thousands of women from all walks of life became active participants in the revolutionary forces. Whether motivated by religious zeal or secular aims, the vast majority of these women had expected to gain new rights and a considerable amount of freedom which they hoped would lead to an era of expanding opportunities under the Islamic Republic regime. At least this is what the leaders of the Islamic Republic had promised to the women of Iran during the crucial days of revolutionary upheaval. However, as soon as the Islamic Republic established itself, the leaders of the revolution changed their attitude towards women and their position in the society.

Within a very short time after the success of the revolution, new rules and regulations concerning all aspects of women's lives were announced. For example, there were restrictions on the type of jobs women could hold. Inclusive among such restrictions was the imposition of compulsory *hijab* on women; it dictated how Muslim women should behave and set forth an ideal image for Muslim women represented by a particular style of *hijab* that is continuously promoted by the government of the Islamic Republic of Iran.

The government of Iran is an active agent in implementing the *hijab* and the code of ethics among its populace. Such rules are conducted through persuasion and specific persuasions are successfully carried out by social movements which employ slogans to create impressions, to alter perceptions, to elicit emotional responses, to make demands and to pressure any type of opposition endangering the government's agendas. The Ministry of Guidance reserves the rights of censorship in all printed, posted or published materials and in all aired programs (television, radio, movies and video films). It is illegal

Figure 7.1 Promotional *hijab* poster by the Islamic Republic of Iran

to distribute any product or provide any services for the public without the written permission of the Ministry of Guidance. Thus any images or messages displayed publicly must have the seal of approval from this department.

The preoccupation of the Islamic Republic of Iran with the protection of woman's sexuality is one of the main issues of concerns for the Office of Guidance. Muslim women's honor and chastity are protected by emphasizing religious morality. Morality is also seen in terms of the woman's conduct and behavior in all aspects of her daily life; this specifically includes her clothing and appearance. This dress code is mentioned in the Preamble of the 1979 Islamic Republic Constitution:

> A woman . . . will no longer be regarded as a "thing" or a tool, serving consumerism and exploitation. In regarding her important duty and most respectful role of mother in the nourishing of human beings who belong to the school of thought, as a pioneer along with men, as a warrior in the active living battlefields, the result will be her accepting higher values and beneficence (Moghadam 1993, p.174).

The preamble is an indication of the importance placed upon the woman's role in the society. Therefore, "exploitation" of her body by displaying her publicly is frowned upon and is considered a sinful act. This "symbolic" and honorable position that has been granted to women by the government is continuously promoted through the propaganda of veiled images of women printed on posters and displayed throughout the country. By law, every business establishment is obliged to have signs displayed at the entry of the shop or immediately in a visible location as one enters into the shop to inform the female customers that "service will be denied to those in improper *hijab*." The following section will explain the importance of the "proper" versus the "improper" *hijab*.

Hijab, its Multiple Dimensions

Clothing can be more than a fashionable or functional entity. The concept and practice of *hijab* may appear to be similar throughout the Islamic world, but in fact, its practice and the reasons for its use varies considerably. Turkish and Palestinian women, for example, have started to re-veil as an outward expression of their anti-Western sentiment, a silent protest against the ruling government (MacLeod, 1992). The same case may be applicable when we

Figure 7.2 Stamp promoting *hijab,* by the Islamic Republic of Iran

note how in recent years, lower-middle-class working women in Cairo and other Egyptian cities have been voluntarily re-veiling. This behavior may be a result of silent protest with symbolic significance, perhaps an indication of a struggle for identity, self-worth; or it may even indicate a new form of women's movement (Zuhur, 1992).

In comparing the Egyptian case to Iran after the establishment of the Islamic Republic regime we arrive at very different reasons for re-veiling. The enforcement of the veiling in Iran is a part of the political reconstruction of Iranian social order into an Islamic central society. The leader of the Islamic revolution, Ayatollah Khomeini, made a reference to the importance of veiling for the Muslim women. According to Khomeini (1990) veiling of women was necessary since it would distinguish revolutionary Islamist women from corrupt (westernized) women from the previous regime.

In the intervening twenty years since the Islamic revolution, two distinct versions of the *hijab* have developed. The orthodox look that established itself as a more severe form of veiling is always black. This style of veiling is derived from the traditional form of Iranian *chador* (in Persian, "tent"), but it incorporates a new additional head piece that was considered a new fashion at the time of its introduction for Iranian women.

The second style of *hijab* can be viewed as a more "western" style of veiling incorporated and modified to meet the demands of veiling requirements in order to be used in public by women. However, there are many recorded documents that indicates the harsh treatment, humiliation and even arrest of women who may have been accused of being improperly veiled, based on their appearance and the choice of adopting a "westernized" form of *hijab*.

At this point I will make a clear difference between these two styles of veiling in the post- revolutionary Iran. Veiling was imposed and revived by the present government in Iran, but veiling always existed in Iranian culture. It has gone through a stylistic evolution thoughout its history. The most common form of veiling in Iran is the *chador* that already was in use by religious women in Iran as proper attire for praying, visiting holy sites and entering mosques and shrines. This particular style of veil is an outerwear floor-length piece of fabric (body and head wrap), cut in semi-circular shape, placed on the head and covering the head and the entire body. The *chador* requires experience and practice in order to handle it properly and gracefully, since it does not have any fastening devices, sleeves or a place for the neck to be slipped into. When the *chador* is worn, a woman must make sure that it is securely placed on the head, properly draped, with its corners leveled at both ends. Perhaps the most difficult part of handling this veil is the fact that at all times, one hand of its wearer is occupied holding it in place. This means a woman carrying babies, grocery bags, or anything under her *chador* must handle everything with one hand. It is not uncommon to see women in the streets carrying a load with both hands and holding the corners of their *chador* with their teeth!

The *maghnae,* an importation (most likely from neighboring Arab nations) of a new piece of head-covering during the first years of the Islamic regime's establishment, was adopted in combination with the *chador* as a part of orthodox veiling worn with other items of clothing. *Maghnae* is also a semicircular sewn garment covering the head, the entire chest and the shoulder areas at the back. This head veil is fitted tightly around the head and loosely around the chest. It resembles the habit of Catholic nuns. The *maghnae* has some sort of fastening device, such as snaps or ties, or it is cut to fit tightly and framing the face preventing slippage. In this manner it securely covers the hair; thus it does not require its wearer to hold it by hand in place. The preferred and common color of the orthodox clothing ensemble is black or navy blue. Black, being a sign of mourning, carries a symbolic meaning in tune with the cause of the Revolution, the Iran/Iraq war and the loss of lives for two causes. Black is a powerful and constant visual reminder for its wearer as a symbolic gesture of the blood shed to establish Islam; veiled women are its other symbolic religious cause. They never forget to mourn for those who lost their lives as martyrs.

On the other hand, the less orthodox style of veiling commonly used in Iran reveals a quite different story. It consists of a head cover called *rusari* (in Persian "placed upon the head"), and an outer gown *rupush* (in Persian "worn outside, or worn over garments"). The *rusari* is a large, square scarf that can be stylishly and loosely draped over the head. It is a fashion statement due to its numerous design patterns, colors, fabric and embellishments such as sewn coins, beads, embroidery, fringes, tassels, pins and pieces of jewelry attached to it. *Rupush,* the outerwear gown that is used along with the headscarf, is another fashion statement. Color and pattern of the fabric used, the length, as well as variations in cut, and other embellishments such as buttons, pockets, lapel width, gathers and slits are indications of fashionable trends or keeping up with "European styles," which the Islamic regime tried to eradicate from the Iranian society. It is this flexibility that has provided an opportunity for a large number of women to keep themselves closer to the European fashions while still adhering to the boundaries of the Islamic dress code. Perhaps the flexibility of what was established at the beginning of the Islamic Revolution as accepted "dress code" has given rise to numerous debates and clashes with chastity patrols. The women's resistance in dropping their fashionable *hijab (rupush,* and *rusari)* and the rejection of the more orthodox style of veil (*chador* and *maghnae)* have opened up new avenues for more detail and in-depth debates that constantly takes a new form.

A woman who adopts the more fashionable form of *rupush* and *rusari* may be publicly projecting her disapproval of the political power in Iran. She understands that she will risk her life and the lives of her loved ones if she protests by not wearing a veil in public. Yet she also understands the power invested in clothing, a silent and "visual" medium of communication, a tool that she uses to demonstrate her ideologies in a small but effective way. In this regard she may try to get by with the minimum possible coverage, still staying within the dress code and silently and effectively showing her disapproval. The dress code as set by the government does not consist of a "uniform" for its citizens, but indicates that all parts of a woman's body should be covered with the exception of her face and hands. Her clothes must be loosely styled and not revealing. The hair, waistline, bosoms, legs and arms should be covered. Yet as evident, women are "innovative" in creating a personal style of *hijab* in a way that is expressive of individuality and carries layers of symbolic messages.

In a recent article published in the *New York Times* Farzaneh Milani explains the multiple layers of meaning. Milani points out the following: "[in Iran] . . . layers upon layers of meaning attached to every word, to every gesture . . . Take make-up. It is as fraught with political meanings and intentions as it has ever been. Women use it to signal their political ideology or to defy authority" (August 19,1999). In her personal account, Milani describes how Mariam, her friend, was deftly wiping off her lipstick with a paper napkin when "The vigilantes have come to the bazaar, . . . the self-appointed moral police, ever obsessed with the dress code for women." She gives a detailed account of what she had to go through in order to escape the unpleasantness that she might have had to face. Milani continues, "I could not believe my eyes. She [Mariam] was reapplying her lipstick. Only half an hour ago she had frantically wiped off all traces of it. The skill and speed with which she had removed her lipstick and her haste and zeal now in reapplying it were astounding." Mariam explained to her, "Lipstick is not just lipstick in Iran . . . It transmits political messages. It is a weapon." Though women in Iran have to cover themselves with a veil, they have become a vibrant political force. They are active participants in the Iranian society and have invaded traditional male territories. Yet, a fashionable modern *hijab* or a dab of lipstick can land them in jail. Milani ended her article with this remark: "Perhaps the next victory will be ownership of their own bodies" (Milani, 1999).

Hijab, Unveiling, Re-veiling and Properly Veiling

In the political history of many Muslim nations including Iran, the woman's body has symbolic meaning for that specific nation. For example, in colonial Algeria under the French rule, Algerian women helped the cause of freedom and participated in the Algerian revolution. They smuggled weapons under their *hijab* until they were exposed and forced not to veil by the French colonial rules. They did not give up their participation in the war against the French colonial rulers. What the Algerian women did was to change their strategies. They dressed themselves as Frenchwomen and smuggled weapons in their bags and purses crossing over to the French quarters, and continued to risk their lives.

Doubts about change, relations with the West, excuses for wars with neighboring countries, civil war and the internal political instabilities and economical problems all can be projected upon a woman's body. A woman's body is, in many instances, the property of her nation. She symbolically represents her nation and its political, religious and cultural ideologies. Her veiled image becomes an ambassador on duty for her nation. In the case of the Islamic republic of Iran, the political and religious agenda has continually redefined the image of a woman's body, her clothes, adornment, make up and attitude.

In the modern history of Iran, there are two instances where women have undergone a drastic visual makeover. The first was during the period known as "un-veiling," or better known in the Iranian history as the *kashfe hejab* episode of Reza Shah, the ruling king at that time. It was done in 1936 in the name of modernization that claimed to emancipate women in Iran. Reza Shah's intentions on "modernization" and "emancipation" of women came under attack decades later by the clerics who saw Reza Shah's "improvements" as nothing more than "westernizing" and secularizing Iran - contrary to the orthodox view of the country.

A change I mentioned earlier occurred again under the order of the revolutionary religious leader of Iran, Ayatollah Khomeini. The Islamic Revolution brought with it numerous changes to the lives of the Iranian people, yet the most visible of all is the drastic change in women's attire and appearances. In 1990, official agencies of the Islamic Republic of Iran published two documents which were classified top secret up until then. These documents contained the correspondences of Reza Shah between 1924 and 1933 and proved most revealing with regard to the process of unveiling under his regime (Khoshonat va Farhang.1990, and Va'egh Kashfe Hejab.1990). The documents revealed that how unfairly and violently the orders of unveiling women in public were carried out. My mother has told me many stories of that period of her life when she still was a young girl. She told me how her own mother chose not to go out in public for a year in order to avoid harassment or violent action by the police who were carrying out the orders by removing a woman's *hijab* by force in public. My grandmother eventually left her house and stepped out into public, but not completely unveiled. She dropped her *chadur* that she was declared forbidden to be seen without in public. Instead she and many other women of her time who did not want to unveil adopted an alternative mode of dress; a large scarf worn on the head and an ankle-length shapeless outer gown worn over other garments. Perhaps it was the birth of our modern *rupush* and *rusari* era, since the model was followed forty years later by the women in the Islamic Republic of Iran. The unveiling of women, which claimed to be an improvement for better life and education, did not encourage women to seek education or make any improvement regarding the illiteracy rate evident among a vast majority of the women, which might have been achieved by adopting instead policies to eradicate such social problems. Woman and her image was used then to announce the task of "visual modernization" of Iran to the world. Again after half a century in the post Revolutionary era in Iran, the veiled image of a woman is a visual announcement of her government's political policies. In many instances around the globe, women have carried out similar burdens for political reasons. They are trained to sacrifice their personal happiness for the sake of others in the family, being made responsible for men's honor and the progress of men's careers. Women are central to patriarchal and cultural attitudes. It is not uncommon to see that they are used and targeted in the name of religion to fulfill the demands of men. This patriarchal attitude is evident in religious practices as well. Islam does not prohibit seeking knowledge, learning of reading or writing by women. But, like other world religions, interpretation of religious texts remains entirely within the male domain – thus it is wrong to stereotype Islamic women as educationally backward. Instead, they are simply denied a role in making decisions regarding the religious customs and laws that govern them. Amina Wadud-Muhsin (1994) a female Muslim scholar, notes that confusion over the role of women abounds. She notes that a large number of scholars have attempted to draw foreign non-Islamic sources to the *Qur'an* rather than extracting from the *Qur'anic* principles and their application to specific problems. In Wadud-Muhsin's view, two significant principles should be applied to the issue of women in the *Qur'an* – first, ". . . the *Qur'an* must be continually re-interpreted. Second, the progress of civilization has been reflected in the extent of the woman's participation in society and the recognition of the significance of her resources" (1994, p. v). In this regard, she has considered the significance of the text of the *Qur'an* as being unique, but the interpretations of the text have come to be held in greater importance than the text itself. Her opinion is fixed on the principle of equality granted to women in Islam. She voices her opinion by stating that it was not the text of the *Qur'an* which restricted women, but its traditional male interpretations. This opinion is shared by a large community of both males and females in Islamic societies, yet it seems that the traditional culture is too powerful a force to be broken down over a short period of time.

Thus, how the religious texts are used or interpreted is at the heart of this drastic makeover of women's appearance. The argument of enforcing the *hijab* based on religious discussion is an important issue that needs special attention. Men and women have both tried to make sense out of a large body of writings dealing with issues of "clothing" in religious contexts. Such religious writings, for example, tend to rely on the old established sacred materials such as the *Qur'an,* the *hadith* (Prophet Mohammad's sayings which served as a moral religious model for the Muslims), and the *shar'ia* (the Islamic law, based on the *Qur'anic* and *hadith* interpretation), as well as more recent opinions of a large body of religious scholars, who have followers everywhere. At this point it will be helpful to discuss how the religious authority can impose legal opinions that emphasize the importance of covering the body. I also wish to mention here that a number of legal opinions on the subject of "dress and adornments" were basically developed out of the questions put to religious authorities. One may assume that such interest in the "clothing and adornment" issue may be the concerns of the elderly, and perhaps less educated, who are concerned about the "hereafter." It is interesting that most of these concerns are from younger generations that are more educated, more religious and conservative compared to their parents. The following section introduces *Qur'anic* verses concerning the issue of *hijab.*

Women are addressed in the *Qur'an* on more than one occasion. In chapters IV *Nisaa* (The Women), XXIV *Nur* (The Light), and XXXIII *Mu'minun* (The Believers), women are exclusively mentioned. It is in the chapter *Nur* that particular verses dealing with veiling is mentioned:

> And say to the believing women
> That they should lower
> Their gaze and guard
> Their modesty; that they
> Should not display their
> Beauty and ornaments except
> What (must ordinarily) appear
> Thereof; that they should
> Draw their veils over
> Their bosoms and not display
> Their beauty except
> To their husbands, their fathers, . . . (XXIV:31)

As evident from the above verse, women are not to be seen without their veils by men to whom they are forbidden. The forbidden men are those with whom she could have potential intimate relationships. Fatemeh Ostad Malek (1989) writes extensively about exclusive *Qur'anic* verses that mentions how obligatory it is for the Muslim women to wear the *hijab* as a part of their religious duty. It is clear that there are women who have firm opinions about the religious obligation and observance of *hijab* (Ostad Malek, 1989, p.174–5). In his earlier speeches Ayatollah Khomeini talked about the issue of *hijab* in a very different tone compared to his later speeches. In a speech delivered in early 1978 Khomeini said:

> . . . yes it is true that woman in Islam must wear *hijab,* but it does not necessarily means that her *hijab* should be a *chadur.* Woman can adopt any form of garment she wants that gives her *"hijab"*. Islam forbids men to look at any woman for sexual pleasure, a toy or an object for play. Islam protects the integrity of all women. We will never allow "our men" To look at "our women" with disrespect, or as a "toy" to become a play thing. (Khomeini, 1990, p. 49)

The quotation cited above, indicating the flexibility of any form of garment chosen by the pious Muslim woman, is in contradiction to the following quotation printed as a *fatwa* (an Islamic legal opinion) on promotional posters for the proper and preferred form of *hijab.*

> The body is the instrument of the soul and the soul is the divine air. This sacred instrument must not become a plaything of the desires, passions, and debauchery of anyone. Respected Ladies of Iran proved that they are a strong fortress of chastity. The best and most superior form of *hijab* is *chadur.*

In the above quotations, there are similarities in terms of respect for the woman, yet there is a major difference in regards to the *"hijab"* issue. While the earlier quote gives a choice to woman, the second promotes *chadur* as the best or most superior form of *hijab.* As we will see later in this chapter, the issue of superior and best form of *hijab* opens a new debate.

The intellectual debates at the beginning of the Islamic regime in regards to veiling were instrumental through the writings of Ayatollah Motahari and the intellectual Ali Shariati. Both rejected Iran's domination by the West by rejecting the "modern" Iranian woman in her western attire and attitude. Both considered "modern" women as embodiments of Western decadence, as "greedy painted under- or overdressed Western dolls." Ayatollah Motahari's approach is religious in nature and relies heavily on the sacred texts in combination with critical viewpoints he presents from the Shah's regime of being greedy and in the name of modernizing and promoting westernization

(Motahari,1995). But Ali Shariati's ground for promotion of the Islamic veil is different. According to him the Iranian woman "actualizes" herself as a believer who negates Western values. She will no longer be a plaything in the hands of foreigners. For Shariati, the *hijab* serves as a symbol of independence from the West, of progress in general. The following quotation from a selection of his writing will illustrates this point:

> A woman who has attained the level of belief chooses her own life, her way of thinking, her very being and even her own form of adornment. She actualizes herself. She does not give herself over to television and passive consumption. She does not do whatever consumerism tells her to do. She is not afraid to choose the colors of dress because it may not be in style this year! She has returned and returned vigorously! To what? To the modest dress of Islam. As what? As a believer and committed human being. (Shariati. n.d. p. 46).

During the summers of 1995 and 1996 when I was in Iran conducting research, I became interested in examining slogans and graffiti displayed all around Tehran stamped or posted on the walls. In a few days it was clear to me that by examining the graffiti and slogans I could examine how popular culture can be distanced from the religious codes of ethics. In reality the popular culture is practiced by the majority. A two-tiered form of orthodoxy exists with reference to wearing of *hijab*; one tier operates in the religious realm and the other in the realm of culture. What has been argued earlier was the level of religious orthodoxy. At this point, through the analysis of collected slogans and graffiti, one can understand how the cultural orthodoxy can be as effective as or even more powerful than the religious orthodoxy when dealing with *hijab*, involving not only women but men as well.

The tone of voice and the nature of content in the graffiti lent themselves to different types of category. I was able to group them as follows. The first category contains positive sentences either in praise of *hijab*, or words of praise for the woman who has chosen this form of dress. In this group, themes of honor, shame and dignity are cited frequently.

- *Hijab* represents your personality and dignity.
- The best adornment for a woman is to preserve her *hijab*.
- My sister, your dignity and honor is in your observing Islamic Cover.
- A woman's *hijab* and chastity show her personality. Your *hijab* is your dignity.
- My sister, add *hijab* to the list of your virtues.
- My sister, adorn your beauty with glory of *hijab*.
- *Hijab* is a divine duty.

– *Hijab* indicates a Muslim woman's dignity.
– Praised be the woman in *hijab*.
– *Hijab* is a sign of her Holiness Fatima Zahra (Prophet Muhammad's daughter).
– *Hijab* is the adornment of Muslim woman.
– The stronghold of the Muslim woman is the *hijab*.
– The worth of a woman is in her *hijab*.

In the second category, the tone of negation is apparent. In this category, the reader is able to understand that the message in graffiti is directed to two people, the woman and the "man" in charge of her. In this respect the men become the target of slanderous remarks because of a woman's misbehavior. The man could be a husband (if she is married) or a brother, father, son or even a paternal uncle. The slanderous remarks aimed at men have deep cultural and orthodox sentiments. It must be understood that the concept of honor and shame affects the honor of a man and therefore it depends upon the chastity, purity and piety of his womenfolk. Thus such indirect insults aimed at "responsible men" is culturally shameful.

– Shame on the man whose woman is in improper *hijab* (*bad hejab*).
– A woman in an improper *hijab* is a toy of Satan.
– A woman in an improper *hijab* is an indication of her improper mind.
– A woman in an improper *hijab* is in need of glance by a stranger.
– Death to a woman in an improper *hijab*.
– A woman's improper *hijab* shows her man's lack of honor.
– Curse on the woman in improper *hijab*.
– A woman in *improper hijab* is the seed of corruption.
– A woman in improper *hijab* is a disgrace for the Islamic Republic of Iran.
– A woman in improper *hijab* is a sign of psychological disorder.
– A woman in an improper *hijab* is a stain on the Islamic Republic of Iran which must be eliminated.

The graffiti texts reveals two interesting issues; first, who is in *bad hejab* (improper *hijab*) and second, what exactly is the act of *bad hejabi* (wearing improper *hijab*)? It is my opinion that the term *bad hejab* has its roots in the modern version form of the veil – the *rupush rusari* combination, discussed earlier in this chapter. The orthodox adherents who have a negative attitude towards the women dressed in the fashionable and trendy western style of "Islamic dress" are opposed to the idea of *rupush rusari* to be included in the same class of the orthodox garb; *chadur* and *maghnae*. *Chadur maghnae* is a symbolic marker of the pious Muslim woman, whose images were promoted by Iran's Islamic regime as the fighter for her religion and by its extension, the supporter of a non-secular political system. The term *bad hejab* opened discussions among the orthodox segment of society. The following statement was published and circulated by "The Public Ministry Opposed to Social Corruption." The question was raised as "What is the difference between the terms of *bad hejabi* and *bi hejabi?*" The writer (no name mentioned) offers the following explanation: "The term *bad hejabi* that has become popular recently [as we already noticed from the graffiti] does not make any sense. The prefix of *bad* [bad in English is the same word in Persian with the same meaning] may not be descriptive of a 'good adjective.' It is like saying that 'bad piety,' 'bad honor,' or 'bad dignity.' Since the term *hijab* is a reference to a positive virtue, it can't be bad. Thus the term of *bad hejabi* is a wrong term and it must be avoided." Thus the term *bi hejabi* (without veil), must be used in place of *bad hejab* for the following reasons: "If a woman exposes her entire body to those forbidden to her, she is considered as naked. If she is clothed, but parts of her body which are forbidden to be exposed publicly such as: part of her hair, her made up face, arms, legs, or neck, then she is referred to as *bi hejab* (without *hijab*), but not a woman in *bad hejab* (improper *hijab*)" (Simaye, 1994, p. 9).

Conclusions

The importance and place of *hijab* in the post-Revolution era of the Iranian culture was established. This observance carefully was orchestrated by examining clerical discussions and a keen interest in the popular culture. In writing this chapter I kept in mind at all times how important a role the symbolic-interaction theory can play as a vehicle in understanding issues discussed here regarding *hijab* and its extensions in terms of religion and politics for the outsiders. In this regard, *hijab* acquired multiple layers of symbolic meanings revealed through my personal interpretations as both the insider and an outsider.

Since the discussion of the terms *bad hejab* and *bi hejab* is already established, I would like to link this dynamic to another aspect of *rupush rusari*, seen as "improper form of coverage" through the eyes of those who are in disagreement of a modern non-orthodox form of dress for a Muslim woman. Along with popularity of the term *bad hejab*, the reference to *hejab e gharbi*, and *hejab e varedati* (Westernized *hijab, and* imported *hijab*) came to be known through the graffiti. The reader must be aware that reminders of "corrupted" Westernized culture must be eradicated as the Islamic Republic claims its establishment of this concept; Islam is its pride in heritage.

Thinking through this ideology, it can be understood why even being covered is not enough anymore. The Muslim women should not only be covered, but must be covered in a certain form of *hijab* as a walking symbol of their pride, piety, national identity to be seen as full supporters of their ruling government, the Islamic Republic that "freed" them from domination of tyranny of the previous monarchic regime and by its extension, the "infidel colonial" Western culture. At this point the most popular slogan during the earlier part of the Revolution is an excellent example of this phenomenon at work: *"na sharghi, va na gharbi, jumhuri e islami,"* neither Eastern, nor Western, only the Islamic Republic. Here, the reference to the East and West is clearly understood by the Iranian people as a rejection of the political and cultural ideologies presented by the communist Eastern bloc nations and the corrupted Western cultures. Thus, the understanding of *hijab* in the complex social atmosphere of the post-Revolution era in Iran may not be easily understood from an outsider's point of view. The messages are coded with symbolic meanings that are only comprehended by those who are completely familiar with the Iranian culture, those who lived and experienced it first-hand. In this respect we can look at this phenomenon from the symbolic-interaction perspective. The debates over *hijab* are by no means near an end. As long as the Iranian society thrives and remains progressive according to the local accepted social norms, we would expect many more new and fascinating fresh ideas and concepts to flourish for years to come. Indeed, issues of women's roles, place in society and *hijab* will occupy a high position in such lively discussions.

Note

1. El Guindi's most recent book on the veil goes into a much deeper and detailed discussion of the word *hijab*. Her work was published after production of this volume had begun, and I could not incorporate her viewpoints into this chapter.

Acknowledgements

I would like to thank Professors Akel Kahera and Kamran Scott Aghaei, The University of Texas at Austin, Department Of Middle Eastern Languages and Cultures, Islamic Studies Program, for the helpful, critical and constructive suggestions offered in reading the first draft of this chapter.

References

Driver, G. R. and Miles, J. C. (Eds.) (1952). *The Babylonian laws*. Oxford: Clarendon Press.

El Guindi, F 1999. *Veil: Modesty, privacy, and resistance*. Oxford: Berg.

Innes, M. (1955). *Ovid, Metamorphoses*. London: Penguin Books.

Kaiser, S. (1990). *The social psychology of clothing: Symbolic appearances in context* (2nd Ed.). New York: Macmillan Company.

Khomrini, A. (1990). *Simaye zan dar kalame Imam Khomaini (Images of women in Imam Khomaini's speeches)*.Tehran: Vezarete Farhang Va Irshade Islami.

Khoshunat va farhang, asnade montasher nashodeh kashfe hejab dar asre Reza Khan. (Violence and Culture, confidential Records about the Abolition of Hijab. 1313–1322). (1990). Tehran: Dept. of Research Publication and Education.

MacLead, A. (1992). *Hegemonic relations and gender resistance: The new veiling as accommodating protest in Cairo*. Signs 17(3): 533–57.

Moghadam, V. (1993). *Modernizing women: Gender and social change in the Middle East*. Boulder: Lynne Rinner.

Milani, F. (1999). "Dress code in Iran." *New York Times*. August 19.

Motahari, M. (1994/1995). *Ma'saleh-ye hejab (The question of hijab)*.Tehran: Sadra Publication.

Ostad Malek, F. (1989). *Hejab va kashfe hejab dar Iran*. Tehran: Moa'sese Matboati Ataei.

Shariati, Ali. (nd.) *Fatima is Fatima*. Trans. Laleh Bakhtiar. Tehran: The Sahriati Foundation.

Shirazi, F. (in press). *The Veil Unveiled: Visual, political, and literary dynamics of the veil*. Gainesville: University Press of Florida.

Shirazi-Mahajan, F. (1993). Islamic dress code in post revolution Iran. Critique, *Journal of Critical studies of Iran and the Middle East*, 2. 54–63.

Simaye, E. (1994). Face of chastity. (A promotional poster published by the Agency for the fight against social corruption.) Tehran: Ministry Opposed to Social Corruption.

Va'qe kashfe hejab, asnade montsher nashodehe kashfe hejab dar asre Reza Khan. (Unpublished documents about unveiling during Reza Khan's time). (1990).Tehran: Agency of Cultural Documents of the Islamic Revolution.

Wadud-Muhsin, A. (1994). *Qur'an and woman*. Kuala Lumpur: Pendrbit Fajar Bakti SDN.BHD.

Zuhur, S. (1992). *Revealing re-veiling, Islamist gender ideology in contemporary Egypt*. New York: State University Press of New York.

8

The Afghan Woman's "Chaadaree": An Evocative Religious Expression?

M. Catherine Daly

Afghan women and their appearance are often the subject of human interest and human rights issues in Afghanistan (Daly, 1999). It is generally presumed that Afghan women's appearance is not the primary issue of contention in Afghanistan. Paradoxically, a review of Afghan history suggests that the "woman question" or "women's issues" referred to in the literature, including women's appearance, is actually a central and visible topic and theme of Afghanistan's social and political struggle to remain independent (Daly, 1999; Dupree, 1998; Maley, 1998; Moghadam, 1994).

Recently practical questions related to women's appearance have been scrutinized internationally because of human rights violations towards Afghan women by the current ruling Taleban Islamic Movement of Afghanistan (TIMA). These questions have focused on and challenged the mandatory head- and body-covering practices that undermine the health, hygiene, education and economic sustainability of Afghan women (Marseden, 1998). These practices attributed to Islamic scripture and jurisprudence by TIMA have tended to be socially critiqued and essentialized by both "insiders" and "outsiders" as a form of religious orthodoxy (Daly, 1999). Following Dupree's lead (1978) at reporting discrepancies in perceptions of women, this chapter provides a historical and cultural overview of the Afghan woman's *chaadaree* and the various explanations for its use that counter religious claims. The research is based on informal interviews of Afghan women living in refugee camps and non-camp settings, Afghan educators and Afghan male shopkeepers in Peshawar, Pakistan during 1998. The major goal of the research was to represent an Afghan point of view, especially that of Afghan women living in Afghanistan and Pakistan.

Afghanistan and the Afghan Diaspora

According to the United Nations High Commission for Refugees in 1998 Afghans were the largest single-caseload refugee population in the world, numbering 2,633,900. During the height of their displacement nearly 20 years ago Afghan refugees numbered 6 million. The total population of Afghans living in areas contiguous to Afghanistan was approximately 3 million; 1.3 million Afghans lived in camp settlements of Pakistan. This figure did not include refugees living in non-camp urban centers of Pakistan nor the 1.4 million Afghans in Iran and the unaccounted number who lived in Tajikistan. Of these refugees some reports suggested that approximately 75 percent of the refugee population were single, separated and widowed women who lived with an average of eight children (ACBAR, 1995). Left unaccounted in this data are those refugees that comprise the Afghan diaspora communities that extend to Western Europe, the Middle East and the United States.

These statistics, however, do not represent the complexity of the internal and external Afghan history and geo-politics of the region that has contributed to the legacy of Afghanistan (Christensen, 1995; Hopkirk, 1994; Miller, 1978). Magnus and Naby in *Afghanistan: Mullah, Marx and Mujahid* (1998) outline six historical time periods in Afghanistan: the Pre-Islamic period; the Medieval and Late Medieval Islamic period; the period of Afghan Empire; the "Great Game" or European Imperial period; the period of the Independent Monarchy and the current political environment.

During the Independent Monarchy period from 1919–1973 and since the Afghan Coup of 1979 to the present, the "woman question" became part of the public discourse documented in colonial, travel and media accounts. During these 80 years, education, social and economic policies toward women, their appearance and their visibility have vacillated between requiring, suggesting and ignoring their wearing of various forms of head and body coverings, (*chaadar* and *chaadaree*); variations of covering (*hijaab*); and secluding (*purdah*) practices. These vacillating policies have been determined by the particular ethnic and/or political party in power and their allegiance to indigenous "tribal" ethnic and/or Islamic perspectives. Magnus and Naby characterize these distinctions as either more "Islamist", based on a particular interpretation of Islam and Sharia religious law or more "Traditionalist" based on local indigenous tribal and ethnic codes of gendered conduct.

El Guindi (1999) questions and cautions us against the Western dualist tendency of interpretation. However, the two perspectives do provide a continuum to compare and contrast social meaning including the economic, religious and political conditions that supported, limited, or restricted women's choice with regard to head- and body-covering practices. Also, an important point to note is the distinction of terminology for head coverings. My preference has been to use indigenous Afghan terms for head coverings.

The two major forms worn by Afghan women are the *chaadar*, or partial head covering and the *chaadaree*, or full body covering.[1] Though the term veil has been seen elsewhere in the literature, throughout this chapter it is used only in reference to texts that use the term. Since the *chaadar* and *chaadaree* are two very different and distinctive forms worn by Afghan women, the challenge is to understand in these texts when the term veil is synonymous with one or the other or both forms of head coverings: the *chaadar* or *chaadaree*.

During the progressive period of King Amanuallah's reign (1919–1929), women were encouraged to come out of seclusion and remove their head coverings or veils. During the tenure of Nadir Shah (1929–1933) and following with his successors till 1959, political alliances were conservative and too weak to challenge the "woman question" so that women returned to seclusion and the full body covering. In the 1960s, Prime Minister Daoud followed and announced the voluntary end of seclusion and the removal of veils and during the 1970s and 1980s Mujahiden encouraged the use of the *chaadaree* (Majrooh, 1989). Only recently have writings in English differentiated between indigenous terms and the forms of head coverings. Dupree describes Afghan women as follows:

> The chadri, though still present, began to disappear from Kabul in 1959, particularly among literate class where Western clothing sometimes from Paris and Rome, had dominated underneath the chadri since at least World War II. The chadri, a sack-like garment of pleated colored silk or rayon, covers the entire body from head to toe, with an embroidered lattice-work eye-mask to permit limited vision (1980, p. 246–7).

What is particularly noteworthy about the current ruling Taleban Islamic Movement led by Mullah M. Omar is that since the autumn of 1996 TIMA has strictly enforced women wearing the *chaadaree* or full body covering. This is the first period in history that a clear definition and distinction has been made about the kind of head and body covering worn as well as the manner in which it is to be worn. The rationale used for wearing the *chaadaree* is based on an Islamist perspective citing more consistently the *suras* and *hadiths* of the Qur'an and Sharia Law in conjunction with the Traditionalist perspective. In this sense then both perspectives, the Islamist and the Traditionalist, are invoked to control the visibility and behaviors of women.

Afghan Women's Head Coverings:
The *Chaadar* and *Chaadaree*

A wide variety of head coverings are worn among Islamic affiliated peoples throughout the world (El Guindi, 1999). From a Western perspective these head and body coverings are usually referred to as "veils" or *burqas* and are perceived as a customary form of Islamic clothing worn by women. However, historically, in most Middle East, Central and South Asian areas head and body coverings or *burqas*, the associated head- and body-covering practices or *hejab* and female seclusion or *purdah* predated the Islamic era. Since knowledge about the indigenous terms for the head and body coverings, the actual forms and their use in a secular environment by observant Muslims are less common in the Western world, there are many misconceptions about their significance. For a more detailed analysis of Arabic Muslim women's head and body coverings and practices see Mernissi (1987, 1991a, 1991b) and El Guindi (1999).

The first misconception is that, rather than singular prototypes of coverings, multiple forms and variations exist throughout the Islamic world. For example, within Afghanistan there are several different styles of head and body covering worn by women which include shaped hats or *kulaa* and draped coverings or *chaadar* and *shawl* and a shaped/draped covering known as a *chaadaree*. However the most commonly worn items are the 2-dimensional *chaadar* and *shawl* and the three-dimensional *chaadaree* (Dupree, 1992, p. 812).

The *chaadar*, made of two to three yards of fabric, is the most traditional and most common draped partial head covering worn by women on a daily basis (Daly, 1999). The shawl is an equivalent *chaadar* but differentiated by wool fiber content worn during more cool seasons by both men and women.

In contrast to the *chaadar* and *shawl*, the *chaadaree* is a three-dimensional, vertically paneled, seamed and pleated garment. It is made from approximately seven plus yards or meters of cotton or silk fabric or synthetic equivalents and is composed of three separate units; the hat or *kulla*, the face or *rooy* band with a region referred to as the eye or *chishim band* and pleated fabric or *teka*.

The *chaadaree* encompasses and encloses the entire body of the wearer, obscuring the entire body from view. It is worn only when in a public context outside the home environment. It is considered a full body/head covering or "veil" worn over an entire ensemble of clothing: dress or *payraahan*, pant or *tumbaan*, head covering or *chaadar*. The *chaadaree* is further distinguished by the *chishim band*, a rectangular area of drawn work hand embroidery that covers the eye and provides limited vision for the wearer as well as minimal view of the wearer by an observer.

Figure 8.1 *Chaadaree* Illustration by Lena Rothman.

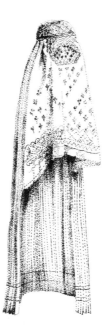

Figure 8.2 *Chaadaree* composed of 3 sewn units; the *kulla, chishim band* and *teka*. Illustration by Lena Rothman.[2]

A Religious or Cultural Perspective?

Burqa, Hejab and Purda

There are several useful terms that are important to understanding the use of the chaadaree in Afghan culture. Since this chapter is an introduction to the Afghan woman these terms will be defined from an Afghan point of view with some inferences to Arabo-Islamic origins. These terms are *burqa, hejab* and *purdah*. El Guindi (1999) provides a linguistic and cultural analysis as well as an "Arabo-Islamic" interpretation of these terms with particular focus on the Middle East. Tarlo notes similar cultural practices in India using linguistically indigenous terms in non-Muslim marital and familial contexts (1996). The intent of this chapter is not to support or dispute El Guindi's and other scholars' definitions from an Arabo-Islamic interpretation or otherwise but rather to understand the validity of using these terms within an Afghan interpretation.

Linguistically, *burqa, hejab* and *purdah* are often cited as Arabic and therefore linked to the Arab Middle East. This geographic association with the Arab Middle East is further strengthened with the Islamic origins in the Middle East. In addition, all three terms if not referenced literally are inferred by scholars from the *Qur'an* which further privileges the association with the religion of Islam, the Arabic language and the Middle East.

Burqa.   For example, the term *burqa* refers to a garment that covers the body and it is generally associated with Muslim women in the Middle East. It is the most consistently used term for Muslim head and body coverings in the media by both Muslim and non-Muslim non-Afghans when referring to Afghan women. Since Afghans speak the Persian languages of Dari or Pashtu they rarely use the Arabic term *burqa* unless invoking Islam when they speak Arabic. Not only does the term for head and body coverings differ from the *burqa* but the form and aesthetics differ: *kulla, chaadar, shawl* and *chaadaree*.

Whether Muslim or otherwise the term *burqa* seems to be used by non-Afghans when referencing any form of head or body covering worn by Afghan women or for that matter any other Muslim woman. In part the use of the term *burqa* presumably but inadvertently gives deference to the religion of Islam and the *burqas* possible origins to the cultures of the Middle East. As scholars have noted Muslim women living elsewhere in the Islamic diaspora wear a variety of head and body coverings that may be used in an equivalent manner to that for the *burqa* but the terms for these items like the Afghan's term *chaadaree* tend to be indigenous linguistic ones. Consequently, neither form of dress, the *chaadar* or the *chaadaree,* is particularly religious when worn in either a public or private, secular or sacred context.

Hejab. However, partial head coverings may take on religious connotations in very specific social contexts. Afghan head coverings worn as *hejaab* may communicate religiosity. Generally among Afghans, the term *hejab* or *hijaab* refers to either specific aesthetic characteristics of head coverings or specialized head- and body-covering practices. The term *hejaab* used in a religious context refers to the concept of covering and the covering practices of both Muslim men and women under Islam (Sheikh Muhammad bin Saleh bin Uthalmeen, 1996). A Muslim man or woman communicates his or her religiosity by either wearing an item of dress considered *hijaab* or dressing in a *hijaab*-like manner.

For example, Afghan women's *hijaab* dress might include wearing *chaadars*. Though not exclusively white, Afghan women frequently wear white *chaadars* during the period of their five daily prayers. Afghan women also tend to wear white *chaadars* following their pilgrimage or Hajj to Mecca. However, non-Hajji Afghan women who are especially observant of Muslim practices wear stylish white *chaadars* because they "go with everything." *Chaadars* worn by Afghan women in both cultural and religious contexts are referred to as *hijaab*. Wearing white *chaadars* therefore is both a cultural-aesthetic and religious-aesthetic choice.

The complexity of interpreting a white *chaadar* as *hejaab* among Afghan women is further complicated in that the color white is also the traditional preferred aesthetic characteristics of secularly worn *chaadars*. Wearing a white *chaadar* not only communicates religiosity but may also communicate social class and virtue. Rural women living in the provinces wear more vibrant as well as dark *chaadars*. To maintain white *chaadars* is more labor- and time-intensive as well as costly in an environment of scarce water resources. For this reason the color white is also associated with the state of purity and the challenge of maintaining purity in the austere environments of refugee and non-refugee settings where cleanliness is associated with virtuousness.

Another example referred to as *hijaab* among Afghans is the style or manner in which a Muslim man or woman dresses. Modesty in dress is referred to as *haya*; to cover the body and conceal it from view is considered a moral commitment under Islam. In everyday practice, therefore, the degree of commitment to Islam is expressed by the amount of the body exposed and the proximity of clothing to the body. A Muslim's *haya* or modesty is simultaneously concealed and revealed in *hijaab*; the body is both modestly covered and concealed while the commitment of the wearer to Islam is visually communicated and therefore revealed to the perceiver. Dressing in or as *hijaab* also refers to the proximity of the clothing to the body. To dress in *hijaab* suggests loose fit of the individual items of clothing whether head or body coverings.

Purdah.   This refers to the practice of seclusion or the demarcation of space that differentiates the private and public nature of male and female social interaction. Whether a strictly Muslim practice or otherwise, *purdah* often refers to the gender-separation of space with the particular designation of female space. There are many nuances of interpretation of seclusion or *purdah* among Afghans and others living in Central and South Asia (Tarlo, 1996).

Some examples of these variations of *purdah* or seclusion follow. For example, actual space may be partitioned within the private domain of a place of residence such as the woman's area. A room may be designated as that space used by women exclusively, such as sleeping quarters or cooking areas. Males in general (both kin and non-kin) as well as non-kin females may or may not be welcome in this space.

Another type of private or woman's space might be the temporal definition of space at a particular moment in time. For example, an otherwise public space in the household might become the private space for females during a female gathering in the household for a specific event. Women might gather for tea or a luncheon to honor female friends and extended family members.

Purdah might also be constructed in a more public environment outside the family residence. In public, *purdah* delineates some space as private, even a very public context. In addition to veiling being used to separate women from men in the public sphere, for example, car windows may be covered to create a sense of privacy or restricted environment as a woman travels.

Regardless of the range of possibilities among Afghan women *purdah* generally refers to the sequestering of women in the private domain of the home environment. Also, dressing in a *burqa* or *chaadaree* provides a sense of privacy or *purdah* as women move freely from the private to the public and maintain privacy when public.

Defining the terms *burqa*, *hijaab* and *purdah* from an indigenous Afghan point of view facilitates an understanding of the current practices imposed on Afghan men and women under the rule of Taleban Islamic Movement of Afghanistan. Do these prescriptions imposed on Afghans represent an Islamist and/or Traditionalist point of view or are they impositions that serve the political orientations of those that rule? Since Afghanistan is a country where women not only far outnumber men but where they are potentially more visible than men, the "the women question" and their human rights is a powerful social issue about control of engendered human resources.

The Woman Question and Appearance

Numerous media report that the Taleban's Ministry for Propagation of Virtue and Prevention of Vice or the Preservation of Virtue and Elimination of Vice declare that the following decrees regarding women are to safeguard the honor and virtue that are essential values of Afghan culture. To ignore these edicts, according to the Taleban, is un-Islamic and punishable by Sharia Law. The severity of punishment ranges from verbal abuse to death.

Women must be covered when leaving the home environment; covering means wearing a *chaadaree* or full-body covering as opposed to the traditionally engendered *chaadar*. In addition to wearing the *chaadaree*, additional items of dress are forbidden in public because they draw attention to specific regions of women's bodies. According to the TIMA it is these regions of the body that are referenced in the chapters and verses of the *Qur'an*.

The rules most consistently mentioned in the media (many can be found on websites) that violate TIMA are those related to the feet; wearing white socks, sandals, high-heeled shoes and ankle bracelets. Other sensory experiences are controlled such as women's behaviors that arouse in public the olfactory and auditory senses of men including wearing perfumes and ankle and wrists bracelets that make noise when walking or moving. In response to alleged human rights violations by TIMA, their website has changed dramatically to counter such claims in support of women's issues.

In some instances certain gendered garments and the origin of their manufacture are unacceptable. For example, women's western-styled fashions are typically more tailored and fitted than the traditional Afghan dress ensemble that is looser fitting. Other unacceptable adornment behaviors considered *tabarruj* by the Taleban under Islam include using finger nail polish and make up. The one item and practice that remains the most distinctive and favored by the Taleban is the *chaadaree* or full-body covering.

Since the Taleban rule began in the Fall of 1996, Afghan women living in villages and cities under Taleban control are required to wear a *chaadaree* when they appear in public outside the home environment. There are reportedly repercussions for women who choose to contradict Taleban policy which range from verbal abuse to physical assault as well as repercussions and male punishment for female behavior. That is, if a woman refuses to cover in the "proper" manner, her husband or other male relatives may be punished for her offensive behavior. Since the ultimate determining factor of family status in any Afghan community is female virtue and honor, the kind of head covering worn and manor in which it is worn visually communicates the degree of covering or *baysatree* and adherence to *hejab* practice by a woman or her extended family.

For example, male family members and men who provide essential services as drivers, shopkeepers and tailors are held accountable for female behavior in public. This current enforced restriction historically contrasts rural and urban practices. Women living in the rural areas of Afghanistan have had more freedom from compulsory head-covering practices than their female counterparts living in urban areas of Afghanistan and in Pakistan. Some women may choose to wear a *chaadar,* or *chaadar* with a *chaadaree,* but may still negotiate head-covering practices with family members.

Afghan Culture, the *Chaadaree* and Social Use

Origins of the Chaadaree

Located in Central Asia, Afghanistan is geographically at the crossroads between the Middle East, Persia and India. Though the *chaadaree* is most frequently associated with Afghan women, according to an article written by Scarce (1974) the *chaadaree* is most likely of non-Afghan but Persian and possibly Moghul origins. Scarce's resources included the "Oriental literary and pictorial records, surviving examples of Oriental costume and European accounts" (1974, p. 4). According to Scarce the *chadri* origins can be traced to the cultural use of head-coverings of the pre-Islamic era of approximately 500 BC, through the period of Arab conquest and conversion to Islam of Persia including Afghanistan, to Afghan independence during the eighteenth century.

Head-covering forms, veiling practices and seclusion appear to have existed prior to Islam in the Middle East and Persia; however, the customs were variable then and continue to be variable into the twenty-first century (Scarce, 1974, p. 4). As stated earlier, since the 1920s the *chaadaree* has been more subject to the prevailing social, economic and political environment of the time. More recently its use depends on the group in political power in Afghanistan and the explanatory interpretation of and degree of conformity to Islam. For this reason the *chaadaree* tends to be more tradition-bound and less subject to aesthetic change and personal preference. The following explanations provide additional historical and speculative information for *chaadaree* survival.

Gender, Function and Utility Explanation

The *chaadaree* is a functional and utilitarian item of clothing. Though most non-Afghans perceive the *chaadaree* as an obtrusive garment most Afghan women cite the protective qualities of wearing a *chaadaree*. In fact they are nonchalant when referring to wearing it. From this standpoint it is nearly equivalent to the Western raincoat. As one woman remarked, "I wear it when I leave my home and market." It is worn throughout seasonal changes and its function changes with respect to fluctuations in temperature and precipitation. Depending on the fiber context it can also protect the wearer from the harsh heat, sun and humidity as well as providing warmth in snowy cold weather.

However, its most noted function is to protect women from the fierce stares of unrelated males, their verbal insults and abuses and, in some instances, physical assault.

Gender, Family and Marriage Explanation

From a historical and traditional point of view, Afghan women customarily wear a *chaadar* as opposed to the *chaadaree* as a gendered garment. It is worn on a daily basis by young women starting at puberty and throughout the female life-course in the context of the home and outside the home environment. Regardless of religious affiliation, all Afghan women wear a *chaadar*.

But like the *chaadar*, the *chaadaree* is first and foremost a garment restricted to the female gender. Women might first receive a *chaadaree* from parents when they attained a marriageable age or they might receive a *chaadaree* from their husbands upon marriage. Some women remarked that "If my husband didn't buy a *chaadaree* for me I would think he didn't appreciate me; that I was not worth protecting or honoring." Gauhari writes a descriptive account of wearing the *chaadaree*:

> I had been wearing the veil for almost a year before the reform came. Dad never told us to wear it, but society forced us to do so. My sister Laila resisted covering her face for a long time, but whenever she walked on the streets, passersby would tell her, "You look old enough to be my mother – and still not covering your face?" To an outsider, a veil looked like a veil, nothing important to it. But to those of us who wore it there were big differences. Some veils were chic and stylish, with special shorter cap designs. Veils also differed in the fineness of the eye mesh, the quality of the material and the way the numerous pleats were set, narrow pleats being considered more stylish than wide ones.
>
> Wearing the veil for the first time was very difficult for me but I came to find that it was not so bad. Under cover, our inner childish feelings came out, released from outside social pressures. In a country like Afghanistan, as soon as a girl enters her early teen years she is considered a mature young woman who must behave. Soon she learns that she must walk gracefully on the streets and not draw attention to herself. She must not ignore or question the preset rules of her society. Otherwise . . . otherwise people will talk about her and it will bring shame to her family. In Afghanistan a woman must carry the family honor. Of course it would be very unwise of a young woman to bring disgrace upon and destroy the good reputation of her family! Concealing your identity behind a veil and watching the world through a four-by-six-inch rectangle of fine mesh had certain advantages, It was a sign of respect, of growing up and womanhood (Gauhari, 1996, p. 14).

As Gauhari indicates the *chaadaree* is and was worn primarily for public social contexts outside the home. Tapper (1977, p. 163) summarizes stereotypes concerning Afghan women and their head-covering practices.

Two different stereotypes about the traditional role of Muslim women prevail in the West. Village women are seen as subjected to men and doomed to a life of unremitting labor, while townswomen are hidden behind their veils and confined in the home to a feminine world where men rarely intrude. The difference between the two is bridged by a third stereotype, this time applied to nomad women, particularly those of Afghanistan. With their unveiled faces and their open-air life, they give an impression of freedom and self-assurance lacking in women of the towns and villages. Like all stereotypes, these are over-simplifications and in many cases misleading.

Gender, Economic and Social Class Explanation

The *chaadaree* seems to have been introduced from either Persia or the Moghul areas to urban centers among the upper classes during the eighteenth century. It was not uncommon for women traveling (then as now) from rural to urban contexts to incorporate wearing a *chaadaree* as a distinctive item of clothing. After all, Afghan women would not want to be misconstrued as rural versus urban dwellers. Majrooh suggests that:

> The veil had been worn by women of the royal clan, urban elites, the landlord class and community and religious leaders. However, since the 1950s the veil lost its significance as an indicator of social status due to two factors: firstly, the royal family and high-ranking government officials began not to wear the veil, followed by the intellectuals and educated middle-class urban dwellers; and secondly, because of the foundation of industrial and construction centers, immigration from rural to urban areas increased. These job seekers were accompanied by veiled women. Thus, contrary to the traditional concept, a veiled woman in the city was considered to be an *"atrafi"* or villager living in the city and belonged to a family with a low socio-economic standard (1989, p. 91).

Majrooh (1989, p. 93) also furthers the discussion of the veil by noting that in urban areas where various ethno-linguistic groups live together, "the feeling of insecurity and alienation makes the wearing of the veil an issue. Therefore, women are obliged to wear a veil while living outside their village or to cover their faces when appearing in front of a stranger." As Tarlo suggests in the following chapter of this book, in India the use of head- and body-coverings denotes complex, fluid and dynamic social practices (1996).

Today, further distinctions in social class can be made through the use of the *chaadaree*. The quality of fabric, the dyed color and cleanliness of the fabric, the number of pleats, the amount and placement of hand embroidery all distinguish an Afghani class status. While I was shopping in the various cloth and women's markets of Peshawar, Pakistan it was not uncommon to see women in *chaadars* and *chaadarees* shopping and purchasing new *chaadaree* or puchasing caps (*kula*), face bands (*rooy band*) or fabrics to replace worn areas of older *chaadaree*. Since most women own only one *chaadaree* but multiple *chaadars*, *chaadarees* are taken to *chaadaree* shopkeepers to be cleaned, re-pleated and re-dyed for continued use.

Gender and Region Explanation

Regional differences also distinguish the wearer of the *chaadaree*. For example, coarsely woven versus finely woven fabrics are associated with rural and urban residence. Specific *chaadaree* colors also differentiate one urban center from another. Specific embroidery patterns and distinctive embroidery stitches also differentiate one ethnic group from another. Dupree notes the following:

> Women in the cities continue to come out of *purdah* (*pardah*) and remove the veil, but a strange reversal of attitudes has occurred in villages becoming towns, brought about by the massive shifts of the transport and communication networks in the 1960s. Village and nomadic women seldom wore the *chadri* in the past because it would have interfered with their many daily economic functions. Now, however, if a village grows to town status, complete with a bazaar and a man gains enough wealth to hire servants, his wife often insists on wearing a *chadri*, for she believes the custom to be sophisticated and citified – not realizing her city cousins have opposite attitudes. In addition, many young girls in cities and towns wear the *chadri* briefly after puberty to indicate they have become bona fide women, ready for marriage.
>
> Actually, the *chadri* originally had two functions: it put all women in public on an equal basis (a plain *chadri* can cover the most inexpensive clothing) and it kept women (i.e., personal property) from being coveted by other men. However, some *chadri* were made in the richest silks and also used for clandestine assignations, thus defeating the original purposes (1980, p. 247).

Gender and Ethnicity Explanation

As mentioned earlier the *chaadaree* was also an additional safeguard of women in social contexts of unknown male non-kin. This has been a particularly important point during the *jihad* experience of Afghans displaced from their village and urban settings of Afghanistan to the refugee camps in areas contiguous to Afghanistan. With the decimation of the male Afghan population more women are forced to sustain themselves economically. In some instances this means seeking employment outside the home. This is problematic, as to work outside the home is considered by some Afghan families as conflicting with Afghan values. Women dress in a *chaadaree* not only to protect their own personal identity but the family identity.

Summary and Implications

The *chaadaree* is a social enigma for both Afghan and non-Afghan alike. It is truly an item of clothing that is a multi-vocal symbol that is dependent on the historic period, the social context, the significant individuals and the role expectations and behavior associated with its use. The most static aspect of the *chaadaree* is its exclusive association as a garment worn by females. The dynamic aspects are familial status, regional and ethnic identity, education and literary, economic and social class, religion and/or religiosity. That it is primarily a symbol of religion is less clear across genders, society and culture.

Notes

1. The transliteration of Afghan and Arabic terms is according to Burhan and Goutierre's *Dari for Foreigners* (1983).
2. Figures 8.1 and 8.2 are composite illustrations from field photographs and actual garments. My preference would have been to use photographs of Afghan women. Though all photographs were taken with their permission, in good conscience, I could not knowingly potentially subject Afghan women and their families further human rights abuses.

References

Afghan Coordinating Body for Afghan Relief (ACBAR) (1995). The role of NGOs in Afghanistan. Peshawar: ACBAR.

Afghan on Online (2000). http://www.afghan-web.com.

Afghanistan Foundation (2000). http://afghanistanfoundation.org.

Afghan Student League International (2000). http://www.afghanmosaic.com.

Burhan, M. & Goutierre, T. (1983). *Dari for foreigners.* Omaha, NE: Center for Afghanistan Studies.

Christensen, A. (1995). *Aiding Afghanistan: The background and prospects for reconstruction in a fragmented society.* Copenhagen: Nordic Institute of Asian Studies.

Daly, M. (1999). The paarda expression of hejaab among Afghan women living in a non-Muslim community. In L. Arthur (Ed.), *Religion, dress and the body* (pp. 147–62). Oxford: Berg Publishers.

Dupree, L. (1980). *Afghanistan.* Princeton, NJ: Princeton University Press.

Dupree, N. (1998). Afghan women under the Taleban. In W. Maley (Ed.), *Fundamentalism reborn?: Afghanistan and the Taleban* (pp. 145–66). New York: New York University Press.

Dupree, N. (1992). Clothing in Afghanistan. In E. Yarshater (Ed.), *Encyclopaedia Iranica* (pp. 811–15). Costa Mesa, CA: Mazda Publishers.

Dupree, N. (1978). Behind the veil in Afghanistan. *Asia*, 1(2), 10–15.

El Guindi, F. (1999). *Veil: Modesty, privacy and resistance*. Oxford: Berg Publishers.

Feminist Majority Foundation (2000). http://www.feminist.org.

Gauhari, F. (1996). *Searching for Saleem: An Afghan woman's odyssey*. Lincoln, NE: University of Nebraska Press.

Hopkirk, P. (1994). *The great game: The struggle for empire in Central Asia*. New York: Kodansha International.

Magnus, R. & Naby, E. (1998). *Afghanistan: Mullah, Marx and Mujahid*. Boulder, CO: Westview Press.

Majrooh, P. (1989). Afghan women between Marxism and Islamic fundamentalism. *Central Asian Survey*. 8 (3), 87–98.

Maley, W. (Ed.). (1998). *Fundamentalism reborn?: Afghanistan and the Taleban*. New York: University Press.

Marseden, P. (1998). The gender policies of the Taleban. *The Taleban: War, religion and the new order in Afghanistan*. Karachi: Oxford University Press.

Mernissi, F. (1987). *Beyond the veil: Male–female dynamics in a modern Muslim society*. Bloomington, IN: Indiana University Press.

Mernissi, F. (1991a). *The veil and the male elite: A feminist interpretation of women's rights in Islam*. Reading, MA: Addison-Wesley Publishing Company.

Mernissi, F. (1991b). *Women and Islam: An historical and theological enquiry*. Oxford: Basil Blackwell.

Miller, N. (1978). *Faces of change, five rural societies in transition: Bolivia, Kenya, Afghanistan, Taiwan, China Coast*. Lebanon, NH: Wheelock Education Resources.

Moghadam, V. (1994). Reform, revolution, & reaction: The trajectory of the 'woman question' in Afghanistan. In V. Moghadam (Ed.), *Gender and national identity: Women and politics in Muslim societies* (pp. 81–109). London: Zed Books Limited.

Physicians for Human Rights (2000). http://phrusa.org.

Revolutionary Association of Women for Afghanistan (2000). http:// rawa.org.

Scarce, J. (1974). The development of women's veils in Persia and Afghanistan. *Costume*, 8, 4–13.

Sheikh Muhammad bin Saleh bin Uthalmeen (1996). *Hijaab*. New Delhi, India: Idara Isha'at–e-Diniyat (P) Ltd.

Taleban Islamic Movement of Afghanistan (2000). http://www.Taleban.com.

Tapper, N. (1977). Pastun nomad women in Afghanistan. *Asian Affairs*. 8(2), 163–70.

Tarlo, E. (1996). *Clothing matters: Dress and identity in India*. Chicago: The University of Chicago Press.

United Nations High Commission for Refugees (2000). http:www.unhcr.ch/statis/98.oview

9

Sartorial Entanglements of a Gujarati Wife

Emma Tarlo

An excerpt from *Clothing Matters: Dress and Identity in India*. London: Hurst, 1996.

Author's introductory note

In rural Gujarat, as in other parts of northern India, clothing plays an essential role in marking a woman's passage through various stages of the life cycle and in defining her relationship to different categories of men. When she marries, a woman is given large quantities of clothing and jewelry from parents and in-laws and it is in the early years of married life that she is entitled and expected to adorn herself most lavishly. Her richly colored clothing, special jewelry and use of colored powders are not only a form of beautification; they are also a sign of *saubhagya*, the auspicious state of having a husband who is alive. In this sense, they declare a woman's privilege and virtue in a context where husbands are ideally perceived as personal deities and where the loss of a husband is marked by the removal of jewelry, make-up and bright clothes. However, if early married life is the period when a woman's body is most adorned, it is also the period when her movements and behavior are most constrained. These restrictions find sartorial expression in the custom of *laj* – the practice of drawing the edge of one's clothing (veil cloth or sari) over the face and at times the entire body, in order to obscure it. *Laj* is a tangible expression of *sharum* – the state of shyness and modesty which women are expected to experience and display in a variety of contexts (cf. Tarlo 1996). *Laj* is practiced most strictly by high-caste women who, once married, are expected to screen themselves in front of all men senior to their husbands in their marital family and village. Although according to ancient Hindu religious prescriptions a woman's dress and behavior are defined by her relationship to her husband, in reality women marry families rather than individuals and their clothing practices have to be understood within the wider context of family and caste relations. The following extract takes us into the house of a Brahman family in the village of Jalia[1] in Saurashtra (Gujarat, in western India). It describes the plight of Hansaben, a young woman from the nearby city of Larabad whose sartorial conflicts with her village in-laws lend some insight into the complex web of issues which clothing evokes and embodies in rural Gujarat.

The Problem of Hansaben's Cardigan

It was midwinter, January 1989 and cold. Those who could afford it draped themselves in shawls and provided cardigans, jumpers and woolly hats for their children. The whole of Jalia took on a wrapped and huddled appearance. Hansaben, the only daughter-in-law in the house of a *Brahman* schoolteacher, opened her cupboard of trousseau gifts, took out a thick warm cardigan given her by her mother and put it on over her sari, continuing her kitchen chores. Her mother-in-law sat close by, huddled in a sari and a woolen shawl and drinking tea from a china saucer. Leriben, daughter of the house, helped Hansaben with the cooking.

At mid-day there was a customary creaking sound from below and a loud and elongated cry of 'Ram' projected up the stairway, reaching the women in the kitchen above. Leriben warned Hansaben in urgent haste that HE was coming and Hansaben swiftly turned her back, sweeping her sari over her head as she swiveled and pulling it down till it hung well over her face and neck in *ardhi laj*.[2] Crouched in the corner of the kitchen, her back turned, her face covered and head tilted downwards, she continued to roll out *roti* (bread) as before.

Sureshkaka, her father-in-law, entered the room and sat cross-legged on the floor while his daughter supplied him with water followed by a large selection of food. A constant supply of hot *rotis* was drafted from Hansa's hot plate to Sureshkaka's *thali* (steel plate) by the intermediary and attentive daughter and wife. But Sureshkaka soon noticed the figure of his veiled daughter-in-law stooping over the fire, dressed in an unfamiliar garment. He demanded with annoyance just what she was wearing and where it had come from. Hansa herself remained mute beneath her veil, but her mother-in-law explained that it was cold and Hansa was wearing a cardigan (*jeket*) that she had brought in her trousseau. Sureshkaka, unimpressed, pointed out that the folds of Hansa's sari were interrupted by this unnecessary addition and that it looked untidy and improper. "No village girl would think it proper to wear such a thing," he remonstrated. "Has she no respect for our traditions? How can she do real *laj* when she looks such a sight with her sari half hidden under her '*jeket*' like that?" He instructed his wife to order Hansaben to get changed. She must put the cardigan underneath her blouse. He did not want to see such a disgraceful sight again. With that he stomped out of the room and went for his rest. His wife and daughter immediately set about telling Hansaben to change her clothes. Hansaben defended herself by saying that her blouse was too tight and the cardigan was too bulky – how could she wear it under her blouse? It was not possible. She could not even fit it beneath her sari, never mind the blouse. Her two advisers reminded her that her father-in-law had ordered it and this alone should make her obey. Hansa stubbornly refused and went on with her tasks.

The next day Hansa continued to wear the offending cardigan as before and her father-in-law lost his temper. He delivered an angry tirade about disobedient daughters-in-law and their lack of respect for their elders. His anger scared all members of the household who knew his short temper and his wife and daughter scolded Hansaben for her stupid disobedience and for deliberately causing trouble to everyone in the house. Intimidated by the situation, Hansaben removed her cardigan, still maintaining to the other women that she could not fit it beneath her sari or her blouse and that she would just have to suffer the cold instead. She would freeze. For the next few days she went about the house shivering and refusing to speak or eat. She did her tasks silently and obediently with the air of a much-abused martyr.

Hansaben was three months pregnant at the time and still breastfeeding her first child, a girl of one and a half years. The family was anxious that she should eat well lest the new baby's health should be affected. When Sureshkaka heard that she was eating virtually nothing, he lost his temper yet again, this time with all the women, leaving the three of them disputing among themselves in the kitchen late at night. Hansaben was crying out in her own defense, saying that her mother had given her the cardigan and that she should be allowed to wear it since it was her own trousseau gift from her parents. Sureshkaka heard this from the next room and flew into the kitchen in an uncontrollable rage. Never before, he claimed, had he heard his daughter-in-law speak. How dare she raise her voice? Had she no *sharum* at all? This was it. He ordered her to leave the house there and then. She caused only trouble to his family. He never wanted to see her again. She should go back to the city if she wanted to behave with so little respect for their revered customs. In Larabad, at her parents' house, she could no doubt wear such a fancy "*jeket*", but not in Jalia.

By now the whole family was involved in trying to placate Sureshkaka's rage. Hansaben's husband (Sureshkaka's eldest son) tried to calm him but to no avail; he was joined by Ramanbhai (the youngest son) who was a little more successful. He pointed out that Hansaben, who spent her days secluded in the house, could not be expected to leave the village alone at midnight. Sureshkaka must rest and think with a cool head in the morning.

Hansaben spent the night in tears, refusing to speak to anyone, including her husband. The next day she continued her tasks of cleaning, washing and cooking in total silence with downcast, tearful eyes and shivering without her cardigan. When no one was looking she slipped across the courtyard and told the neighbor that if it were not for her child, she would kill herself. There was kerosene in the kitchen. How quick and easy it would be to set herself alight. She had thought of it many times.

The neighbor, who was sure to gossip, quickly reported this back to Sureshkaka's wife and soon the whole family was anxious about the threat of a suicide in the household. Everyone knew that Sureshkaka had gone too far this time. Even Sureshkaka himself seemed to realize that. He agreed to send a message to Hansaben's family in Larabad, saying that Hansa was unhappy just now and needed encouragement to eat. The next day her brother arrived from the city and she was able to confide her problems and explain how her father-in-law had ordered her out of the house in the middle of the night just because she had worn her cardigan when she was cold. Her brother left after a polite and strained saucer of tea with his in-laws, but the next day a short note was delivered to the house by a stranger who used the local bus. It was from Hansaben's father, saying that he was currently ill and required his daughter to look after him for one month. His son would arrive to fetch her from the village the following morning and escort her back to her parental home in Larabad.

There was no protest. Hansaben packed three saris and her controversial cardigan and left the house with her young daughter in her arms and her brother by her side. The female in-laws and her husband waved her good-bye and told her to come back soon. They hoped her father was not too ill.

The incidents described here were spread over a period of seven days. But it was eight months before Hansaben was to return to the village, much to the consternation of her in-laws. During these months another minor dispute arose, this time concerning Hansaben's saris.

Hansaben's Saris

Hansaben had been gone three months, already far longer than the initial request in her father's note and long enough to set other villagers gossiping and speculating about this errant daughter-in-law, when a letter appeared written by Hansaben herself and addressed to her husband. In it she greeted other members of the family politely and gave news of her daughter's well-being. But she proceeded to say that her father was still very ill and needed her assistance. She was therefore writing to request that they send her saris to Larabad as she had to attend a wedding and had nothing suitable to wear. All her best saris were in Jalia and besides she needed her ordinary ones too since she had only taken three of them when she left the village.

This letter was met with grim resentment and much discussion among her in-laws. Three points emerged. First, Hansaben's father was not really ill, for only three days earlier the goldsmith's son had met him in the city and he seemed fine. Secondly, Hansa's request showed her intention to remain at her *pir* (natal home) for longer still, humiliating her in-laws in the process and forcing her mother-in-law to do the cooking and household chores which were Hansa's duty. It was argued that if she asked for her saris one day, then she would be demanding her jewelry the next, then her cupboard, her vessels, the ceiling fan, the bed. In short she would try to win back the whole of her trousseau. Then she would never return to the village. It was therefore decided that not one sari would be sent to her, for with her saris still in the village, she would be forced to return to Jalia soon.

The third objection was to the idea that she should be allowed to dress up and attend a wedding at all in the circumstances. This was only proof of her lack of *sharum* and her desire to wander aimlessly about, which was inappropriate to her married status. It also highlighted the irresponsibility of her parents in allowing their married daughter to go out and enjoy herself. What business did she have to go to a celebration? How could she be a good mother to her child when all she wanted to do was to dress up and wander about? How could she pretend that her father needed looking after when she was going off to weddings? That only showed the type of cunning and dishonest people her family were.

The Jalia family therefore decided to ignore Hansaben's request for her saris altogether and their bitterness was expressed in the fact that her mother-in-law began to wear Hansa's saris during the day. These were stored in Hansa's personal cupboard, also a trousseau gift from her parents. Her mother-in-law had ensured that Hansa handed over the key to the cupboard before leaving on the grounds that a few communal things were stored there. This gave her access to Hansa's saris, though not to her jewelry which was locked in a separate compartment from her clothes.

A second letter requesting Hansa's saris arrived a fortnight after the first and seemed only to aggravate the mounting tensions between her and her in-laws, making reunion difficult. As the months passed the Jalia family became more and more desperate for her return, yet personal pride and cultural etiquette prevented them from lowering themselves to demand it.

Family Delegations: How to Get Hansaben Back

Late one evening in the fifth month of Hansaben's departure some surprise visitors arrived at Sureshkaka's house. They were his two elder brothers (a priest and a trader), his eldest brother's son (a doctor) and a cousin (a teacher). Although they all lived in Jalia, they rarely visited Sureshkaka's house owing to long-term family tensions. The priest's wife and Sureshkaka's wife claimed not to have spoken to each other for twenty-six years and had lived separately for more than twenty. The trading brother and Sureshkaka had remained together for longer but now blamed each other and in particular each other's wives, for the split in the joint family some eight years before. A visit from these men could not be interpreted as a casual call, nor was it. They had come with a purpose. They wanted Hansaben back. A lengthy and heated discussion ensued between these five men. Hansaben's husband was excluded from this and fell asleep outside on the verandah. However his mother, well wrapped beneath her veil, was straining to hear the discussion and posted her daughter just outside the main room to convey the gist of it.

It seemed that rumors were circulating via the goldsmith's son and his family that Hansaben would only return if she could live alone with her husband, separate from her mother-in-law, who caused her sorrow and treated her badly. The family delegation was concerned and horrified that such gossip should be conveyed by other people in the village and not even through personal relatives. Hansa, it seemed, was talking to her neighbors in Larabad, some of whom had relatives in Jalia who were talking in the village. One rumor claimed that her in-laws had threatened to burn her. The delegation was concerned about the ramifications of all this for both the family and the caste reputation. It was disgrace enough that Hansaben had left, bringing shame on them all and now these rumors made it worse. It was time, they felt, for direct action. Hansaben must be recalled and must be well treated.

This led to a second, highly sensitive issue which was raised by Sureshkaka's eldest brother, the priest. If Sureshkaka were not so lax in maintaining old traditions, he argued, then this type of behavior in a daughter-in-law would never have occurred. But Sureshkaka had tried to improve himself too far and by "becoming a *Vaniya* (businessman)" he was losing sight of their own caste traditions. Most respected families in Jalia were content to educate their daughters up to seventh standard in the village school. This meant they could read and write and why should they need more? But for Sureshkaka this was not enough. He sent his daughter to high school on the bus where "anything might happen". Then there was question of her being dressed in a *shalwar kamiz* (loose trouser and tunic). It was not right for a Hindu girl to put on the trousers of a Muslim.[3] Did he know how people talked when they saw her at the bus stop? Only the other day their cousin the *panwala* (betel-nut seller) had exclaimed at the sight: 'See, the *Vaghran* is coming.[4] Look, the prostitute!' Sureshkaka owed it to his family and his caste to keep up his standards. His daughter should cease her education right away and this would save her from the disgrace of using the bus, roaming alone in town and dressing in clothes that were unsuitable for any Hindu village girl. But most important of all, Sureshkaka must send his son to fetch Hansaben back at all costs, even if this meant a split in the household. For just now Sureshkaka's family brought disgrace on all his brothers in the village.

The meeting ended with Sureshkaka losing his temper and the delegation leaving in haste. He did not want a split in his own household, particularly since he had another son and a daughter whose marriages were yet to be arranged. These would be costly affairs for which he required the financial assistance of his eldest son (Hansaben's husband), who ran the shop. Hansaben's husband in fact hoped to escape this burden, particularly in the case of his brother's wedding. Not only did he want the financial independence of running his own house, but he also felt resentment that his younger brother was more respected by their father; for the elder brother this seemed unjust, since it was he who contributed to the family income while his younger brother merely "played around at college", costing them money and contributing nothing.

A few weeks after the visit of the first family delegation a second family delegation was planned. This time, much to my surprise, it involved my own family. My parents had come to visit Jalia for one day and, shortly after their arrival, it became clear that they were to be sent with me and Ramanbhai to Hansaben's house in Larabad as a gesture of reconciliation. As older-generation white educated people, they were greeted with considerable respect in Jalia and by sharing the honor of their brief visit the Jalia family were making a gesture of goodwill to Hansaben's family without having to lower themselves to actually asking for her return. My parents, who were entirely unable to communicate in linguistic terms, were essentially to act as peace envoys. They sat obediently on a bed drinking tea and smiling at appropriate moments while I was beckoned into the kitchen by Hansaben, who was keen to hear what havoc her departure might be causing to her in-laws. When I asked about her plans, it soon became clear that her problem was not so much *whether* to return as *when*. She explained her position as follows:

> I am married and must stay married. It is my misfortune to be married with those people, but what can I do? I know my life is there in the village and all my trousseau things are there. I asked them for my saris and they sent not one, not even one. My jewelry, my vessels, everything is there. I have nothing here in my parents' place. My life is not here. Soon things will get better in Jalia. Ramanbhai will marry and a new wife will come to the house. She will help me with the work and she will judge who is honest in the house. She will know that I am good.

Hansaben never feared that her in-laws would not take her back for, as she explained, they needed her not just for the housework but for their reputation. Ramanbhai, their youngest son, would never be able to find a really good wife if there was already a divorce in his family. Even at this moment their reputation was being discussed because, according to Hansaben's interpretation, everyone always wanted to know who was treating their daughter-in-law so badly as to make her leave. Hansa perceived her sojourn with her parents not merely as a refuge but also as a good revenge for her in-laws' unpleasantness. She demanded to know how difficult her absence had made things in the village and expressed particular pleasure that her mother-in-law, who disliked cooking, was now doing so every day. Hansa would play hard to get. She wanted her in-laws to apologize and ask her back but her own parents would not make the approaches. They were waiting for her in-laws to call her and in the meantime she was enjoying the comfort and pleasure of being in her parental home.

When one day, her husband finally visited her in Larabad, requesting her return, she refused to speak with him and denied him access to their daughter, but her parents told him that Hansa would return to the village for a two-week trial period. Her husband refused this humiliating offer and left. As far as he was concerned this was a sign that she was intending to return and he was not going to receive her on *their* terms. If she was coming back to Jalia, she must come and she must stay.

Hansaben's Return

In the sixth month of her departure, Hansaben gave birth to their second child, another daughter. Two months later her father wrote to Sureshkaka saying that Hansaben was ready to return, having recovered from the birth. Since it is customary for women to give birth to their first child and occasionally their second at their parents' house, the birth provided a suitable time for her reappearance in the village, giving it some façade of normality. She arrived with her daughter and new baby girl and was greeted with much affection and lavish displays of love from her mother-in-law and sister-in-law. The family was back to its customary state of precarious stability and the cardigan returned to the cupboard.

At first sight it might appear that the seemingly exaggerated response of Sureshkaka to a mere cardigan tells more about the temperament of one particular man than it does about the significance of clothes. The cardigan might, for example, have been simply a random catalyst which happened to spark off flames in what was already a tense relationship. But closer investigation of the meaning and value of clothing to the people of Jalia suggests that the nature of the catalyst was by no means arbitrary. To gain some insight into the labyrinth of tensions which this clothing dispute seemed to evoke and embody, it is necessary to examine briefly certain aspects of the giving and receiving, wearing and possessing of clothes.

Giving and Receiving Clothing and Adornment

Giving and receiving gifts forms a vital element of every major life-cycle rite in Jalia. The most important of these rites is the giving of a virgin daughter (*kanyadan*) in marriage. Around this central rite a whole series of other gift-giving obligations is organized. Clothing and jewelry are, along with food, the most important components of these gift-giving rituals, accompanying marriages, pregnancies, births, deaths, arrivals and departures. Werbner has shown how Pakistani migrants from Manchester, visiting their relatives in Pakistan, often pay excess luggage charges owing to the enormous quantities of clothing they carry back and forth as gifts for kinsmen and women. Such gifts tie immigrants to their natal homes and objectify social relations between families (Werbner,1990). In Jalia, gifts of clothing hold a similar importance, binding together individuals and groups, ratifying agreements, confirming commitments, ascribing social roles and protecting future interests. As Evans-Pritchard once commented in the African context, "material culture may be regarded as part of social relations, for material objects are the chains along which social relationships run" (1967, p. 89). In India the major links of such chains are often forged in cloth.

Although both men and women give and receive clothes, these gifts have a special and particular importance for women. Large stocks of clothing are accumulated in preparation for a daughter's wedding and after marriage a wife usually keeps her trousseau clothes in her personal dowry chest or cupboard to which she generally keeps the key. Men never acquire the large stocks of clothing that women receive from their parents, nor do they discuss clothes with the same enthusiasm and eye for detail. Clothing is for women a frequent topic of conversation as they compare and inspect each other's apparel and even display their entire clothing collection to visitors and friends (Gold-Grodzins, 1988).

For women clothing is not merely a question of adornment but also a form of property, particularly in a village context where women's rights of inheritance to other forms of property such as land are rarely recognized (Goody and Tambiah, 1973). If they get the opportunity, women hoard clothes, often in excess of their apparent requirements (Chaudhuri, 1976). Clothing, carefully locked away and jewelry, worn or safely stored, are often the only parts of a new wife's trousseau over which she has primary access and control. It is not therefore surprising to find that women take more interest in accumulating and comparing clothes than men who inherit other, more permanent forms of wealth.

A brief examination of the gifts of clothing and adornment given to a woman in connection with her marriage reveals her gradual assimilation into her in-laws' home.

Betrothal (*Sagai*)

Following the agreement between parents that their children should marry, the father of the prospective groom offers the future bride a veil-cloth (*chundadi*), one outfit of clothes and a selection of jewelry, usually comprising a nose-ring, anklets and earrings. He paints a vermilion mark (*chandlo*) on her forehead and places the veil over her head. There is no written contract at the time of betrothal but the offering of the veil and the painting of vermilion are seen as a concrete agreement on the part of the groom's parents to take on responsibility for the girl's future. It is a contract written, as it were, on the girl herself.

This became clear in the case of the *Brahman* girl who suffered rejection by her future husband only one week after the engagement ceremony had taken place. This caused great outrage among her relatives who had witnessed the offering of the *chundadi* and *chandlo* and who remonstrated that the groom's father had already given the veil and therefore could not "cut it now". Broken engagements, although they sometimes occurred, were rare and considered highly inauspicious. The offering of the *chundadi* usually served as a formal acknowledgement of the intention of the groom's family to accept the gift of the bride.

Marriage (*Lugan*)

During the marriage ceremony the bride is dressed in a new set of clothes given by her parents, consisting usually of petticoat, blouse and *paneter* (special red and white tie-dyed wedding sari). As she enters the marriage booth, however, one of her in-laws (usually the mother-in-law) covers her face and head with a *gharcholu*, a special marriage veil, usually green with yellow and red tie-dyed dots. She therefore simultaneously wears the veil given by her parents and that from her in-laws, symbolizing her passing from the protection of one household to another. The colors red and green are associated with fertility and auspiciousness and are worn mainly by young women, married or unmarried.

Along with the *gharcholu*, a bride also receives jewelry from her in-laws, including the *mangalsutra* necklace and ivory bangles which she will wear throughout her married life. As the ceremony begins, the bride's brother declares in Sanskrit: "This maiden, decorated with ornaments and robed in twin apparel, I give to you." The priest joins together the hands of the bridal pair and leads them to the central marriage square (*chori*). Here their upper garments are tied together and the couple take four turns around the sacred fire, physically united by the knot in their clothes and a long cotton thread (*mala*) which binds them together. The knotting of garments and the tying of thread are a metaphoric enactment of physical union and it is through these actions that the permanence of the union is stated.

The Sending Away (*Anu*) Ceremony

The customs surrounding sending away (*anu*) ceremonies vary greatly according to the community and the age of the bride at the time of marriage. If she is young and there is a gap of some years between the marriage and the main *anu* ceremony, then the groom's parents are often expected to send one outfit of clothes to the bride every year to reaffirm the wedding contract. Often they are also expected to give money to the bride's parents to cover the stitching charges incurred at the tailors during the preparation of the bride's *anu* clothes.

The number of *anu* ceremonies may vary from one to three according to the particular preferences of different individuals or castes. The main *anu*, however, takes place when the mature girl first goes to live in her husband's home, rather than simply visiting it. On this occasion she receives a large collection of clothes from her parents, consisting usually of at least twenty-one outfits and a few items of jewelry. After being carefully displayed to friends and neighbors, these are placed in a cupboard or dowry chest, along with a selection of steel kitchen vessels contributed by all her near relatives and small items of household furniture and ornaments which vary considerably according to family wealth and caste expectations.

The final *anu*, called *jianu*, occurs when a woman returns to her marital home after giving birth to her first child at her parental home. When she returns to her in-laws' house, she receives from her parents a few outfits of clothing and a number of outfits for the baby, along with a baby's cot and quilt. For the rest of her life she will usually receive a gift of clothing from her parents each time she visits her parental home. She will also be expected to provide gifts for her in-laws, but these are secondary to those she receives herself. Her in-laws will in turn provide her with clothes and jewelry from time to time, particularly on festive occasions; thus a woman can accumulate clothes even after marriage.

Social relations between two families are therefore expressed and reconfirmed through a series of gifts of clothing and adornment which bind the two groups together through the conversion of daughters into wives. The knotting of garments acts as the central pivot around which such gift-giving takes place. In the case of Hansaben and her in-laws, the contractual aspect of these gifts was particularly apparent. They belong to a *Brahman* subgroup that is numerically small, with a severe shortage of marriageable girls. When Sureshkaka first discovered Hansaben, she was only fifteen and her parents had considered her too young to marry for at least another three years. She was pretty, fair-skinned, intelligent and well-bred, which had made Sureshkaka particularly anxious to procure her for his son. One of her strongest attributes was that she came from the city of Larabad, where he himself hoped eventually to settle. This, he felt, made her refined and greatly preferable to the less educated girls found in villages. All in all, Hansa had seemed too good to lose and the Jalia family had wanted to fix the betrothal right away. Hansa's family had been apprehensive because this meant a three-year gap between betrothal and marriage. Finally they were persuaded by Sureshkaka's offer of twenty-one saris which would be given to Hansaben at the engagement ceremony. These revealed his family's commitment to the future marriage. They also acted as a deposit which guaranteed that Hansaben would be reserved exclusively for them, even if other more appetizing offers presented themselves in the three years before the marriage.

When Hansaben married three years later, she received another twenty-one saris from her own parents in her trousseau, making her the owner of forty-two saris and a fine selection of gold jewelry, mostly given by her in-laws. These were her own property and were kept separately from the other women's clothes in her new home. She had, as we have seen, her own steel cupboard which was used almost exclusively by her.

In theory, the forty-two saris belonged to Hansaben, yet during her absence they were kept by her in-laws as hostages to ensure her return. When I asked Hansaben why she had taken so few saris with her to Larabad in the first place, she replied that her mother-in-law had been watching over her while she was packing and had told her she did not need to take much. Her mother-in-law was suspicious, so Hansa had left with only three saris. In other words, if she had taken too many saris with her, she would have been seen to be breaking the contract under which those clothes had been given by expressing her intention to stay away from the marital home as long as possible. But her departure, though obviously based on just such a desire to get away, had to be made to look like a departure of necessity, an obedience to her sick father's wishes rather than her own.

During Hansa's absence, the topic of the twenty-one saris given at betrothal was frequently raised by the Jalia family. Their deposit seemed to have proved worthless and they felt cheated. It was apparently in a spirit of bitterness and vindictiveness that the mother-in-law began to wear the saris herself. When I first saw her dressed in one of them, it was not entirely obvious that they were not her own since she had selected a fairly subdued color. But she seemed self-conscious and immediately confessed, with a laugh, that she was dressed in Hansa's clothes which were really more suitable for a younger woman. Wearing Hansa's saris seemed a way of reclaiming the remnants of a broken agreement.

Although Hansa possessed a large collection of saris, it was clear that her rights of ownership were constrained by the context in which the clothes had been given. Owning clothes seemed to require the acceptance of certain conditions. The saris were hers so long as she was prepared to fulfill her wifely duties, but they ceased to be so the moment she appeared to step outside the role of wife, a role which, after all, justified her entitlement to the saris in the first place. It has been suggested (Jacobson, 1976) that a woman's control over her own jewelry varies according to her relationship to the donor. Just as a woman's kinship bonds with her parents are strong and permanent, so her ownership over jewelry from her natal kin is absolute, but in the same way that her relationship with her in-laws is vulnerable and precarious, so too is her control over jewelry given by them. A dissatisfied in-law can reclaim jewelry in the same way that Hansa's mother-in-law reclaimed her saris. Such gifts from in-laws are conditional on the daughter-in-law's obedience and good behavior. This raises interesting questions about what it means to own and receive clothes as a woman in Indian society.

Women as Owners and Recipients of Clothes

Women receive and accumulate clothes more than men and this is one of the privileges of becoming a wife. While a woman's control over the gifts from her own parents is more secure than that over gifts from her in-laws, it must be remembered that both sets of gifts are conditional on her marrying; only through making the transition from daughter to wife does a woman become entitled to a large stock of clothes at all. Girls who never marry never receive the trousseau items that their parents accumulated for them in their youth. Indeed such unmarried women, who are in themselves a rarity, do not receive more than the basic requirements of clothing from their parents. Women who are separated or widowed, on the other hand, sometimes retrieve their trousseau clothing, but this is often at the discretion of their in-laws and cannot easily be enforced. If they return to their parental homes with their trousseau clothes, these are usually given in remarriage or distributed among other family members if remarriage is unacceptable. One *Brahman* woman who returned to her parents after prolonged maltreatment by her husband regained her saris yet contributed all but three to her younger sister's trousseau as it was no longer thought necessary or appropriate for her to posses such clothes now that her marriage was over. She accepted this as her contribution to the parental home.

Young married life is, as we have seen, the only time when a woman is expected to adorn herself extravagantly and possess fine clothes. Great emphasis is placed on the beauty and adornment of the youthful bride and wife who symbolizes prosperity and auspiciousness. The finer her clothes and the more lavish her jewelry, the greater her resemblance to Lakshmi, the goddess of wealth and prosperity. She should dress brightly and have smooth oiled hair, lampback round her eyes, polish on her nails, vermilion in her parting and an abundance of gold jewelry on her wrists, round her neck and in her ears. But if an unmarried girl adorns herself too beautifully, she is immediately thought disreputable, attracting unsuitable attention. Before marriage she must dress plainly except for special festivals when she can wear her finest apparel. Similarly, in old age a woman is supposed to tone down her appearance until finally, if widowed, she loses her entitlement to look beautiful altogether, casting aside the symbols of happy married life. *Brahman* widows usually wear white clothes, farming widows dull red and shepherd widows black. Excessive adornment worn either before marriage or after a marriage has ended is associated with immorality and even prostitution.

This suggests that the adornment of women is closely related to the celebration and control of their fertility – which must not be emphasized before marriage. Nor should it be expressed in old age, even though some of the women who called themselves "old" were only in their thirties and clearly still capable of conception. Such "old" women risked the accusation of trying to "be" their daughters-in-law if they dressed too lavishly. Once their daughters-in-law had come to the house, they themselves were expected to cease producing children and to begin to divest themselves of excess ornament. It is therefore only the child-producing years that entitle a woman to dress brightly, lavishly and decoratively. These are the years when her beauty can be safely expressed within the context of her relationship with her husband. Yet if a woman's freedom to dress lavishly reaches its highest expression during this period, it is also the time when her behavior is most constrained and her physical presence is most hidden. She must absent herself behind her veil, hiding her powers of allurement from other men of the household and the village and *Brahman* wives like Hansaben usually cannot leave the house or enter the village, even when screened by their veils. The privilege of receiving clothes and displaying one's beauty is therefore closely linked with the need to conceal it. Conversely, for men the act of providing clothes for their women entitles them to expect certain displays of *sharum* and obedience from them. To husbands and fathers the obligation to give is as much a part of the masculine role as the privilege of receiving and obeying is part of the feminine wifely role.

Men as Givers of Clothes

For parents giving clothes is an obligation, a duty and a necessity. Much time is spent on deciding precisely how much should be spent on the clothing and jewelry for a daughter's wedding. It is sometimes suggested that women control the distribution of goods while men control financial transactions (Sharma, 1984). This is true to some extent but the distinction is not rigid (Vatuk, 1975). Furthermore, while the mother of the bride does indeed play the major role in organizing the trousseau and selecting appropriate items of dress, among most castes it is the father who takes the financial responsibility. And although it is women who inspect and assess a girl's trousseau display, it is the man's reputation that is at stake if her provisions are thought to be lacking. Nirad Chaudhuri sums up the situation when he writes that men give enthusiastically because their own position and prestige depend on the clothes of their women. He quotes the lines from *Manu Samhita* (ancient Brahminical legal code) which read:

> Women must be honored and adorned by their fathers, brothers and husbands and brothers in law for their own welfare . . . The houses on which female relations, not being duly honored, pronounce a curse, perish completely as if destroyed by magic. Hence men who seek their own welfare should always honor women on holidays and festivals with ornaments, clothes and food (1976, p. 42).

Often the obligation to give reaches unfortunate proportions, particularly for men with a predominance of daughters, whose marriages and trousseaux cause many families financial difficulties. But the obligation to provide and to be seen to provide, is stronger than any purely financial consideration; it is part of the duty of fatherhood and an indicator of a man's worthiness of respect. Gifts are often given in public situations where there is a large audience of kinsmen and women to impress (Werbner, 1990). Displaying one's wealth and generosity, establishing and reconfirming social bonds, providing for daughters and fulfilling the duty of fatherhood are all features that are intermeshed in the giving to the trousseau.

The intensity of the obligation to clothe a daughter is expressed in Jalia in the annual ritual of *Tulsi Vivah* (Basil Wedding) when Tulsima, the holy basil plant which grows in every courtyard, is formally married to Takadada (Lord Krishna) in a ceremony which marks the end of the austere monsoon season and the beginning of the more festive winter period. The ceremony takes place on the eleventh day of the bright half of *Kartik* (mid-November) and only after this sacred marriage can mortals in the village celebrate their own weddings.

The marriage of Tulsima with Takadada resembles a human marriage in most ways, since it contains the essential elements of any Hindu wedding, including the setting up of a marriage booth (*mandap*), a central square (*chori*), a sacred fire (*agni*) and so on. Tulsima (the basil plant) receives all the privileges of the bride, including a full set of marriage clothing which is wrapped around her leaves. When I witnessed the ceremony, a nose-ring and earrings provided by the substitute parents of the bride were attached with difficulty to a paper face which had been inserted at the top of the plant. Takadada, in the form of a small statue of Krishna, was dressed in a *dhoti* (waist-cloth) and seated beneath a canopy. The couple were linked by a cotton thread (*mala*). Responsibility for the cost and equipment necessary for the wedding is taken every year by a married couple who have no daughter. They become the parents of Tulsima for the night and give her away. It is significant that they not only provide her with bridal clothes but also with an entire trousseau of saris. The year I attended the wedding, Tulsima was promised twenty-one saris, which were to be taken by the *Brahman* priest and distributed to female ascetics.

Taking the financial responsibility for this event is considered a privilege and is meritorious to couples without daughters. It is said that a man cannot fulfil his full duty of fatherhood if he has only sons. Although sons are as a rule greatly preferred, people feel it necessary to have at least one daughter whom they can give away in marriage. The *Kanbi*[5] man who acted the role of father explained this as follows: "It is only after obtaining wives for our sons and giving away our daughters with the provisions of a good trousseau that we can say we have completed our duty as fathers. Before today I had no daughter, but now I have given Tulsima, my daughter, to our god Takadada and I can become old quietly." When I questioned him about the necessity of providing Tulsima with twenty-one saris, he looked me askance and answered: "Who would give away a daughter without a trousseau of fine clothes? What kind of father is that?"

The nature of the relationship between the sexes is restated in the female privilege of receiving clothes and the male privilege of providing them. This is particularly true among high-caste groups. Where women are secluded, as in Sureshkaka's family, the man's obligation to provide is at its strongest but so too is his ability to control the clothing and behavior of the women of the house. Sureshkaka's wife claimed (somewhat exaggeratedly) not to have been shopping since before her marriage some twenty-six years earlier. If she needed clothes, then she asked her husband or her son to provide them. She said she would like to shop but her husband would get angry if she left the house. She only went out for funerals, weddings and special events. When Leriben, her daughter, came to marry, then she would be able to shop with her husband for Leriben's trousseau, but this would be an exceptional event for which they would make a special trip to the major city of Ahmedabad.

Leriben herself, being unmarried, was not so restricted in her movements as her mother. She was able to visit the cloth shops of Larabad with her brother and choose the material for her own clothes. It was considered acceptable for her to have clothes made by a tailor so long as he did not take her body measurements. But this "freedom" did not exempt her from her father's criticism and overriding choice. He wanted her to look like an educated city girl, which meant wearing a *shalwar kamiz* of shiny synthetic fabric. In the sweltering heat of the summer she had tried to explain that cotton would be cooler and more comfortable, but her father had objected: "What will people say if they see you dressed in *sada kapda* [plain cloth]? They will say that your father is so mean and poor that he dresses his daughter like a *Vaghri*. People talk." And people, usually relatives, did talk about Leriben's clothing. Her uncle, the priest, felt it indecent for a respectable Hindu girl to wear a *shalwar kamiz* which was suitable only for Muslims or fancy city people. His own unmarried daughter, who was more or less confined to the house, wore simple long "maxis" and, on the rare occasions of her entering the village, a sari. The *panwala* (betel-nut seller), Sureshkaka's cousin, called Leriben insulting names as she stood at the bus stop. But Leriben waited quietly for the bus and went to college despite the objections of her extended family, some of whom thought she was dressed above her station while others thought she was dressed below it. As the heat of the summer increased, her father gave her permission to wear cotton "maxis" inside the house and even agreed to her having a cotton *shalwar kamiz*. But these were strictly for indoor use and she was severely chastised when an unexpected guest arrived at the house and saw her wearing cotton. Cotton was too *deshi* (local, unsophisticated); as far as Sureshkaka was concerned, it was the cloth of rough, uneducated, backward farming people.

Finally, as we have seen, Hansaben had little control over her own apparel. She too relied on the choice of her husband if new clothes were required. But she resented the limitations of the village. She wanted to dress like a city woman with her sari tied in the "Bengali style" with the end hanging down her back rather than over her front. But her in-laws argued that she would not be able to perform proper *laj* dressed in that style. Why, they asked, did she feel the need to look like a *sarawala* (well-to-do person) when she was living in a village? She also wanted to wear a bra, but her mother-in-law had forbidden it on the grounds that she would not be able to feed her baby easily. Hansa resented this for there were, as she told me, front-fastening bras available in Larabad. She did not see why Leriben, who was younger and unmarried, should be allowed to wear a bra when she, who was older and married, was forbidden to do so.

The Cardigan Reconsidered

Examination of the importance of giving and receiving clothes helps to explain the apparently extreme reactions of Sureshkaka and Hansaben to what at first glance seems like the trivial matter of a mere cardigan. Because clothes are given in the context of specific relationships and events, they embody the relationships between individuals, families and groups (cf. Cohn, 1989, Werbner, 1990) with the result that each item of clothing that a person possesses has a very specific history which becomes embedded within the garment itself. Hansa's cardigan had been made by her mother and given by her parents in her trousseau and therefore evoked a whole series of associations: parents, home and Larabad, where her life had seemed happier and freer. This accounts in part for her extremely emotional attachment to the garment and her reluctance to remove it, but it cannot fully account for her persistence in wearing it even after her father-in-law's initial objection. Before addressing this particular problem, it is worth considering exactly what Sureshkaka's objections were really about. This is difficult to assess since he refused to discuss the incident in any detail, but his wife claimed that he felt the cardigan was too modern, being a city style and one which no married woman would wear in a village. Other women, if they needed warmth, wore shawls.

The city style of Hansa's cardigan was symptomatic of Hansaben in general. She came from a well-to-do police inspector's family in Larabad city where her parents had a modern concrete house, well equipped with furniture and items of urban living. Members of Sureshkaka's family seemed at once to admire and resent this. It was in many ways what they themselves aspired to for they felt oppressed by the village and referred to "village people" as if they were something entirely different from themselves. But Sureshkaka was unable to find work in the city and therefore remained frustrated in Jalia, hoping for a way out. That the daughter-in-law was so obviously city-bred seemed to rile the household. The women of the house would often inform me that Hansaben was a *shaher wala* (city type), used to fine things, with a high-level cooker in the kitchen, a fridge and much else besides. This would be said with an air of sarcasm and jest and Hansa would deny it with a laugh, saying that things in Jalia were good too. In private, however, she confessed that she hated the village with all its restrictions. She wanted to be a school-teacher, not to cook and clean all day inside the house. She had studied to tenth grade, which was four years more than her husband. When Hansa's in-laws felt that she thought herself superior and above the village, they were in a sense right. How many of these more general household tensions were evoked by the sight of that modern city-styled cardigan it is difficult to tell, but it is at least likely that they lurked in the background, adding poignancy to the event.

Thus the clothing style and what it represented were in themselves a means of provocation, which was enhanced by the fact that Hansa's sari had not hung straight on account of her cardigan. This meant that instead of being the absent, unnoticed figure draped in the corner of the room, she was notice-able and in Sureshkaka's mind unsightly. The mere fact of being so visible was, he thought, a sign of immodesty since it attracted inappropriate attention. He had immediately accused her of lack of *sharum* even though her face was properly hidden and her back well turned. In other words Hansa in her cardigan was too modern and too visible.

This leads to the second question of why Hansaben persisted in wearing the cardigan even after Sureshkaka had made his objections clear. Her refusal to remove it was more than a case of personal attachment. It was, as she well knew, a denial of Sureshkaka's authority. By keeping her cardigan on, despite being fully veiled, she was showing her autonomy in a situation where she should have been meek and unnoticed. No one was more aware of this than Sureshkaka himself, who reacted with due fury, causing her finally to remove the garment and lapse into silence and resentment.

Hansa's actions are worth examining in more detail. Everything she did was indirect but highly effective, illustrating how even a daughter-in-law can carefully circumvent the apparently rigid system of senior male authority. If she had chosen a more confrontational approach, such as answering back to Sureshkaka or lifting her veil, this would have been viewed so badly that it is doubtful if she would ever have obtained her parents' sympathy or support. But in choosing the apparently innocent gesture of wearing a cardigan, she was in the advantageous position of appearing like an innocent victim, denied a basic right and forced to go cold. Her refusal either to eat or to speak played on the guilty conscience and ultimate helplessness of her in-laws, as did her threat of suicide which was delivered to the neighbor and to me, on the assumption that it would get back via one of us to the rest of the family. This it did and she was soon able to speak to her brother and leave the house on the pretext of her father's supposed illness. Unhappy though she was with the oppressively patriarchal environment in which she lived, Hansa was by no means the helpless victim of the incident. She was carefully manipulating events in her own subtle way.

This raises interesting questions about the role of clothes in female disputes generally. Where women are confined to the house in an essentially male-dominated culture, control of their own bodies – whether through starving, becoming mute, withdrawing sexual favors or dressing in a provocative way – becomes one of the few means by which they can assert their wishes, sorrows and desires. As actors, inventive women can even find means of reworking the very institutions that stand against them. For example, their own dependence on their men for jewelry and clothes can be exploited by women who try to bribe their husbands into providing such adornment. Similarly the restrictive custom of *laj*, in which a woman is expected to withdraw herself from view, can be used at times when a woman is expected to be on display but does not wish to be seen. Although the veil conceals women, it does not deprive them of a means of expression (Sharma, 1978). It can be drawn out of defiance and flirtation as much as modesty. This was beautifully illustrated by a popular song performed in a local drama in a neighboring village. It depicted a desperate man with two wives who were denying him access to their bodies unless he gave them each the most expensive gold necklace available in the city. He was trying to approach them with offers of mere bangles and earrings, but they swiveled away from him every time, both flirting and taking refuge under their veils, swearing that they would never come out until their wish for the necklaces was fulfilled. Finally the man, exasperated by these two shrouded women, was forced to agree to the purchases.

Despite the numerous prescriptions and restrictions concerning how a woman should dress, it is clear that some women do not blindly follow the expectations of their seniors and, like Hansaben, are prepared to put up a challenge. Similarly, some women in central India siphon off money in their conjugal homes and then purchase jewelry which they later pretend has been given to them by their parents (Jacobson, 1976). Using such indirect methods, they can accumulate new apparel without their in-laws' approval or consent. In Hindi movies clothing often arises as a subversive issue for women, as for example when an urban girl defiantly appears in jeans instead of a sari when her undesirable prospective husband pays her a visit. Just as Gandhi had used clothes in the colonial and nationalist context to challenge British authority (Tarlo 1996), so Hansaben in the confinement of the domestic context was asserting at least a little independence by rebelling through the apparently innocent medium of dress.

Notes

1. Place names have been disguised in the interest of preserving the anonymity of the people whose clothing disputes are described in this extract. In 1988–9 I spent time and conducted fieldwork in this village.

2. *ardhi laj*: This translates literally as "half shame" and refers to the practice of screening the head and face as opposed to *akhi laj* ("whole shame") in which the entire body is obscured by cloth.

3. Although the *shalwar kamiz* worn with a *dupatta* (large scarf) is considered the standard dress of both Hindus and Muslims in some parts of northern India, in rural Gujarat it is worn mainly by Muslim women and is considered a form of Muslim dress. Rural Hindu women dress either in saris or in one of the many older regional styles of embroidered skirt, backless bodice and veil cloth. (For further details cf. Tarlo 1996.) However the *shalwar kamiz* has become popular among students and educated young women in urban areas throughout north India, including Gujarat. By wearing a *shalwar kamiz* when she went to high school in the local city of Larabad, Sureshkaka's daughter was following urban fashion to the disgruntlement of her village relatives.

4. This is reference to the Vaghri community which is held in low repute by most Gujaratis.

5. A prominent agricultural caste in Gujarat.

References

Chaudhuri, N. (1976). *Culture in the vanity bag*. Bombay: Jaico.

Cohn, B. (1989). Cloth, clothes and colonialism: India in the nineteenth century. In A. Weiner and J. Schneider, (Eds.) *Cloth and human experience*. Washington: Smithsonian Institution Press.

Evans-Pritchard, E. (1967). *The Nuer*. Oxford: Clarendon Press.

Gold-Grodzins, A. (1988). *Fruitful journeys: The ways of Rajasthani pilgrims*. Berkeley: University of California Press.

Goody, J. and S. J. Tambiah (1973). *Bridewealth and dowry*. Cambridge: Cambridge University Press.

Jacobsen, D.(1976). Women and jewelry in rural India. In G. R. Gupta (Ed.), *Family and social change in modern India*. Dehli: Vikas.

Sharma, U. (1978). Women and their affines: The veil as a symbol of separation. *Man*, 13, pp. 218–33.

Sharma, U. (1984). Dowry in India and its consequences for women. In R. Hirschon, *Women and property, women as property*. London: Croom Helm.

Vatuk, S. (1975). Gifts and affines in north India. *Contributions to Indian Sociology*, vol. 9, no. 2, pp. 155-96.

Werbner, P. (1990). Economic rationality and hierarchical gift economies: Value and ranking among British Pakistanis, *Man*, 25(2), pp. 266–86.

10

Veiling and Unveiling: Reconstructing Malay Female Identity in Singapore

Joseph Stimpfl

In the last two decades, Malay women in Singapore and Malaysia, like women in many societies throughout the world, have faced challenges to their traditional roles and identities. These challenges have required a number of adjustments in relationships and, in many cases, a redefinition of identity. Such changes are clearly reflected in patterns of dress. This chapter deals with young educated Malay women in Singapore and their interpretation of Muslim women's veiling practices as articulated in Malay cultural forms.

In interviews with a dozen Malay university students and professional women from Singapore, I identified an emerging identity reflected in dress patterns that appear to be an adaptation of traditional forms to modern demands. The result seems to be a version of Islamic feminism based upon the variety of roles for a modern urban woman.

Malays in Singapore

Malays are a Muslim people indigenous to Southeast Asia who have a tradition of subsistence based on farming and fishing. Malay residence is traditionally in a village (*kampung*). Malay villages are usually structured around the practice of Islam expressed through local custom (*adat*). Each village has a common prayer site (*surau* or *mesjid*) and is hierarchical in structure with a village headman (*ketua*). Traditional behavior offers respect to a political hierarchy outside the *kampung* but resists outside interference in local affairs.

Malay culture emphasizes social obligation, most dramatically in the form of participation in formal occasions such as marriage and religious activities, in particular religious holidays. Participation in village and community rituals, inevitably associated with Islam, is seen as an absolute obligation. Family ties are important and carry certain expectations of support; however, community membership and cooperation, particularly at the village level, are absolutely necessary for the individual to maintain standing in the community and thus preserve Malay identity.

Women have clearly defined roles in these activities and have established broad community relations within the village based upon age and kinship. The frequent incidence of daily prayer also allows women to maintain close communication with each other through attendance at public prayers which are segregated by gender and traditional women's activities such as marketing. In things such as the preparation of food for religious celebrations (*kenduri*), specific duties are ritually defined (Firth, 1966). Women's roles are situated in village contexts with clear responsibilities absolutely demarcated from those of men. The social activities of both males and females are largely demarcated by gender. In a traditional household, women's responsibilities are mostly domestic while men's are mostly public (Strange, 1981; Karim, 1992). It would be a mistake to assume that women are without power and influence (Raybeck, 1974).

The traditional village pattern has been adjusted by the realities of modern Singapore. The majority of Malays in Singapore have been resettled in public housing estates mainly composed of high-rise apartments where limits on the number of Malays in a given building are strictly regulated. Resettlement from traditional Malay housing in Singapore has been random, with no attempt to maintain the integrity of former residence groups. Malays are widely dispersed in public housing dominated by Chinese. Yet, even though Malays have been displaced from the *kampung*, they have attempted to adapt a community social structure based on the rural village. This preservation of village structure is usually tied to the area mosque and its various associations. Participation in traditional Malay social activities remains an important and integral part of daily life.

Malays feel they must make tremendous adjustments to be active participants in the economic and political structure of Singapore. "The widespread and deeply held belief among Malays in Singapore is that their problems and disadvantages have been imposed on them on a racial basis by the Chinese majority" (Li, 1989, p. 179). Many Malays feel that conceding to the urban state that is Singapore constitutes embracing Chinese culture and abandoning traditional Malay culture.

As a result, Malays are especially resistant to the loss of traditional cultural forms. In the past, authors cited Malay resistance to change as a reason for the failure of economic growth and development among Malays, particularly those in Malaysia (Wilkinson, 1957; Swift, 1965; Parkinson, 1967). Certainly the reproduction of village culture in an urban environment is a necessary adaptation to preserve identity. Many Chinese view Malays as lazy and unproductive social outsiders who are uninterested in Singapore's achievement orientation (Clammer, 1985). Malays appear mostly immune to this disdain.

> Malays tend in Singapore to have a less rigid system of social classification . . . than the other groups and are thus less influenced by pressures to become assimilated to the urban, industrialized, time conscious and competitive world of many Singaporeans. They are thus more marginal to the mainstream ideology than any other group . . . and that, at the margins of the mainstream society, people express their marginality by, amongst other things, the slackening of physical control, made manifest by longer hair and a more unkept appearance than the average citizen. (Clammer, 1985, pp. 25–6).

Resistance to the state culture of Singapore (because of its perceived Chinese character) is exacerbated by traditional tensions in the Malay community. Since the advent of the British colonial administration, there has been tension between central administration, usually under the auspices of the king or sultan and local leaders who adhere to traditional custom that includes a localized form of Islam. In recent times, this tension has extended to include centralized or state-sponsored Islam and cultural individualism. This is very apparent in intra-Malay relations in Singapore. Singapore Malays feel pressure not only to conform to behavioral patterns prescribed by the secular government but to those norms identified as "proper behavior" by the governmentally sanctioned Islamic central authority in Singapore that administers the Syariah or Islamic court and hands down Islamic dogmatic guidelines (*fatwa*). In discussions with me, several prominent Islamic figures in Singapore cited that this tension is a major problem among Malays even in the relatively small confines of Singapore.

Malay Women and Dress

The *kampung*, like many villages in subsistence societies, assumes the role of an extended family. Relations are formally prescribed between women and men according to real and fictive kinship frames of reference (Banks, 1983). Dress for women is situational and reflects relationships and contexts. Female children have a great deal of leeway in the forms of dress for play and interaction in the village. Children generally move easily between households with the assumption of kin relationships. As little girls grow older, particularly with the approach of menses, there is a higher expectation of modesty (*kesopanan*). This idea of purity or modesty is also associated with the observance of proper behavior and the adherence to a code of moderation (*sederhana*). Women are expected to be shy and reserved (*malu*) (Stivens, 1996). An ideal Malay woman is modest, retiring and compliant (Laderman, 1996).

Yet although the concepts may appear simple, there can be quite a bit of complexity to the everyday reality of dress and behavior. Whereas older traditional dress (*sarung kebaya*, Figure 10.1) is modestly conceived, it leaves a great deal of room for sexual expression. The *kebaya* or blouse may be diaphanous to near-transparent. It may also be pleated significantly above and below the bodice. The *sarung* is a skirt hemmed into a cylindrical shape that is stepped into, folded right to left and tucked into the waist. While normally worn with a blouse or pull-over top, it can be worn by itself. This is commonly done for sleeping or bathing. The *sarung* can be worn to accentuate the body. The final piece associated with traditional dress is a head scarf (*selendang*) which, although it can serve as a veil, can also be worn in a number of ways, e.g. draped over the shoulders, around the neck or loosely over the head. This all reflects a juxtaposition of the religious and the sexual. A head scarf is to cover a woman's

Figure 10.1 Woman in a traditional *selendang* and *sarung* with *baju kebaya*. She has been shopping in the market.

hair, considered to be an erotic feature, but it could also be used as a means of flirtation (Ong, 1995).

The public and private in the *kampung* are closely juxtaposed. It would not be uncommon for males and females (males also wear *sarung*) to catch glimpses of each other while bathing (village bathing is often done using a bucket at a well situated behind a residence). Males may also catch glimpses of females in homes where they are more informally attired since village residences are traditionally quite open in construction to provide for liberal flow of air in the humid tropical climate. Discreet flirtation is commonplace (Karim, 1992).

On the other hand, females are very careful to conform to public forms of dress in the market or the mosque or various celebrations in the village. The more accepted contemporary form of public village dress is the *kain tudung*. Commonly, this consists of matching a long-sleeved tunic and floor-length skirt (*baju kurung*, Figure 10.2), accompanied by a head scarf (*anak tudung*). It is not uncommon for women to mix and match long skirts and a variety

Figure 10.2 Mother wearing a full *baju kurung* with a *tudung*. She has come to fetch her children from religious instruction at the mosque.

of tunics, even substituting short-sleeved blouses or tee-shirts (Figure 10.3). The *baju kurung* is often made from very colorful cloth which may also be patterned. In recent times, the *sarung kebaya* has fallen into disrepute as a public garment and been replaced by the more moderate clothing, although sometimes one will catch a glimpse of an older woman so attired in public. The *sarung* itself, however, continues to be a staple of the *kampung*.

With the advent of better international travel and communication during the last 50 years, worldwide Islamic interaction has increased. The first result has often been a tension between the local customary law (*adat*) and centralized religion (*agama*). This tension is often articulated in changes in dress, most particularly among women. For those women who have acknowledged the non-Islamic aspects of local culture (central religious authorities have always claimed that localized Islam is strongly and improperly influenced by animism), there is often an attempt to change patterns of dress. In place of brightly colored *baju kurung* and head scarf, they may wear a much more unshaped gown of a more

Figure 10.3 Young woman in front of her home in the *kampung* wearing an informal combination of *baju kurung* blouse, *sarung* and *tudung*.

subdued color, with a more effusive head covering similar to a wimple (*mini telekung*, Figure 10.4). In some cases the head covering extends all the way to the floor (*telekung*). The mini telekung would be worn with a baju kurung, often in plain dark colors. In some cases, Arabic dress patterns were used, either long flowing robes (*hijab*) or even a full-body covering (*jubah*).

The spread of the popularity of the *mini telekung* is closely related to the rise of the Islamic revivalism known as the *dakwa* movement (see Nagata, 1984). A fundamental concept of veiling in *dakwa* is the principle that women represent passion (*nafsu*) and men reason (*akal*). Although men and women have both characteristics women are predisposed to passion and evoke eroticism (see Peletz, 1996). A man must struggle to maintain reason and control women's eroticism. Women's dress can cause the ascendancy of passion over reason. Because of this, women must dress carefully and de-emphasize their erotic potential.

Figure 10.4 Older woman returning home from the market. She is wearing a *selendang* and *sarung* with a *baju kurung*.

The movement was very popular among women at Malaysian universities (Karim, 1992; Ong, 1995). Veiling in the new and conservative sense is mostly centered among highly-educated women who are career-oriented and articulate about their religious world view and lifestyle (Nagata,1995). Nagata describes the rise of religious conservatism among university-educated women and its accompanying dress characteristics as a way to resolve two cultural hegemonies. On one hand is the "Western technocratic educational and professional culture" and on the other hand is the "domestic ideal grounded in a larger sacred tradition with ethnic (Malay) and religious charters of legitimacy" (1995, p. 115). Ong believes that veiling relates to controlling women's bodily and social movements. It reflects the "nationwide struggles over a crisis of cultural identity, development, class formation and the changing kinds of imagined communities" (1995, p. 187).

The dress style is regarded by many Malays as an urban affectation. Nagata points out it's as much a class issue as a gender one. Such clothing has become associated with highly educated women and thus becomes a status marker. "An elder woman explained that her granddaughter, clothed in *mini-telekung* and *hijab*, was dressed in the way of an educated woman" (Ong, 1995, p. 180). But veiling remains situational (Karim, 1992). Most villagers consider the clothing inappropriate for the *kampung*. It is often abandoned by students when they return to a village environment (Nagata, 1995).

There may be more than simple questions of status or religious peer pressure. Brenner (1996), in studying veiling (*jilbab*) associated with the "Islamic resurgence" in Indonesia among young educated women, found it had more to do with personal and religious awareness (*kesadaran*) than status or social change. This awareness is not just knowledge but rather a "new subjectivity" in which a woman "believes that she is ultimately responsible for her own actions" (p. 684). Although the movement draws its strength from the broader Islamic movement, women who choose *jilbab* "view it as a self-conscious move toward personal and social change" (p. 682). The purpose of awareness is the "construction of a new society" (p. 685). It is not simply accepting the hegemony of male authority or even acknowledging the influence of Middle Eastern Islam. "By wearing *jilbab*, a young woman declares a certain self-mastery, even if she is, in the end, submitting herself to the greater authority of God and Islam" (p. 686). The practice of veiling provides women with "a sense of identity, self-mastery and purpose" (p. 691).

Dress Adaptation in Singapore

The dichotomy between public and private dress so obvious in the *kampung* becomes quite complex in an urban environment. Although custom may be similar in Singapore and Malaysia (many Singapore Malays have relatives in Malaysia), the circumstances of customary dress are quite different. The *syariah* court in Malaysia holds a great deal of influence over the day-to-day lives of Malays. In Singapore, a Malay may choose to disregard Islam even to the point of marrying only in a secular venue, publicly failing to practice Islam or even converting to another religion. This would not be possible in Malaysia.

> I am from Malaysia. I was born and raised in the *kampung*. When I go there I can dress very informally. This is not possible in Kuala Lumpur [capital of Malaysia]. I must be very careful what I wear in public there. But in Singapore I can wear quite western dress in public if I want. It is more free [*bebas*] there, like the *kampung* (Malay professional woman).

It is important not to gloss this comment superficially. The term *bebas* is a common and important one. It does not mean freedom in a political sense and it is probable that Singapore Malays would say just the opposite. What it means to a Malay is the ability to act more informally and to participate actively in social activities. It is to be relaxed and at home in the community. It is also an expression that acknowledges control of your life.

Bebas for women is a new concept and men are often concerned with its ramifications. This is particularly true of the recent phenomenon of female factory workers (Ong, 1987). It has become a "romantic" alternative to village life and has resulted in an erosion of the control of women (Stivens, 1996). Freedom (*kebebaskan*) has resulted in new patterns of dress and behavior (Ong, 1987; Karim, 1992). Women who comfortably enter the public (male) realm provide a threat to the status quo (Ong, 1990).

Freedom is clearly an important principle for educated women in Singapore. They have learned that they have choices and like the idea. This particularly applies to dress. All the women interviewed agreed that dress in Singapore was a function of the situation.

> My mother is from a *kampung* in Johor. My grandmother too. She used to wear a *kebaya* in the village. In Singapore, my mother wears a *baju kurung*. I was raised in Singapore. I sometimes wear western dress or traditional Malay clothes. It depends upon where I am or where I am going (university student).

The heavily populated urban environment in which Malays are in the minority and most women follow western fashions affords Malay women greater flexibility in dress. Given the wide variety of tourists and Asians living in Singapore, a Malay woman in western dress is little noticed. In fact, as was pointed out to me by several informants, women in Malay dress would be conspicuous in many of the shopping areas in the city.

> I used to go to "tea dances" when I was in secondary school. You know, those places where Malay teenagers go in the afternoon to listen to music and meet other Malays. Of course we couldn't wear *baju kurung* or anything like that. We had to dress western (university student).

Several of the Malay women who were attending or had attended the university in Singapore had changed their dress habits as a result of the university experience.

> Most of us come from close families. We haven't spent much time even in other parts of the city. The university is a new experience. We become very conscious of being Malay. It is important that other students recognize us as Malays (former university student).

Family and extended family are very important. There are many more Malay women than men in post-secondary education in Singapore. One important attribute of university women is a feeling of solidarity or even a form of fictive kinship (*kaum*) which is commonplace in Malay schooling situations (Karim, 1992).

Although the dress adopted at the university might appear to be conservative and religious in nature, this would be an oversimplification of the situation. Ong (1990) found that university women in Malaysia conformed to a hybrid religious dress code because of a complex system of intimidation and persuasion. This is not the case in Singapore. Although many women adopt a new type of head covering it appears an expression of solidarity and support rather than one of coercion. Educated women seem to be creating a new identity that acknowledges a new status and new set of responsibilities.

> For me wearing a *tudung* changes your life. But I don't criticize others for not doing it. As long as you do what is right, it is O.K. It is between you and God. It is not up to others but only a matter to each one of us. We can help each other but each of us must answer to God alone.

The concerns of these women are not necessarily religious in nature but oriented toward protection of an achieved status: Malay women who have navigated their way through the competitive educational system of Singapore and been accepted at the university. All the women were very conscious of this responsibility and wanted foremost to be recognized as Malays.

> It is not easy for a Malay to get into university in Singapore. We are a minority in the city and an even smaller minority in the university. I think it makes us more responsible for the way others feel about Malays, particularly the Chinese.

Veiling does not necessarily mean heightened religious awareness or a rejection of the secular. In several cases I observed, what initially appeared to be conservative head coverings turned out to be expensive silk scarves (Liz Claiborne, Ralph Lauren, Anne Klein) folded in unique ways that resembled the *mini-telekung*. In fact, women would often wear this complex head covering with non-Malay clothes such as fashionable jeans, pants and shirts. It is also important to note that not all Malay women wore head coverings at the university.

In every interview I was struck by the concern of the women not only to be properly attired but also fashionably attired. Women did not only concern themselves with Western designs and trends. They also reminded me that there are several women's magazines produced in Singapore and Malaysia (*Jelita*, *Wanita*, *Perempuan*) that catered to middle-class Malay women and contained substantial sections on Malay fashion. There was no one fashion, no one form of dress and no one way to act.

My assumption that veiled women in Singapore are religious conservatives who do not have normal concerns with socio-economic status was much mistaken. Women who attend the religious schools in Singapore and Malaysia are very different from university women. University-educated Malay women knew Paris fashions. They were familiar with popular music (favorites included Metallica and Bon Jovi). They followed movies and movie stars. In fact, they were much like their Chinese classmates except by virtue of dress and association.

I do not mean to make light of this difference. It is a considerable gap. Malay women understand that being (and acting) Malay is an important part of their identity. They understand that Islam and Islamic belief are a considerable part of being Malay. Tradition and family responsibility were not to be ignored. And yet, at the same time, they are finding that in common association they are discovering a new and vitally important Malay female identity: one that is completely within their control to define and develop.

We Malays believe in the will of God and the fate that God assigns to each of us (*rezeki*). We do not want to be too ambitious or greedy about our future. But coming to the university changes you and makes you see things you didn't see before. Possibilities. My father is a driver for a company. My brother works in a hotel as a bellboy. I can be a lawyer. Things change. If God wills it I will do something no one in my family has done before.

Singapore Malays very clearly distinguish between themselves and other Malays. They accept the achievement orientation that is clearly part of Singaporean culture. University-educated women believe that Malay achievement and a change in the perception of Malays by non-Malays is dependent upon them. They also believe that this new Malay identity is an opportunity for women, one that has not been possible before. They look to each other for support and assistance in defining this identity: one that includes a level of freedom not available to their mothers and grandmothers.

Conclusion

Malay women in Singapore who adopt the hybrid form of veiling practiced in Singapore universities are not necessarily bearing a burden of honor, acknowledging shame over their erotic natures or conceding the hegemony of men over women. Rather, veiling can be, as Fadwa El Guindi (1999) points out, an expression of liberation and a symbol of resistance that works to demarginalize women. In Singapore, adopting non-traditional dress with religious overtones is an expression of new status. It reflects an expanded self-awareness and indicates that the wearer is free of traditional constraints while at the same time rejecting the intrusion of western values and practices so prominent in that city state. It is not ideological in nature as some authors surmise, but rather the articulation of a new identity. Women who adopt the veil are expressing a hybrid feminism that celebrates the solidarity of educated Muslim women who recognize their new power and status, but also their responsibility to become key actors in social change.

The practice of Islam has no inherent religious principle that marginalizes women. Rather it celebrates the importance of women and their equal responsibility with men. Muslim women have never been powerless. Furthermore, there is no conflict between the basic teachings of Islam and social change (Al-Lail, 1996). The idea that feminism would be rejected out of hand by Islamic teaching is absurd. However, feminism for Muslims would be unique and idiosyncratic. It would not mirror western forms of feminism and certainly would draw heavily on Islamic teachings.

Regardless of the origins or influences of the hybrid form of veiling that one finds among university-educated Malay women in Singapore, it now represents a new identity that is available to women who in the past were relegated to the domestic and the shared experience of other women. Singapore Malay women are now both domestic and public, modern and traditional, religious and revolutionary, feminist and Muslim. Nagata and Ong are insightful and precise in their observations of the phenomenon of veiling but have failed to recognize that Muslim women are in the grip of radical change that reflects a new self-empowerment. It is not a retreat from modernity (Nagata, 1995) or a concession to the control of men (Ong, 1990). Karim was correct when she pointed out that veiling is a rejection of Westernization in favor of a mix of *adat* and Islam in a "bold display of self-identity." As a result, women become the symbols of "self-containment and self-definition" (Karim, 1992, p. 231). It promises new freedoms and new control that is as yet undefined.

References

Al-Lail, H. R. J. (1996). Muslim women between tradition and modernity: The Islamic perspective. *Journal of Muslim Minority Affairs.*16: 1, 99–110.

Banks, D. J. (1983). *Malay kinship.* Philadelphia: Institute for the Study of Human Issues.

Brenner, S. (1996). Reconstructing self and society: Javanese Muslim women and the veil. *American Ethnologist, 23:* 4, 673–97.

Clammer, J. (1985). *Singapore: Ideology, society and culture.* Singapore: Chopmen Publishers.

El Guindi, F. (1999). *Veil: Modesty, privacy and resistance.* Oxford: Berg Publishers.

Firth, R. (1966). *Housekeeping among Malay peasants.* New York: Humanities Press.

Karim, W. J. (1992). *Women and culture: Between Malay Adat and Islam.* Boulder: Westview Press.

Laderman, C. C. (1996). Putting Malay women in their place. In P. Van Esterik (Ed.), *Women of Southeast Asia.* (pp. 62–77). DeKalb: Northern Illinois University Press.

Li, T. (1989). *Malays in Singapore: Culture, economy and ideology.* Singapore: Oxford University Press.

Nagata, J. (1984). *The reflowering of Malaysian Islam: Modern religion radicals and their roots.* Vancouver: University of British Columbia Press.

Nagata, J. (1995). Modern Malay women and the message of the veil. In W. J. Karim (Ed.), *'Male' and 'Female' in developing Southeast Asia* (pp. 101–20). Oxford: Berg Publishers.

Ong, A. (1987). *Spirits of resistance and capitalist discipline: Factory women in Malaysia.* Albany: State University of New York Press.

Ong, A. (1990). State versus Islam: Malay families, women's bodies and the body politic in Malaysia. *American Ethnologist, 17:* 2, 258–76.

Ong, A. (1995). State versus Islam: Malay families, women's bodies and the body politic in Malaysia. In A. Ong and M. G. Peletz (Eds.), *Bewitching women, pious men: Gender and body politics in Southeast Asia* (pp. 159–94). Berkeley: University of California Press.

Parkinson, B. K. (1967). Non-economic factors in retardation of the rural Malays. *Modern Asian Studies,*1: 1, January.

Peletz, M. G. (1996). *Reason and passion: Representations of gender in a Malay society.* Berkeley: University of California Press.

Raybeck, D. A. (1974). Social stress and social structure in Kelantan village life. In W. R. Roff (Ed.), Kelantan: Religion, society and politics in a Malay state (pp. 225–42). Kuala Lumpur: Oxford University Press.

Stivens, M. (1996). *Matriliny and modernity: Sexual politics and social change in rural Malaysia*. St. Leonards, Australia: Allen & Unwin.

Strange, H. (1981). *Rural Malay women in tradition and transition*. New York: Praeger.

Swift, M. G. (1965). *Malay peasant society in Jelebu*. New York: Athlone Press.

Wilkinson, R. J. (1957). Malay customs and beliefs. *Journal of the Royal Asiatic Society, Malayan Branch*, 30: 4.

11

Continuation and Change in Tenganan Pegeringsingan, Bali

L. Kaye Crippen and Patricia M. Mulready

Cultural change coexists with tradition in Tenganan Pegeringsingan, Bali, an area long known for technically complex textiles which are used to create subtly elegant ceremonial ritual dress. A description of change in ceremonial ritual dress and in the production of traditional resist-dyed *geringsing* textiles, an integral part of Balinese ceremonial ritual dress, is presented in this chapter. Ceremonial ritual dress refers to the broad spectrum of textiles and other ornamentation used to create ritual dress for the religious practices and ceremonies found in Tenganan Pegeringsingan, Bali.

Fieldwork in this village was conducted from 1985 to 1999. Most scholarly field research on the village, in relation to textiles and dress, occurred before 1985 at which time ceremonial dress was becoming institutionalized with few or no changes. Many scholars studying the village did not predict the revival of *geringsing* production or changes in ceremonial dress that has taken place and accelerated since 1985, particularly during 1995-1999. The focus of this chapter is on continuation and change in ceremonial dress and *geringsing* textiles in Tenganan Pegeringsingan. This study focuses on the key changes observed in the use of *geringsing* textiles by unmarried adults and the additions and changes to the ceremonial ensembles during 1985-1999. In addition, key reasons for change are discussed.

Increased tourism and other Western and nation-building influences usually cause traditional dress to be codified into national or regional dress. When this happens, dress style remains static and few changes are allowed (Gellner, 1987). Simultaneously, introduction of a monetary economy necessitates changes in income production; often this causes youth to leave the village in search of employment. In Tenganan Pegeringsingan, most people live in the village except during their youth when they attend school outside the village.

The major festival in Tenganan is the *Usaba Samba*, which starts during the fifth month according to their calendar (which is different from Balinese, Javanese and Gregorian calendars). It lasts about a month and features numerous ceremonies with prescribed ceremonial dress. The festival reaches its zenith with the *mekaré*, a two-day mock battle among unmarried men. During this event, there are other ceremonies in the temple, in meeting places for the women's and men's clubs and in homes where feasts are served. This study examines ceremonial ritual dress during these two days during the fifteen-year period 1984–1999.

Methodology

Crippen conducted this investigation from 1985 to 1999; she attended the key days of the fifth month ceremony almost every year. She used triangulated methods for data collection, including a review of the written literature, oral history, in-depth interviews, participant and pictorial observation of religious and cultural ceremonies, review of pictorial documentation and case studies.

Historic records served as an initial source of comparison. Korn's (1933) early photographs and descriptions of ceremonial dress allowed comparison of early ceremonial dress with that of today. Other historical photographs were also used (Buhler *et al.*, 1975; Gittinger, 1979).

In-depth interviews provided insight to the current production of traditional double *ikat* textiles. Notes were made during the ceremonies and expanded immediately. The long period of research observation allowed for verification of information. Since most villagers speak Balinese in their homes, this research was greatly aided by the assistance of a translator, I. Komang Sumanta, a member of a weaving family from the village.

Observation was a key factor to verification of changes in process – some weavers were more traditional than others. For example, some informants said the production process had changed in that the first color step where the candlenut oil is applied to the yarns was no longer aged about six months. However, visual observation of storage of this yarn with ashes on it (lye, which allows for a better red because the oil is a mordant) contradicted these assertions in at least some cases.

Photographs taken by Crippen at major ceremonies were later examined to verify impressions and to seek additional information. There were hundreds of persons at ceremonies such as the *Usaba Samba*, which makes it difficult to directly observe all changes in dress. For example, in 1999, platform sandals were seen for the first and only time in ceremonies – but not seen outside ceremonies – from pictorial analysis rather than first-hand observation. The photographic analysis also allowed for verification of when and where certain dress items were worn, i.e. in the temple or village.

Cultural Background

Tenganan Villages and Religion

The small, ancient *Bali Aga* villages of Tenganan Pegeringsingan and Tenganan Dau Tukad, on the eastern coast of Bali, are where double *ikat* textiles called *geringsing* are produced. (See below at page 186 for a description of how single and double *ikat* textiles are made.) This area is the only Indonesian site, one of three countries worldwide, where these extremely difficult-to-make textiles are produced. This study focuses only on Tenganan Pegeringsingan, which has a population of several hundred.

The origins of the *Bali Aga* or *Bali Mula* peoples are obscure (Hobart *et al.*, 1986). The *Usana Bali*, the *Bali Aga* peoples' sacred chronicles of Bali, is a book of myth and history which indicates they lived in Eastern Bali by the tenth century (Ramseyer, 1983). The village of Tenganan Pegeringsingan is known to pre-date the flight of Javanese Hindus into Bali in the sixteenth century, which resulted from the dominance of Islam in Java.

In Indonesia, all persons must belong to one of five official religions. Thus, while the religion in Tenganan Pegeringsingan is officially classified as Hindu, villagers refer to their religion as Hindu Indra (Indrah). Their religious beliefs, practices and ceremonies derive from the *Usana Bali* and village traditions and differ from those of the Hindu majority of Bali. For example, there is no caste system in the village, nor do they cremate the dead or perform tooth-filing ceremonies that are done by other Balinese Hindus.

The Chosen People – Beliefs, Ritual Ceremonies and Textiles

Mystical powers and the spirit world are interwoven in Tenganan Pegeringsingan. The village-creation and weaving mythology indicates that the God Indra was responsible for the creation of the village as well as for teaching the complex art of making double *ikat* textiles. The villagers are the "chosen people," whose main responsibilities are to participate in a large number of religious and ceremonial days in order to keep the village pure and safe. The Gods are welcomed to the village during many of the ceremonies. The village priest determines the ceremonial days. (There are 79 in the year 2000.) Other family and outside community ceremonies are in addition to the official ceremonial days.

Wearing prescribed protective ceremonial dress suitable for age, gender, marital and social status are very visible elements of the rituals. Two key textile types are used for ceremonies, the *geringsing* and the *gotia*, both of which are made from handspun yarns. The *geringsing* textiles are said to have magical or protective properties; the name *geringsing* means illness- averting. Many old *geringsing* cloths have a small section cut out that was used for curative purposes. Uncut *geringsing* cloths are offered to the gods on certain occasions. People wear clothing from textiles whose warp yarns have been cut after weaving.

Ceremonial textiles and dress are worn to honor the presence of the gods, to protect the villagers while performing potent ceremonies and to assist in keeping the village pure. They also can denote membership in the village and identify age, sex, marital and village status. For example, women prepare refreshments for visitors on the raised platform called a *balé*. Marriage status is shown by the way the women wear the ceremonial ceremonial ritual dress.[1] All women, including most guests, should wear a breast wrapper with their shoulders uncovered. Men on the *balé* keep their chests bare.

Geringsing textiles worn in village ceremonies denote membership in the village. Villagers and knowledgeable viewers would also judge the overall quality of the textiles by the execution of the *ikatting* and weaving to give sharp clear motifs, the sheerness of the cloth, color depth, motif and age of *geringsing*. Old, high-quality complex pieces transmit the most status. New *geringsing* textiles are also used in ceremonies today.

In this very traditional community there are many ceremonies to learn and participate in and many rules that must be followed because of their importance to the well-being of the village. Youth learn about rituals and the use of traditional sacred dress by participating in ceremonies from an early age when they become members of one of six youth groups for boys and girls (three each for boys and girls); these are supervised by a village elder of the same sex.

Production and Marketing of *Geringsing* Textiles

The production of *geringsing* textiles is central to achieving the traditional ceremonial dress. Various sizes of textiles are folded, draped and pinned to achieve ritual dress. Double *ikats* are complex to make since both the warp and weft yarns are *ikatted*. This requires tying off yarn sections to resist the color penetration of each dyebath before weaving occurs. The resulting colors in both the warp and weft should be well-aligned to show a clear pattern. This cloth is much more difficult to make than a single *ikat*. Numerous *geringsing* patterns have been documented (Buhler *et al.*, 1975), including both rectilinear and curvilinear motifs (the latter being more complex to produce). Motifs used in Tenganan Pegeringsingan include geometric florals, architectural and temple elements, figures such as priests and worshipers, *mandelas* and star-like representations with cosmic connotations. No new motifs have been developed for ceremonial ritual dress since written records started, although there has been one recently developed exclusively for the tourist trade.

The *geringsing* weavers continue to use the traditional production methods of back strap looms for weaving and three natural dye materials to create color (Buhler, 1959; Crippen & Mulready, 1994). The taboo of using indigo dye in the village remains today, thus the neighboring BugBug villagers continue to perform this process (Hauser-Schaublin *et al.*, 1991). The resulting colors, which are subtle and muted, include yellow or beige with red, red-purple and in some cases deep orange or blue-black (these latter colors were almost lost but are being revived).

The use of cotton instead of silk also contributes to a muted effect instead of the shiny, lustrous images created when silk is used in the double *ikat patola* of India. Many of these *patola* were used in Indonesia as ceremonial textiles and some think Indian textiles influenced the *geringsing*.

Traditionally, the young, unmarried women in the village learned and practiced the complex process of double *ikat* production in the girls' clubs. The multi-staged process involves preparing the yarn then tying and dyeing it, followed by weaving on the backstrap loom. In 1985, a master middle-aged weaver who had some of the young women's equipment in her home, which was their meeting place, said that the young women were no longer interested in learning the process. This was the last time weaving items were seen by Crippen in the meeting areas of the unmarried women. Today, women wanting to learn select a teacher and weave at her house.

In 1985, several women were still weaving; one was unmarried, three were elderly and the rest were middle-aged. In 1986, all of the older women had stopped production due to age. *Geringsing* production was in severe decline and many thought it was in danger of disappearing. However, as more tourists started coming and buying *geringsing* cloths, more women started weaving again and more young women started learning the technique (Crippen and Mulready, 1994).

In addition, women from neighboring Pandai Sikit are learning to produce *geringsing* textiles. Some of these women are originally from Tenganan Pegeringsingan weaving families, but broke the marriage laws and therefore reside in Pandai Sikit. This is a major change – allowing "outsiders" and "renegades" to make *geringsing* textiles which are traditionally sacred and also sold to outsiders.

Tenganan Pegeringsingan had functioned mainly on the barter system before the arrival of collectors and tourists. Prior to 1985, villagers and outside dealers sold textiles directly to museums and private collectors. In 1985, there were about five home shops selling *geringsing* textiles. Since the end of the 1980s there has been a large increase in income generated by selling items to tourists. Now most homes are also shops selling high quality art objects such as *geringsing* textiles, other textiles from all over Indonesia, *lontar* books (pictograms) and basketry items made from the same technique as the shields used in the *mekaré* (see Figure 11.1). This has given many more villagers access to hard cash and some have done very well financially (Crippen & Mulready, 1995). These new sources of cash have been used to send more of the youth to school outside the village as well as to purchase ceremonial and everyday food, clothing and consumer items.

Some families have chosen to retain their high-quality old cloths and many use them in ceremonies. These high-quality older *geringsing* are very powerful and also serve as status markers. Their possession indicates that the family had ancestors who were very good weavers, and may indicate that they have enough wealth or integrity to keep them.

Figure 11.1 Several men on left side wear *geringsing* hip wraps over a cotton batik or *endek*, while the men on the right wear the silk *rembang* with *loken* motif for the second day of the *mekaré*. Photo by Kaye Crippen.

Usaba Samba – Fifth Month Ceremony

Usaba Samba is one of the two most important groups of ceremonies in the Tenganan Pegeringsingan calendar. *Usaba Samba* lasts about a month. This study focuses on the two most important days featuring two of the most widely known *Usaba Samba* ceremonies – the *mekaré* ritual mock battle and the *rejang* temple dance.

The general purposes and meanings of the *Usaba Samba* are to invite the gods to visit the village to provide protection and to remove evil spirits. Specific meanings of many of the various sub-ceremonies have been lost for the most part; thus the actual precise performance of the rituals becomes of great importance because it is considered the right way to satisfy the gods. However, changes to the rituals, including dress, are allowed in some cases.

The villagers in Tenganan Pegeringsingan consider themselves to be the chosen people of the gods, entrusted by them to maintain purity, goodness and protection. They have been promised that so long as the villagers perform the rituals appropriately there will be an absence of evil. Ritual performers belong to "clubs," divided by sex, age, marital status and clan status. Generally, only persons with no physical or spiritual defects are allowed to participate in the ceremonies (Ramseyer, 1984). The ceremonies are performed within the boundaries of the village. Many are performed in the temple and on the temple grounds. In addition, ceremonies are performed on *balés* (raised platforms) constructed in the main street by each boys' club. These are named for the directions they face – Seaside, Middle and Mountain – and are on the main street in a straight line at three different levels, giving a terraced effect.

Mekaré – Ancient *Pandanus* Leaf War

The *mekaré*, also called the *karé-karé*, is a ritualized version of the ancient *Pandanus* Leaf War. It is performed on both of the two important days of the *Usaba Samba* by the unmarried young males using swords made of *pandanus* leaves, which are sharp and spikey and shields made of a basketry technique (see Figure 11.1). The *mekaré* is performed on the ground in front of the *balés* and begins around 2:00 p.m. On the second day the *mekaré* starts after musicians and others circumambulate the village three times.

Mekaré Ritual Mock Battle – Unmarried Young Men Prior to the 1990s

Traditionally, the young unmarried men wore a hip wrapper from a large *geringsing* cloth, often with a cotton wrapper worn underneath it. A waist wrapper was tied from a hand-woven black and white cloth with large white blocks and very fine black lines which look like stripes going in both directions.

Another smaller *geringsing* can also be worn as a waist wrapper instead of this cloth. Some men also wear *endeks*, cotton single-weft *ikats* produced elsewhere in Bali. Batiks, either handmade, stamped, or machine-produced, are also worn as lower-body coverings or hip wrappers.

Men have specified dress codes for specific ceremonies and all unmarried men must wear a *keris* (ceremonial dagger) in their sarongs while in ceremonial dress in the village. In 1985, most villagers wore some *geringsing* when participating in the *mekaré*. They wore *geringsing* as a lower-body covering and a waist wrapper. Unmarried young men generally wore complete outfits of *geringsing*.

Mekaré Ritual Mock Battle – Young Unmarried Men in the 1990s

The first hint of youthful rebellion regarding ceremonial dress noticed by Crippen was in the early 1990s when a young unmarried male wore a nose ring and chain to the *Usaba Samba* ceremonies. The last day of the fighting he did not wear it; his reason was that his mother did not like it. This small form of rebellion was one of the few that youth are permitted in this conservative culture. One of the most interesting changes observed in 1999 was the decrease in the use of *geringsing* dress by unmarried men performing the *mekaré* ritual mock battle. This year on the first day of the two days of fighting, only one man appeared with a *geringsing* around his waist.

In 1999, many more unmarried young men and women wore silk batik *rembang* cloths with the *lokan* motif.[2] They were worn in a variety of ways, such as hip wrappers by males. In Figure 11.1, the three men on the right wear the *rembang* as a hip wrapper instead of the traditional *geringsing*. The man to the left of these three men wears a *rembang* as a waist wrapper. Several men to the left wear hip wrappers of *geringsing* textiles. In this photo, the men are pouring palm wine libations on the platform before the start of the ritual mock battle on the second day of the fighting. Note they are wearing longer hip wrappers of *endek* or batik under the ceremonial textiles.

Photo-analysis showed several men wearing the large *rembang* sarong in a manner that would be considered improper in Java or Sumatra. They wore what is considered the head, the *kepala*, on the side or back; the *kepala* is generally centered in the front. In Figure 11.1, all the men on the right are wearing the *kepala* on their left hips. Other photographs showed the *kepala* in the back, so this was not an isolated event. None of the cotton batiks previously seen in Tenganan Pegeringsingan had a *kepala* section, hence they are unfamiliar with the way the Javanese wear these batiks. Previously, their batiks have been the same on both ends. Other textiles now worn as hip wrappers include inexpensive brightly-colored *batiks* with thick wax lines as found in modern Malaysian *batiks*; plain woven plaids with shiny gold Lurex threads; and high quality *songkets* (richly patterned brocaded silks, made with supplemental weft threads of gold, silver and/or brightly colored metallic threads). Clearly, the ceremonial dress for unmarried men at the *mekaré* is changing. On day two of the ritual mock battle more men appeared wearing some *geringsing* cloth.

Mekaré Ritual Mock Battle – Unmarried Young Women Prior to the 1990s

Unmarried women wear many different ceremonial ritual dress during the *Usaba Samba*. During the *mekaré*, they watch the unmarried men from the far north side of the *balé*. Prior to 1985, the unmarried women wore the complete *geringsing* ensemble on the *balé* with gold head dresses, sandals and gold jewelry such as rings, pendants, gold coins and pins. In 1985, they wore the complete *geringsing* ensemble which consisted of a *geringsing* hip wrapper, breast wrapper and long *geringsing* front panel which emanates from the bodice and hangs freely down the front of the garment. By 1985, this free hanging piece shifted from off-center to center. Photographs in Korn (1933), Ramseyer (1984), Buhler (1959) and Gittinger (1979) all showed this piece worn off-center, but we do not know when or why this change occurred. This same ensemble was worn in the temple after the *mekaré* when selected young un-married women performed the *rejang* dance. Ramseyer (1984) also mentions that he had noted some changes as early as ten or so years before; he cited the replacement of the underslips of *gotia*, hand-woven checked cloth, with machine-made cotton prints purchased in stores.

Mekaré Ritual Mock Battle – Young Unmarried Women in the 1990s

In 1998, several women departed from the traditional ritual dress while on the *balé* watching the *mekaré*. They wore breast wrappers of traditional weft *ikat* textiles with supplemental weft patterning and fringe, from the eastern Indonesian island of Sumba. This was the first time that coordination of non-traditional textiles was noticed. Since several women were wearing this style, there must have been planning and coordinating of outfits of these textiles among those available from shops around the village which sell textiles from other islands.

Rejang Dance

The *rejang* dance is performed on several occasions at various locations using a variety of ceremonial ritual dress. This discussion centers around the dance performed about 5:00 p.m. in the main temple courtyard on the second day of the *mekaré*. Young unmarried women in lines perform a brief dance of limited motion consisting of arm extensions. Worshipers in ceremonial dress take offerings into the main temple where they worship. The young unmarried women generally wore *geringsing* for the breast and hip wrapper up till the mid-1980s. They wore either *geringsing* or *songket* for the front center panel.

Slowly changes started to occur in ceremonial dress during the 1990s. In 1998 and 1999 several changes were seen in ceremonial ritual dress for the *rejang* dance in the temple. In 1998, several young unmarried women wore other types of textiles for hip wrappers. One woman wore *prada*, a gilded cloth worn by Balinese dancers as a waist wrapper. In 1999, three more women were seen wearing this style which is tightly wrapped in a spiral fashion around the waist (refer to Figures 11.2 and 11.3) as worn by some Balinese dancers.

In 1999, unmarried women who were selected to dance in the temple wore a much greater variety of dress than ever before (see Figure 11.2). In addition, they performed a new variation of the *rejang* dance with more motion. One dance movement was to extend the right hand and arm which held a long *rembang* sash worn below the waist wrapper. Thus they have added a new element to the ensemble. All women who were selected to dance had to be able to afford or borrow this silk batik. The choreographer and dance leader, who was from Pandai Sikit and thus not a villager, was in front so the women could follow along. She wore a bright orange *kebaya* (lace jacket), with a very bright orange

Figure 11.2 Temple dance by unmarried women who are wearing *geringsing* breast wraps, a variety of hip wraps including some multi-colored, supplemental weft fabrics and a new element – the long waist wrapper of silk *rembang* which serves as a dance prop. Photo by Kaye Crippen.

and green *songket* cloth as a hip wrapper. The woman in the front left (Figure 11.2) has combined a *geringsing* breast wrapper, a gold waist wrap of *prada* (gold leaf applied in a floral pattern on cotton) in the style of that used in other types of Balinese dances, and a Balinese *songket* hip wrapper and has topped it off with the long *rembang* sash. Further photo-analysis showed she was wearing platform sandals with her ensemble. She appears to be the "fashion" leader. Her *songket* was probably specially commissioned. It used at least nine different colors in motifs which appeared over the complete textile. Most *songkets* used in village ceremonies feature bright gold or silver threads.

In Figure 11.3, two young unmarried women exit from the upper part of the temple after worship. Their ensembles exhibit several changes and took considerable planning to coordinate. Although they wear the breast wrapper of *geringsing*, *sanan empeg* motif, they have made it much shorter by folding the top part over further. Generally, the women fold a small part down so that both white selvages show. These folded white selvages were also shown in photographs in Korn (1933). This was probably done so they could show more of their *prada*, gilded cloth which is worn by Balinese dancers. They added a shiny rayon Jacquard hip wrapper as worn by male musicians.

Figure 11.3 Two young women wear identical outfits as they exit the main part of the temple following worship after day two of the *mekaré* in 1999. The gold leaf *prada* cloth, used as a waist wrap, is worn by some Balinese dancers. Photo by Kaye Crippen.

Continuity and Change

There have been many changes in Tenganan Pegeringsingan since 1985. Key change agents impacting the village include 1) increased tourism; 2) increased use of money in the village; 3) better transportation; 4) availability of television in the village; 5) availability and promotion of expensive traditional textiles and inexpensive ceremonial ritual dress produced throughout Indonesia; and 6) increased numbers of young people with concurrent enhanced education and increased contact with other Balinese youth when villagers attend schools outside the village. The most significant impact has been tourism, as it stimulated a shift toward a cash-based economy while at the same time revitalizing *geringsing* production.

These change agents, including those imposed or supported by the Indonesian government and those with no apparent origin, worked synergistically to cause rapid social change in some aspects of Balinese life, including the villagers'. This chapter notes these, but focuses on the more surprising continuance and growth of traditional production of *geringsing* textiles and ceremonial dress.

Before the mid-1980s, most tourists who came to Tenganan Pegeringsingan could be described as cultural tourists who were interested in either the traditional village culture and/or the complex weaving. Articles describing this were published by Alfred Buhler (1959) and later work by Buhler *et al.*, (1975). Tourist books mentioned this village and it was the basis for numerous articles in airline publications.

The initial tourism strategy by the Balinese was to contain tourists to the southern part of the island. There was no public transportation to other parts of Bali. Transportation remained difficult and even in the 1980s one generally had to hire a car to get to the east side of the island, traveling on two-lane roads. Now there are more hotels and cars for hire so it is easier to get to the village; large tour buses also visit.

Bali continues to be the main tourist destination in Indonesia. Bali experienced dramatic growth in tourism in the 1980s and 1990s due to an increase in new, huge four- and five-star hotels and promotions by the Indonesian Ministry of Tourism. Public transportation and phone service to and within Bali has improved, facilitating the tourist industry. More tourists and journalists (including photographers) who publish articles in the international press come to Tenganan Pegeringsingan to photograph the *Usaba Samba* and other ceremonies.

The traditional cycle of ceremonies continues and the *adat* tradition is still practiced. There are no stores in the village selling tee-shirts or apparel, food or other consumer items, but more ready-to-wear and other consumer goods are available at the market in neighboring Klungkung than in the mid-1980s. There are no real shops selling consumer goods near the village and consumption of modern products is not particularly high.

The previous barter system still exists in the village. However, as more Balinese started working in the tourist industry, either directly or indirectly, they had more disposable income. In this village, many families are obtaining money from the sale of items to tourists from their home shops. The sale of textiles for money has played a dramatic role in revitalizing the production of *geringsing* textiles and other items for tourists, concurrently revitalizing it for ceremonial usage.

As can be noted in other contexts, before traditional dress becomes institutionalized there are usually slow changes; these stop when dress is worn only by a few older persons but is adopted by a culture at large to reinforce group identity (Gellner, 1987). One example of this is traditional dress in Volendam, Netherlands, which Mulready (1990) has studied since 1984. Volendam is not isolated geographically, but is culturally unique in numerous ways. Each year, millions of tourists visit Volendam to see the traditional dress and other sights. Older women still wear the traditional dress both in public and at home. The women receive a small national historic trust stipend to continue to wear it. Young people often will have the ceremonial ritual dress made for them but don't usually wear it. It is usually seen only on young people who work in the tourist industry. Any deviation from the prescribed dress can be easily recognized by a Volendamer.

The Dutch government started promoting Volendam as a tourist destination during the 1930s, to replace the declining fishing industry. The men abandoned traditional dress altogether, as they encountered ridicule when they migrated to Amsterdam in search of work. This is when Volendam's traditional dress started showing little change; by the 1950s no further changes developed.

Contrast this with Tenganan Pegeringsingan where traditional dress continues to be worn. The Indonesian government has promoted tourism, particularly in Bali, the most visited island of Indonesia. There has been a huge influx of tourists and a monetary economy has replaced much of the barter system. In the early 1980s, many scholars stopped studying textiles and dress in Tenganan Pegeringsingan because they believed it had become stagnant, that the artistic quality had declined and that the effects of modernization would cause the traditional weaving practices to eventually die out. This has not happened in Tenganan Pegeringsingan, where older people have not changed their traditional dress but young people are changing and developing new ceremonial ritual dress for their gods, ceremonies, village and families, not for tourists. This shows a dynamism not usually found under these circumstances. Modifications in everyday dress (such as sarongs) and ceremonial ceremonial ritual dress continue to take place in Tenganan Pegeringsingan at a slightly accelerating pace of change.

Why is this change so slow and limited? Huge hotels and resorts continue to be built close enough to Tenganan Pegeringsingan to bring thousands of tourists each year. Television is increasingly prevalent in the village. These and other change agents have greatly sped up the drive to modernization in other cultures where they have been introduced.

Probably the most important reason is the Tenganan Pegeringsinganers' world view of themselves as the chosen people of the gods, whose life-work is to continue the ceremonies and practices which purify and protect the village. As Ramseyer notes: "Thus it becomes understandable that costumes have evolved into an essential part of the sacred order, *adat*, on which religious ideas, ritual, law and the social system are based. Dressing according to *adat* is religiously and socially required behavior" (1984, p. 157).

Another reason is that desired change is easier to implement. Most modernization in dress has involved less restrictive ceremonial ritual dress, with greater comfort and easy care (Rosencranz, 1972; Roach & Eicher, 1965). This is obviously not the case in Bali. Most Balinese wear batik or *endek* hip wrappers or sarongs at home. The everyday sarong, with or without breast/chest covering, is probably the most comfortable garment ever made. It is perfect for the hot Balinese weather, whether rainy or dry and offers easy care.

The media have had an impact on Bali. Very few villagers had television in their homes in 1985; today many more have television. International and Indonesian television shows might expose youth and adults to current styles popular both in Jakarta and internationally. Few Balinese seem to aspire to emulate the latest Western fashions but television may have some influence on certain dress trends. Indonesian cultural performances such as dance and drama are important as changes in traditional ceremonial ritual dress seem to be influenced by the dress of other Indonesian performers.

Bali and greater Indonesia produce both traditional, handmade textiles and apparel for the domestic, tourist and international mass markets. The appearance of imported machine-produced textiles originally contributed to the decline in the production of traditional textiles in Bali. In 1980, the Balinese governor supported expansion of the traditional textile trade throughout Bali; subsequently beautiful textiles such as *songkets* became available for purchase. A new aesthetic has been created by the new combinations of motifs and patterns as well as the intensity and number of colors used when compared with previous *geringsing* ceremonial ritual dress which formerly used subtle colors. The new combination of motifs and bright colors gives a very different look.

Theoretically, one would expect greater change among young people (Rosencranz, 1972). Currently there are more unmarried young men and women than there were at the start of this research. Children have to leave their villages to go to schools past the first grades. Many live outside the village while completing secondary school. More attend universities or professional schools, including many more women, in part due to the village economics of tourism. This brings the young men and women in contact with other students and gives them a view beyond their village. They may also see ceremonies outside their village which would give them new ideas for how other Balinese dress. The youth are also marrying later, which would allow women more time to think about fashion. It is logical they would be concerned with fashion as it relates to ceremonial dress since this is the key time that women in this culture want to look their best. These and other change agents have greatly sped up the drive to modernization in other cultures where they have been introduced. In Tenganan Pegeringsingan, they seem to have just touched the surface of village life.

Conclusion

In Tenganan Pegerinsingan there are an exceptionally large number of ceremonial days requiring the use of ceremonial dress. Complex ceremonies have pre-scribed textile and dress requirements that are based mainly on the *geringsing* double *ikat* and *gotia* textiles. The *geringsing* textiles and ceremonial ritual dress are the most well-known outside the community; they also continue to be produced exclusively in Tenganan Pegerinsingan. *Geringsing* textiles can be combined to make a complete ensemble of *geringsing* which traditionally has been worn for the *mekaré* ritual mock battle and *rejang* temple dance. The textiles and therefore the ceremonial ritual dress, have protective elements, hence their importance in powerful ceremonies which invite the gods to visit and help secure prosperity for the village. This ritual dress designates member-ship in the ancient village as well as marital, sex and age status.

During the period of this research, little change was observed in ceremonial dress until the early 1990s. The most radical change was observed in 1999 for ceremonial dress of both unmarried men and unmarried women. Ceremonial dress of married adults remains unchanged; thus it was not discussed.

Geringsing textiles are a crucial, sacred part of the ceremonies, the double *ikat* techniques taught to the villagers directly from the god Indra. Thus it is critical that women in the village continue to weave them. When most of the older weavers stopped weaving in 1986 and few young women started weaving, there was concern for who would continue to weave the sacred ceremonial textiles for future generations in order to assure the purity and prosperity of the village. Today, *geringsing* textiles are more frequently combined with other high-status textiles such as the silk *rembang* or *songket* to make the complete ensemble for certain ceremonies such as the *rejang* temple dance. This change, which has developed over the very short period of fifteen years, seems to have evolved for both practical and aesthetic reasons.

Increased tourism brought increased sales of *geringsing* textiles which has helped to revive the complex weaving skills. Today, new *geringsing* textiles are produced for both ceremonial use and tourists. Revenue from sale of *geringsing* and other items to tourists has helped to fund the purchase of new high-quality ceremonial textiles.

Although today's process is not as complex as previously, it is still very labor-intensive and takes a long time (up to six years) to finish making a *geringsing* cloth. Good weavers do not appear to put less effort into making textiles for sale to tourists than into ceremonial textiles. However some lesser-quality textiles are sold to tourists that would not be used for ceremonial purposes.

Several older motifs such as the *peparé*, which have not been produced for a long time, are now being made in the village again. No new *geringsing* motifs are used for ceremonial textiles or ceremonial ritual dress; one new motif has been developed for the tourists by one weaver but is not readily available. There are more new students learning the weaving process, but in the homes of their teachers instead of the young women's clubs.

Interestingly, during a time of increased production of *geringsing* cloths in the village, this research found changes in ceremonial dress including the introduction of some new ceremonial cloths. The changes observed since 1985 may not seem to be dramatic to persons used to rapid fashion change. However, they are very dramatic in the context of a culture that has previously had very little change as verified by photographic comparisons with Korn (1933) and others.

Since the early 1990s subtle changes have started to occur, then a major break from the past in 1998 and 1999. Instead of becoming a static form of regional dress there have been changes with the introduction of new ceremonial textiles, i.e., the *rembang* and new elements such as the long *rembang* worn below the waist wrapper for the new version of the *rejang* dance in 1999.

The increase in tourism has brought more cash into the village for many families, thus they can often afford to purchase new types of beautiful textiles, such as the *rembang* and elaborate *songket*, for use in ceremonies. Such textiles as the *rembang* are more available in village textile shops or near the village than before. Others, like the *songket*, can be commissioned.

It is difficult without more research to determine why these changes are taking place. It will be interesting to continue to monitor future changes to determine whether change will continue to occur or is short-lived. Future research will include further study of written guidelines for dress in the village and in the material in *Usana Balı*, which contains some information on ceremonial costume. The scarcity of textiles will be examined as well. A shortage of textiles has occurred because they have been sold and there is an increased number of young people needing *geringsing* textiles for ceremonies. As such, the scarcity of *geringsing* may well have led to an easing of ceremonial-dress codes. In addition, more interviews will be conducted with villagers, one-on-one, to determine additional reasons for these recent changes in ceremonial garment.

Notes

1. Marriage to persons outside Tenganan Pegeringsingan is generally not allowed. However, in certain cases, males may take a wife from outside the village if the village council approves based on the woman's clan. If a woman marries outside the village she follows her husband since Hindus outside the village are patriarchal.
2. *Rembang* cloths are made of silk batik and commonly come from the North shore of Java; the most common form of *rembang* is much like a large *selendang* (shoulder cloth).

Acknowledgements

The authors would like to thank Puspita Wibisono, Public Relations Manager-Dinas Jakarta and formerly Director Museum Tekstil in Jakarta and Lembaga Ilmu Pengetahuan Indonesia (LIPI) who were the research sponsors. Kaye Crippen had a research permit from 1997-1999. I. Komang Sumanta from Tenganan Pegeringsingan served as the local guide and interpreter throughout the project. We also thank the villagers, especially the weavers.

References

Buhler, A. (1959). *Patola* influences in Southeast Asia. *Journal of Indian Textile History, 4,* 4–46.
Buhler, A., Ramseyer, U. & Ramseyer-Gygi, N. (1975/76). *Patola und geringsing: zeremonial tücher aus Indien und Indonesien.* Basel: Austellungsführer Museum für Völkerkunde.
Crippen, K. & Mulready, P. (1994). Continuation and change in *"geringsing"* double *ikat* weaving in Tenganan, Bali. *Proceedings, Indonesian and other Asian textiles: a common heritage.* Jakarta, Indonesia.

Crippen, K. & Mulready, P. (1995). Textile traditions and quality of life concerns in Southeast Asia. In H. L. Meadow, J. M. Sirgy, & D. R. Rahtz (Eds.), *Developments in quality-of-life studies in marketing, V* (pp. 26-34). DeKalb, IL: Academy of Marketing Science.

Gellner, E. (1987). *Culture, identity and politics.* Cambridge: Cambridge University Press.

Gittinger, M. (1979). *Splendid symbols: textiles and tradition in Indonesia.* Washington, D.C.: The Textile Museum.

Hauser-Schaublin, B., Nabholz-Kartaschoff, M. & Ramseyer, U. (1991). *Textiles in Bali.* Berkeley–Singapore: Periplus Editions.

Hobart, A., Ramseyer, U. & Leemann, A. (1986). *The peoples of Bali.* Oxford: Blackwell.

Korn, V. E. (1933). *De Dorpsrepubliek Tenganan Pagringsingan.* Santpoort: K.N.I.

Mulready, P. (1990). *The relationship between market economy and traditional dress in Volendam, Holland.* Paper presented at the Popular Culture Association Annual Meeting, Toronto, Canada.

Ramseyer, U. (1983). Double ikat ceremonial cloths in Tenganan Pegeringsingan. *Indonesia Circle, 30,* 17–26. London, School of Oriental and African Studies.

Ramseyer, U. (1984). *Clothing, ritual and society in Tenganan, Pegeringsingan.* Basel: Verhandlungen der Naturforschenden Gesellschaft.

Roach, M. E. & Eicher, J. (1965). *Dress, adornment and the social order.* Boston: Wiley.

Rosencranz, M. L. (1972). *Social psychological aspects of dress.* New York: Macmillan.

12

School Uniforms as a Symbolic Metaphor For Competing Ideologies in Indonesia

Linda B. Arthur

In a metaphorical sense, dress and dressing are themes relevant to a wider set of related phenomena. Nation-states dress themselves not only through uniforms, but also by way of architecture, street names, postage stamps, monuments and rituals (Nordholt, 1997).

Competing Ideologies

States have used varied forms of material culture, including dress codes, to create powerful appearances of state control, nationality and group solidarity. In doing so, they have built their esprit de corps on the backs of their citizens through dress. Similarly, social classes, ethnic groups, religious movements and political associations tend to use dress as a means of identity expression (Comaroff and Comaroff, 1992). Though the Comaroffs suggest that states actually manage to colonize the bodies of their subjects, Nordholt (1997) reminds us that there will always be room for individuals to give expression to their own identities.

In terms of display, clothing is a most visible marker of status, identity and ethnicity. As such, it is a potent symbol used by civil religions to express religio-political identity. In Indonesia, traditional dress and uniforms have come to express religious affiliation, ethnic identity and nationalism/civil religion.

Western dress arrived in Indonesia in the sixteenth century and it has been one of the many sources of tension between the indigenous groups and colonizers. This long history was summarized by Van Dijk (1997) as falling into chronological, but simultaneously socio-historic categories of time, based on dress as an indicator of cultural change. These three periods refer to eras categorized by dress terms: *sarong* (local dress), *jubbah* (Islamic influences) and trousers (Western influences).

Restrictive rules with regard to clothing were in place during the colonial period but changed somewhat with Indonesian independence. Under the New Order (which began in the late 1960s), while there was a constant trend toward westernization in dress, this period was characterized by the use of uniforms for much of the citizenry (Danandjaja, 1997). Sekimoto (1997) referred to a "uniform fever" that accompanied the rise of the New Order.

The function of dress in Indonesia, with a population that is primarily Muslim, is quite complex. Although Islam had an impact on Indonesia prior to that of the Europeans, after centuries of Dutch domination, dress in Indonesia has become a way to express attitudes toward foreign, cultural, political and religious influences. The subject of dress, particularly of head coverings, points to conflict over the struggle for cultural hegemony which started after the arrival of Islam (Nordholt, 1997).

Indonesia has undergone great change in the twentieth century, becoming a rapidly developing heavyweight among the Southeast Asian nations. During that time, traditional Indonesian culture interacted with both Islamic and Western concepts. These competing influences have been visibly manifest in the dress of Indonesian citizens. The veil, a particularly potent metaphor, has served as both an expression of ethno-religious identity and as a source of conflict within Indonesian society. As Hassan *et al.* (1985) noted, in the 1930s most women from the Javanese religious elite did not wear a head shawl. In fact during that era, open hostility was shown against people who followed the Islamic practice of head-covering. In Bandung, for instance, stones were thrown at houses of Muslim women who wore head shawls (Van Dijk, 1997). Attitudes toward the practice of wearing head-coverings shifted radically following the rise of the New Order and its focus on uniforms as an expression of Pancasila, the state-instituted civil religion of Indonesia. This ideology stresses nationalism, exemplified by ritual and material culture. Pancasila is a civil religion in Indonesia, where Islam is the formal religion for the vast majority (86.9 percent in 1992) of the population (Worden and Worden, 1993).

Indonesia's Islamic Political Culture

With a population of 180 million, Indonesia was the largest Islamic country in the world by the 1990s, though it was not an Islamic nation ruled by religion. In Indonesia, there are four officially sanctioned religions; by law, each person must proclaim adherence to one of these four religions.

Though most of the Indonesian population is Islamic, there exists a wide range of expression with regard to compliance with Islamic principles and law in the Indonesian population. Islam is a religion based on high moral principles and an important part of being a Muslim is commitment to these principles. Islamic law (*sharia*) is based on the Koran. While Islam is practiced in a much less austere form in Indonesia than in the Middle East, the striking variations in the practice and interpretation of Islam in various parts of Indonesia reflect its long and complex history in Indonesia beginning from about the twelfth century (Worden and Worden, 1993).

One of the tensions dividing Indonesian Muslims was the conflict between traditionalism and modernism. The nature of these differences was complex, confusing and a matter of considerable debate in the early 1990s, but traditionalists generally rejected the modernists' interest in absorbing educational and organizational principles from the West. Specifically, traditionalists were suspicious of modernists' support of the urban *madrasa,* a reformist school that included the teaching of secular topics. The modernists' goal of taking Islam out of the *pesantren* (school of Koranic studies) and carrying it to the people was opposed by the traditionalists because it threatened to undermine the authority of the *kyai* (religious leaders). Traditionalists also sought, unsuccessfully, to add a clause to the first tenet of the Pancasila state ideology requiring that, in effect, all Muslims adhere to Islamic law, the *sharia* (Worden and Worden, 1993).

The appeal of Islam was not weakened when it was supplanted by modern secular nationalism, the civil religion of Pancasila, as the basis for the independent Indonesian state in 1945. In fact, given the prominence of Islamic proselytization and reinvigoration, the people's desire to maintain Islamic institutions and moral values arguably was at an all-time high in Indonesia. There was, however, a separation between Islam as a cultural value system and Islam as a political movement (Worden and Worden, 1993).

Pancasila and Civil Religion

In its preamble, the 1945 constitution sets forth the Pancasila as the embodiment of basic principles of an independent Indonesian state. These five principles were announced by Sukarno (Indonesia's first president) as 1) belief in one supreme God; 2) humanitarianism; 3) nationalism expressed in the unity of Indonesia; 4) consultative democracy; and 5) social justice. Sukarno's statement of the Pancasila, while simple in form, resulted from a complex and sophisticated appreciation of the ideological needs of the new nation. The Pancasila has been used as an instrument of social (and political) control. To oppose the government was to oppose the Pancasila, because such opposition was interpreted as undermining the foundation of the state. The effort to force conformity to the government's interpretation of Pancasila ideological correctness was not without controversy. After the election of Indonesia's second president, Suharto, the New Order's emphasis on the Pancasila was viewed by orthodox Muslim groups as an effort to subordinate Islam to a secular state ideology, even a "civil religion" manipulated by a regime inherently biased against the full expression of Muslim life. Indeed, in 1985 the government capped its effort to domesticate all elements in society to the Pancasila with legislation requiring all voluntary organizations to adopt the Pancasila as their sole ideological principle. It provided for measures to guarantee compliance. For some Muslims, this decision was the last straw. The government's assurance that Muslims were not threatened by the law seemed hollow because the new law restricted the practices of Islam to family, mosque and prayer, rather than allowing Islam to enfold the fullness of human activity, including politics.

On the other hand, by the 1980s, within the legal and politically acceptable boundaries of Muslim involvement, the state had become a major promoter of Islamic institutions. The government even subsidized numerous Muslim community activities. Although by then Islam was a state-favored religion in Indonesia, it was not a state religion (Worden and Worden, 1993); Islam may have been the formal religion in the archipelago, but Pancasila had become the civil religion of the Indonesian nation.

At about the same time that the New Order began in Indonesia, Bellah (1967) published "Civil Religion in America" and set off a firestorm of controversy with his notion that political and religious ideologies can be fused to further the goals of modern nation states. He defined civil religion as "a collection of beliefs, symbols and rituals with respect to sacred things and institutionalized in a collectivity to serve . . . as a genuine vehicle of national religious self-understanding" (Bellah, 1967, pp. 8, 12). Civil religion is conceived as a belief system that draws on religious ideologies and common historical experiences; it exists somewhat independently from formal religion within the culture to unify disparate groups (Cristi and Dawson, 1996).

Indonesian politics and the state ideology of Pancasila have influenced a Muslim theology of religion that in Indonesia is anti-fundamentalist and anti-totalitarian (Steenbrink, 1993). The government of Indonesia saw itself in the early 1990s as having a responsibility to advance a national culture devoted to national development and political integration. As more of the Indonesian population sought employment in large, poorly integrated cities consisting of diverse ethnic groups, the concept of a national culture had great appeal as a way of regulating the population. The central government attempted to guide the formation of this culture through education curricula, national-holiday celebrations and careful control of the national media, including control of popular art and print media (Worden and Worden, 1993). Most importantly, however, there was the central control of television. This medium was commonly found in homes throughout the nation before the 1980s and governmental control of information that came across Indonesian airwaves led to a homogeneity of thought with regard to the civil religion. In addition to the control of media, the Indonesian government had a large proportion of the population directly under its control as much of the population was employed as civil servants for whom Pancasila was their guiding philosophy (Arthur and Solyom, 1995). As a consequence, civil religion appeared in numerous forms, including an attempt to unify the many ethnic groups by the use of the official national language, Bahasa Indonesia; patterns of eating and preparing food; the viewing of team sports, such as soccer, badminton and volleyball; motion pictures; and material displays of wealth (Worden and Worden, 1993).

Clothing, Uniforms and Head-coverings

Although western dress is most commonly worn in Indonesia today, traditional dress continues to be important in Indonesia, where varied forms of traditional dress testify to the wide variety of sub-cultural groups in the nation. Traditional dress is still seen in rural areas and is especially important throughout Indonesia for national ceremonial occasions. For both sexes, traditional dress in Indonesia includes a wrap-around lower-body cover (*kain*, generally worn on Java) or a *sarong* (in which the ends are stitched together forming a tube) (Solyom, 2000). Indonesia is noted for its textiles made with complex resist-dyed techniques. The *kain* is generally made of *batik*, while a *sarong* may commonly be made of *ikat*. For particularly important occasions, sometimes a special fabric called *songket* is made with a supplementary weft of gold or silver (and more recently a metallic tinsel). Women in Java and Bali wear *sarongs* and *kain* with a *kebaya*, a tight, often sheer, long-sleeved blouse (Arthur and Solyom, 1995). In addition, women may have a *selendang* draped over the shoulder (Java) (on less formal occasions a large *selendang* is used to carry babies or objects), or on Bali the *selendang* is worn around the waist. Indonesian men generally wear *kain* or *sarongs* only in the home or on informal occasions. A black felt cap or *peci*, is occasionally worn; though it was once associated with Islam it has acquired a more secular, national meaning in the post-independence period (Worden and Worden, 1993). These ensembles have become national dress in Indonesia because the vast majority of the populations lives on Java and Bali. Although *kebaya* and *batik kain* are considered Indonesia's national dress for women and *teluk beskap*, a combination of the Javanese jacket and *kain* are national dress for Indonesian men (*Jakarta Post*, 1993), many Indonesians can't afford to own their own national dress (Solyom, 2000).

Fieldwork[1] done on the island of Java in 1994 included numerous structured observations over a three-week period. Seventy-three percent of men wore western dress, followed by six percent in *batik* or *ikat* shirts, another six percent in sarongs with western shirts, five percent in uniforms and four percent in traditional *sarong* with *peci*. For women, 42 percent were in western dress, followed by 26 percent in the traditional *sarong* and *kebaya*, 16 percent in a combination of traditional sarong and selendang with a western blouse and seven percent were veiled Muslim women wearing head-coverings. Only one percent wore uniforms (Arthur and Solyom, 1995; Arthur *et al.*, 1995).

Uniforms and Civil Religion in Indonesia

A large percentage of the civilian workforce and all schoolchildren wear uniforms in Indonesia. The rise of the uniform can be attributed to what has been called a "uniform fever" accompanying the rise of Suharto in the late 1960s. A veritable "flood of uniforms" inundated Indonesia in the 1980s (Shiraishi, 1986). Weiner and Schneider note that political elites "depend on cloth to mobilize human emotions in support of . . . nation states" (1989, pp. 10–11) and while this is true to some extent in Indonesia, it is equally true that the adoption of uniforms was also a voluntary act on the part of people showing their support of the New Order state (Nordholt, 1997) and acceptance of its ideology, Pancasila, as a form of civil religion. Van Dijk notes that:

> Indonesians like – or are forced – to show to what group they belong by their clothing. Civilian uniforms are very much in fashion . . . Civil occupations, or so-called "functional groups" tend to have their own uniforms as well. It may be an official one like the one members of the association of civil servants, the KORPRI, wear on Fridays; or an informal one, such as the white, frequently ill-fitting frocks worn by nursemaids. Batik shirts (and skirts) featuring either traditional or modern patterns facilitate the opportunity for developing uniforms for such groups and even for special occasions. The mere fact that one participates jointly in a meeting or celebration nowadays is at times expressed by the wearing of batik with a special design by most or all of the people present, although they are from different organizations and walks of life. At important manifestations one may witness, for instance Suharto and his ministers and their wives and at least part of the audience wearing batik shirts and blouses, all with the same pattern.

In relation to the weeks of preparation for the Independence Day celebration of 1975, Sekimoto noted that the community worked long and hard to prepare for the celebration; "the communal work was framed in a national context which belonged to the domain of *bahasa Indonesia* . . . the village looked neat and clean with national symbols everywhere" (1997, pp. 315–6). On Independence Day, the community turned out in a variety of uniforms in order to participate in the ceremonies:

> Especially noteworthy are the uniforms of those who attended the ceremony. The village officials were in safari suits decorated with the golden badges of the Indonesian Civil Service Corps (KORPRI) on their breast and their black velvet caps (*peci*) indicated the formality of the occasion. The safari suit is not a uniform in a strict sense, but it has been the dress of government officials on duty throughout Indonesia since the early years of the New Order. Most village officials in the area also habitually wore the safari attire following the custom of government officials, in spite of the fact that village officials were not government employees and thus not subject of any specific regulations as to their attire. The safari suit clearly marked out those in power. Usually village officials wore safari suits of varied cuts, colors and materials for daily use. However, on this particular day, at the village headman's suggestion, all the village officials of Darman were wearing the same light-brown suits. Thus, while most of the officials from other villages came to the ceremony in safari suits of various styles, only those from Darman and one other village had a uniform appearance.
>
> The wives of the Darman officials also [were] in uniform. It had previously been arranged that all wives of local and village officials were to wear the uniform of the Pembinaan Kesejahteraan Keluarga (PKK, Family Welfare Guidance), a government-led women's organization . . . The PKK uniform in the area was not very different from the full dress of Javanese women for formal occasions: a thin blouse, shoulder cloth, batik wrap-around skirt and high-heeled sandals. However, unlike outfits for personal use, the blouse and shoulder cloth were uniformly tailored and of the same material and colour: light green blouse and dark green shoulder cloth. The wives of the Darman officials further extended this idea to include uniform batik skirts with a yellow motif. This addition made them highly visible at the Independence Day ceremony (Van Dijk 1997, pp. 319–20).

Under Indonesia's New Order, the uniform has acquired a special significance. For members of centralized institutions such as the army, police and schools, uniforms are a fact of life. For others, wearing uniforms is a completely voluntary act.

> The uniforms functioned, therefore, as a sign of the wearer's closeness to the state. In order to wear a uniform in the era of the New Order, a person had to be a member of an organization that was officially recognized . . . Wearing uniforms is convenient way for people on the fringes of the state machinery to distinguish themselves from the anonymous masses that have no uniform and are assumed to have no part in the workings of the state and the nation (Sekimoto, 1997, pp. 321–3).

The uniform has thus become a metaphor for Indonesian civil religion.

School Uniforms

The penchant for uniforms, so clearly manifest in the adult population from the time of the New Order to the present, extends to Indonesian children as well. The great majority of Indonesia's 50 million schoolchildren wear uniforms; regardless of whether the school is public or private these uniforms are the same throughout the country. The uniform habit and the national characteristics of it are established early in life, through the requirement that all school children wear specific uniforms (Arthur and Solyom, 1995).

School uniforms come in different forms and colors, depending on the age and grade of the student. The basic uniform is composed of white shirts and colored pants and skirts. In primary school, the short pants or knee-length skirts are red, while in junior high the color of pants and skirts changes to dark blue. In high school, grey full-length trousers and knee-length skirts are worn (Danandjaja, 1997). (See figure 12.1).

Figure 12. 1 High school uniforms, after Decree 52 in 1982. Illustration by Kelly Pak.

Dress regulations were outlined in a formal decree (No. 052/C/Kep/D82) issued in 1982 from the Department of Education and Culture by the Director General of Primary and Secondary Education. It is worth noting that this decree begins with a statement of philosophy indicating that uniforms are necessary for "a good and healthy atmosphere and etiquette in school life such that it will insure the carrying out of studying and teaching in the context of uplifting Indonesian humanity as a whole . . . [for] shaping schools as the center of culture" (Keputusan Direktur, [1982] 1986). The decree sets forth stipulations that clearly indicate the role of the uniform as a metaphor for social control in the society. "Wearing school uniforms requires order and discipline . . . self-discipline grows from within [and it will] shape group discipline and strengthen national discipline (Keputusan Direktur, [1982] 1986).

In elementary school, the patriotic intent of the white top and red slacks or skirt is obvious. The idea of everyday and formal outfits is introduced, the latter achieved by addition of tie and cap. In junior high school, colors become more sedate with the introduction of dark blue; caps and ties add formality to the uniform. Colors become more subdued and conservative in high school, where the uniform color is gray (Arthur and Solyom, 1995).

The manual on school uniforms issued in the decree (Keputusan Direktur, 1982), presents ideas common to many schools in many countries. The perception is that the dress code will develop the feeling of unity among students and strengthen esprit de corps. While wearing the school uniform, every student is responsible for good behavior and guarding the image of the school and that this is a moral responsibility that should be (and is) heavily felt. The uniform will also reduce "excessive pride and return a proper sense of pride regarding the respective school" and will "heighten the student image in general and the good name of the school." To achieve this, the desired treatment of school uniforms is described as clean and better if ironed; neat, with shirt inside skirt/trousers, no faded colors or tears; shirt buttons done up, with a belt and no unapproved added items (Keputusan Direktur, [1982] 1986).

Although there is little room for the expression of individuality, there are a few officially sanctioned variations that include batik shirts for the school band and for street processions. For students chosen to be standard bearers on formal occasions, all-white shirts and skirts or trousers are worn. Boy Scouts and Girl Scouts wear brown and yellow uniforms. In Indonesia, scouting is a quasi-government organization with a similar, centrally controlled administrative hierarchy and the uniform is identical all over the country (Arthur and Solyom, 1995). Consequently, scouting is one of the many manifestations of civil religion in Indonesia, so it may come as no surprise that even youngsters who are not members of scouting organizations would attempt to emulate them through uniform dress. As Sekimoto (1997) noted, in Darman, where the government had not yet set up official youth groups, the youth leaders organized the village youth by developing a uniform for them. These quasi-uniforms (Joseph, 1986) were composed of long-sleeved white shirts, beige pants and black ties for boys and orange blouses with grey wrap-around skirts for girls. The informal use of uniforms for ritual attire is customary in the village (Sekimoto, 1997).

Islamization, Dress and Uniforms

The interaction between Indonesian, Western and Muslim ways of thought, manners and dress is actually indicative of competition in Indonesia between these three divergent interests; this tension has recently manifested itself in a renewed emphasis on Islamic ideology. As a symbol of religious piety, expression and subjugation to the rules of Islam, headcoverings are of particular concern throughout much of the Islamic world. In Java, a proper Muslim man covers his head with the *peci and* a conservative Muslim woman wears a veil. Recently, globalization has been hotly debated in Indonesia and Islamic leaders warn their followers about the dangers of following western fashions. Consequently, a great deal of attention is now focused on dress for Muslim women (Van Dijk, 1997).

During the 1980s there emerged a new trend among Muslim women, particularly among high school girls, to put on dresses that covered their bodies from head to toe. This trend has increased to include older women as well.

> Over the last couple of years there has been a tendency among Muslim women to wear Arab costumes, after they return from the *hajj* [a pilgrimage to the sacred places in and around Mecca]. Most of them only put that kind of attire on for about forty days and then return to their western dress, but some keep on wearing it permanently (Danandjaja, 1997).

While this use of dress indicates that visible manifestations of religiosity can be used as a symbol of a person's spirituality, the concurrent role of status symbolism must also be acknowledged. Neatness and cleanliness of clothing, in addition to the wearing of expensive jewelry and shoes have long been signs of high social status in Indonesia. In addition, the wearing of dress that has religious meaning such as the dress Danandjaja recounts above, is also a symbolic statement that the wearer was financially able to pay for the expenses associated with a pilgrimage to Mecca. After the *hajj* the continued use of conservative Muslim dress may attest to the wearer's projection of an affluent lifestyle guided by Islamic principles.

Female dress in Indonesia was a hotly debated topic in the 1980s and that debate continues unabated. While Islam requires that women be modestly dressed, some conservative Muslims interpret this requirement to mean that women should wear a head shawl at all times. Islamic fundamentalists advocate that women take it a step farther and wear a *jilbab*, a long loose dress and head-covering as an expression of Islamic ideology. In doing so, women use their bodies to visually express their commitment to Indonesia's dominant religion. The mounting emphasis on a Muslim lifestyle is mirrored in the number of articles and books devoted to Muslim dress codes for women. Many give religious arguments for adopting such a style of dress and give specific details as to what shall be worn, in addition to how it should fit and how long the garments must be. "A growing stress on Islam is making the hemline drop; some women's bodies are now almost completely covered " (Van Dijk, 1997, p. 75).

Uniforms for Muslim Girls

In a 1992 article about Muslim apparel, a good description was presented of the unrest in the early 1980s over the attempt to introduce head-coverings into Indonesia's school uniforms. This situation was a result of the conflict between two competing ideologies; that of the civil religion of Indonesia, the Pancasila and the formal religion, Islam. While the debate seemed to be about a superficial aspect of dress, an item of cloth, in reality girls' bodies were the site of a conflict over the expression of Indonesian identity. By the early 1980s it was no longer feasible for the Ministry of Education to deny Muslim school girls the right to use clothing to give expression to their formal religious ideology.

> The call of Islam made its first tentative sounds heard once again a little over a decade ago (1982) when young girls of school going age suddenly developed a taste for wearing the Muslim veil and refused to go without it anywhere, even to school.

> At the time it stirred up quite a fuss, because Muslim wear just did not fit in with the standard school uniform that students must wear. Education Minister Daoed Yoesoef, of unbendable character, issued a regulation that students were not to put on any other clothes than school uniforms during school hours. Around the same time, Muslim students in Europe had to face the same problem but were more lucky when the French authorities, after considerable deliberating, allowed female students to cover their heads at school.

> Now, more than ten years and two education ministers later, the Muslim veil or kerudung has finally found acceptance in the classrooms (*Muslim apparel* 1992, p. 33).

There was an intense amount of pressure placed on the Ministry of Education and this office was persuaded to allow some alteration of the uniform code. In 1982, Decree No. 52 allowed for the use of Muslim dress in school uniforms. In Chapter five, Paragraph five of Decree No. 52 (Keputusan Direktur [1982] 1986), an allowance was made for female students who wanted to express their Islamic religion. By default, no allowance was considered necessary for Muslim boys' uniforms. Starting in junior high, adolescent Muslim girls can wear a short headscarf, three-quarter sleeves and a shirt worn outside the skirt (to obscure the waistline). By high school, full coverage is an option for Muslim girls who generally wear a full headscarf, long over-blouse with long sleeves and long skirt. Female modesty is a sign of both religiosity and high social status, so the high school uniform for observant Muslim girls is a visible symbol of family values and status. The result has been that by allowing for a

Figure 12. 2 Girls at lunchtime, outside an Islamic school in Jakarta. Photo by L. B. Arthur.

change in the fit, length and head-coverings for Muslim girls, their uniforms, while similar to those worn by their less religious classmates, have a remarkably different overall appearance. (See figures 12. 2 and 12.3).

Pancasila Today

The New Order under Suharto made Pancasila courses compulsory not only for students but also for government officials, editors and others. With that level of central control, Pancasila left the realm of ideology and became civil religion with a touch of totalitarianism. Dissenters were labeled "anti-Pancasila" or "communists" (Magnis-Suseno, 2000). Under Pancasila, homogeneity was a value and was expressed with the use of uniforms throughout the population.

Figure 12. 3 High school students leaving class. Bogor, Indonesia.

The New Order ended with the ouster of Suharto, followed by the immediate (but short-lived) appointment of B. J. Habibie as third president. An election was held in October 1999 and Indonesia's fourth president, Abdurrahman Wahid was brought into power. Interestingly, this president is a moderate Muslim cleric who supports the right of all Indonesians to learn any ideology. He is not overly invested in Pancasila as a civil religion. As Franz Magnis-Suseno recently noted (4/28/2000), since the country's independence, Pancasila evolved into a totalitarian teaching that excluded other opinions. "Pancasila was used by the New Order to crush communism, the Islamic political movement and the growth of democracy itself which was labeled as liberal democracy and unfitting to the culture," said the professor at the University of Indonesia. Magnis-Suseno (2000) suggested that the five principles of Pancasila should be used as fundamental values of government policy but discarded as the state ideology. Whether or not this occurs, I would anticipate that there will continue to be tension between civil and secular religions in Indonesia. Perhaps continued observation as to the role of uniforms in this society may lead to an awareness of societal shifts in social roles and personal identities. As the state lessens its hold on individuals, this shift may become symbolically manifest in changes in incidence of uniforms worn by the Indonesian population.

Conclusion

This chapter presents an investigation into the use of the uniform as an expression of religious identity in two domains; that of Indonesia's civil religion (Pancasila) and of its dominant formal religion, Islam. Uniforms are shown to be an expression of commitment to both nationalist and religious ideologies.

Rather than examining uniforms merely as an instrument of social control, the existence of agency with regard to self-presentation is seen to exist simultaneously with the cultural system of social control. Ambivalence between conformity and individuality, agency and control is seen in women's self-presentations. Expression of individuality, family status and family values with regard to religion can be seen in spite of the domination of the uniform.

Note

1. The research project involved participant observation and routine counts of people alongside the roads on Java and Bali. These counts were taken three times per day for three weeks in the summer of 1994. A total of 3021 women were observed and 3466 men were observed. Dress was categorized into types based on a continuum from traditional to western dress (Arthur, 1995).

References

Achjadi, J. (1976). Traditional costumes of Indonesia. *Arts of Asia,* 6(5), pp. 74–9.

Arthur, L. B. (1994). Cultural highlights: Focus on Indonesia. *Asia Pacific Exporter,* 1(7), 10–13.

Arthur, L. B. & Solyom, B. (1995). Uniforms and social control in Indonesia. Paper presented at the annual meetings of the International Textiles and Apparel Association.

Arthur, L. B. & Solyom, B. (1998). From gold to lurex: The commodification of Indonesian songket. *Costume Society of America Annual Meeting Symposium Abstracts.* Madison, WI: Omnipress.

Arthur, L. B., Boehlke, H., Cerny, C., Des Jarlais, M., Douglas, S., Hyllegard, K., Michelman, S., Niessen, S. & Solyom, B. (1995). Indonesian images: Textiles and clothing as material culture. *International Textiles and Apparel Association Proceedings* (pp. 23–4). Monument, CO: International Textiles and Apparel Association.

Bellah, R. (1967). Civil religion in America. *Daedalus,* 96, 1–21.

Chriss, J. (1993). Durkheim's cult of the individual as civil religion: its appropriation by Erving Goffman. *Sociological Spectrum,* 13, pp. 251–75.

Comaroff, J. & Comaroff, J. (1992). *Ethnography and the historical imagination.* Boulder: Westview.

Cristi, M. & Dawson, L. (1996). Civil religion in comparative perspective: Chile under Pinochet (1973–1989). *Social Compass* 43 (3), pp. 319–38.

Danandjaja, J. (1997). From hansop to safari. In Nordholt, H. S. (Ed.) *Outward appearances: Dressing state and society in Indonesia.* pp. 249–58. Leiden: KITLV Press.

Hassan A., Masaum, M., & Aziz, H. M. (1985). *Soal jawab mas-alah agama.* Bangil: Persatuan.

Jakarta Post (1993). Indonesian fashion. May 15.

Joseph, N. (1986). *Uniforms and non-uniforms: Communication through clothing.* New York; Greenwood.

Keputusan Direktur Jenderal Pendidikan Dasar dan Menengah Departmen Pendidikan dan Kebudayaan No. 052/C/Kep/D82 (1982). Tentang Pendoman Pakaian Seragam Sekolah Dasar, in *Informasi pedidikan dan kebudayaan.* Jakarta. Departemen Pendidikan dan Kebudayaan, Republik Indonesia.

Muslim apparel: Prospective export earner. (1992). *Indonesia Magazine,* 23(2), pp. 33–7.

Magnis-Suseno, F. (2000). Scrap Pancasila as state ideology. *Jakarta Post.* (April 28).

Nordholt, H. S. (Ed.), (1997). Introduction. In Nordholt, H. S. (Ed.). *Outward appearances: Dressing state and society in Indonesia.* pp. 1–37. Leiden: KITLV Press.

Sekimoto, T. (1997). Uniforms and concrete walls: Dressing the village under the New Order in the 1970s and 1980s. In Nordholt, H. S. (Ed.) *Outward appearances: Dressing state and society in Indonesia.* p. 336–8. Leiden: KITLV Press.

Shiraishi, T. (1986). Gakko shoka, siefuku, dorakyura; Indonesia no kokumin togo. [School songs, uniforms and Dracula; On Indonesian national integration], In Yonosuke, H. (Ed.), *Tonah ajia kara no chiteki boken* [*intellectual adventures in southeast Asia*] pp. 69–108. Tokyo: Libroport.

Steenbrink, K. (1993). Indonesian politics and a Muslim theology of religions: 1965-1990. *Islam and Christian Muslim Relations*, 5(2), Dec. pp. 223–46.

Solyom, B. (2000). Personal communication.

Van Dijk, K. (1997). Sarong, jubbah and trousers: Appearance as a means of distinction and discrimination. In Nordholt, H. S. (Ed.) *Outward appearances: Dressing state and society in Indonesia.* pp. 39–83. Leiden: KITLV Press.

Weiner, A., & Schneider, J. (Eds.) (1989). *Cloth and human experience.* Washington DC: Smithsonian Institution Press.

Worden, F. & Worden, R. (1993). Indonesia, a country study. Area handbook series, Federal Research Division, Library of Congress. Washington, DC. Superintendent of Documents, USGPO.

Index